Leadership And Human Development

Oscar Arias
Ergün Olgun
Harriet Mayor Fulbright
Howard Berry
Mansour Yousef Elaagab
Bernard M. Bass
Bruce Lloyd
Carol Allais
Mahy Abdel Latif
Anjelika Baravikova
Jiang Xuewen
Hafiza Golandaz
Fathi El Shazly
Ingmar Karlsson
Halil Güven
Adel Safty

Edited by

Adel Safty
Halil Güven

With a Preface by
Oscar Arias

The International Institute of Leadership and Public Affairs, Bahcesehir University. Istanbul.

Leadership for Human Development
The International Leadership Series (Book Four)

Sponsored by:
The International Institute of Leadership and Public Affairs
Bahcesehir University, Istanbul, Turkey, 2002

First edition published by the International Institute of
Leadership and Public Affairs, of the University of
Bahcesehir. Istanbul. Turkey. 2003.

Copyright © 2002 Adel Safty and Halil Güven
All rights reserved. No unauthorized photocopying.

Published by:
Universal Publishers/upublish.com
USA • 2003

ISBN: 1-58112-614-X

www.upublish.com/books/safty4.htm

Table of Contents

Chapter	Page
Preface **Oscar Arias**	3
Introduction **Adel Safty**	6
Leadership for Human Development **Adel Safty**	24
Leadership for Peace and Dialogue **Oscar Arias**	51
Ripeness in the Resolution of International Conflicts: the Significance of Leadership **Erg‚n Olgun**	63
Leadership and Human Progress **Harriet Mayor Fulbright**	68
Constructing the World Anew **Howard Berry**	80
Leadership and Human Rights **Mansour Yousel Elaagab**	89

II

New Paradigm and Ethics of Leadership **Bernard M. Bass**	117
Leadership, Globalisation And the New Economy **Bruce Lloyd**	136
Leadership for Nation-building in South Africa **Carol Allais**	148
Leadership and Conflict in Africa **Mahy Abdel Latif**	159
Leadership in Russia: The case of Mr. Putin **Anjelika Baravikova**	191
Leadership in China Social Stability v. Freedom of Expression **Jiang Xuewen**	218
Leadership for Creativity: The case of Indian Emperor Akbar **Hafiza Golandaz**	242
Clash of Civilisations: A Muslim Perspective **Fathi El Shazly**	261

III

Clash of Civilisation: A European Perspective **Ingmar Karlsson**	276
Civilisations and Natural Laws **Halil Güven**	289
Dialogue of Civilisations **Halil Güven**	306
Leadership in Education **Halil Güven**	322

Acknowledgement

This book is the result of the contributions of many distinguished leaders and scholars who came from over the world in response to my call to address the issue of Leadership for Human Development. The Conference was also the inaugural conference of the International Institute of Leadership and Public Affairs (IILPA), which was established at Bahcesehir University in Istanbul. The Global Leadership Forum, and therefore this book, and for that matter the IILPA itself, would not have been possible without the leadership, vision, and support of Mr. Enver Y‚cel, Chairman of the Board of Trustees of the University of Bahcesehir and of Prof. Halil G‚ven, President of the university. To them goes my first debt of gratitude and appreciation.

The holding of a major international conference is always a demanding affair and a necessary teamwork. In the six months that I worked preparing for this Global Leadership Forum, I was ably assisted and helped by Dr. Halil G‚ven, the President of Bahcesehir University who actively participated in every aspect of the organisation, providing leadership and valuable can-do-attitude. I also wish to thank Dr. Tamer Atabarut who acted as my personal assistant, and who kept a smile under all circumstances. I was naturally assisted by a host of helpers from the University of Bahcesehir who gave of their time and energy to ensure the success of an international conference of this magnitude. I wish to thank them all and record my debt of gratitude and appreciation to them. These people are: Ercan Akin, Prof.

Dr. Zafer Dogan, and Murat ˆp ,. From Public Relations: Faika B,rkan and Havva Salman. From The School of Foreign Languages: Dr. Olga Atacanova, Beatrice Vanni, Anna Meskhi, Arzu Karakurt. Beldan zant, Canan Mendi, Kˆsker. Fehime Muhaffel, Kemal Karagˆl, Mehran Shahid, M,r,vvet olakoglu, Nilay Oguz, Sibel Erkman, and Vafa Kazdal. From the administrative assistance department: Aynur Imer, Burcu Alarslan, Alev Durmusoglu, Yasemin zdemir, Sezen G,lsen, Senay Mutlu, Fatma akiroglu, Murat ˆp ,, and Engin G,ner. From the camera department: Ozan Konrot, and B,lent G,ven. From the graphics department: Meral Hi sˆnmez and Tayfun Akman, and from the Information Technology department: Yal in eki , Ferhat Konakoglu, Ersun Aydin, and Safak B,lb,l. Thank you to you all.

I also wish to thank my able assistants from the United Nations Leadership Conference Committee who came from all over the world to participate and assist in yet another international gathering concerned with the ideas and activities of leadership. Their contribution and commitment are testimony to their own leadership. I wish to thank them one by one: Dr. Mahy Abdel Latif (Egypt), Dr. Carol Allais (South Africa), Ms. Marina Tyasto (Russia), Ms. Anjelika Borokovic (Austria), Mr. Fïsan Bankale (Nigeria), Congressman Jose Gomez (Venezuela), Mr. Rupert-Douglas Bates (England), Mr. Leong Sze Hian (Singapore), Mr. Jiang Xuewen (China), Dr. Mansour Elaagab (Sudan) and Professor Hafiza Golandaz (India). I appreciate their support and value their friendship.

Adel Safty
Istanbul, July 2002

Preface

Oscar Arias

It is a pleasure to be here at this grand occasion celebrating one of the most important concepts, and certainly one of the most needed qualities, in the world today: leadership. I had the privilege of participating in one of Dr. Saftyís United Nations leadership programs in 1998, and so I am very aware of the high standards and quality of his work. For that reason, I gladly accepted when he asked me to come halfway across the world once more to talk about what it means to be a leader.

Leadership, my friends, is something, which has many definitions. We can speak of political leadership, business leadership, and educational leadership, among many other areas. We can speak of visionary leadership, effective leadership, magnetic leadership, or efficient leadership, and each of these phrases might bring to mind a different type of individual. In reality, leaders come in all shapes, sizes and colours, and with many different personalities, styles, and convictions. So how do we recognize a leader when we meet one? By the fruits of their labours. Just as the sweetness of the fruit indicates the health of the tree, the results produced indicate the quality of the leader. Judging by these standards, I would say that Professor Adel Safty has proven himself time and time again to be both a philosopher and an achiever, a learner and an educator, a person of both flexibility and conviction--in sum, an outstanding leader. For all of your achievements, Professor Safty, and especially for the opening of this promising institution, which we are here to inaugurate today, I heartily congratulate you.

What is the significance of the International Institute of Leadership and Public Affairs? Standing here in Istanbul, a city both ancient and modern, a place which from the beginning of civilization has been at the crossroads of East and West, North and South; and synthesizing leadership perspectives from the fields of governance, management, and multilateral cooperation, this institution stands for authentic leadership for the twenty-first century. For the leadership that the world requires today is based on ancient wisdom but open to innovation, rooted in a home culture, but reaching out to all people; it is a leadership, which is not afraid to learn and is equally eager to teach. It is leadership, my friends, that not only proclaims a vision, but also makes that vision a reality. It is my hope and my belief that this institution will serve as a greenhouse for the incubation of the seeds of this type of leadership, seeds which will later be planted, cultivated, and brought to flower and bear fruit in different lands around the world.

More than thirty years ago, Martin Luther King Jr. had this to say about leaders, and it still applies today: "The urgency of the hour calls for leaders of wise judgment and sound integrity leaders not in love with money, but in love with justice; leaders not in love with publicity, but in love with humanity; leaders who can subject their particular egos to the greatness of the cause." I am confident that many women and men who fit this description will be passing through the doors of the International Institute of Leadership and Public Affairs, in order to develop, debate, and refine their ideas and practice of leadership. May this institution serve them well, so that they may serve humanity well.

Introduction

Adel Safty

This book continues the leadership series, which I started shortly after I set out to organise the United Nations Leadership conferences in 1996. It follows, therefore, Leadership and the United Nations, Leadership and Global Governance, and Leadership and Conflict Resolution. In this latest volume, Leadership and Human Development, I include the presentations made by distinguished leaders and scholars of leadership at the Global Leadership Forum I organised in Istanbul in June 2001, as well as presentations made by two distinguished diplomats after the Global Leadership Forum. The Forum brought together distinguished leaders and scholars from around the world, as well as representatives of more than 20 international organisations. It also brought together my United Nations Leadership Conference Support Committee, which I first set up in 1997, with representatives from the United States, Venezuela, England, Russia, Austria, Egypt, Nigeria, South Africa, Singapore, India and China.

In his preface, Dr. Oscar Arias, Noble Peace Laureate and former President of Costa Rica, argues that the leadership that the world requires today is based on ancient wisdom but open to innovation, rooted in a home culture, but reaching out to all people; it is a leadership, which is not afraid to learn and is equally eager to teach. It is leadership that not only proclaims a vision, but also makes that vision a reality.

Although I proposed leadership for human development as the theme of the Global Leadership Forum, the participants were free to define leadership and human development from their own perspective. For me for instance, all leadership activities, whether in the private or public sector, whether in the academy or in citizensí associations, are ultimately about human development. In his/her concern for the professional and personal development of the companyís staff, in the national leaderís responsibility to serve his people, in the United Nationsí and global civil societyís efforts to promote peace and development worldwide, the effective leaders are in the final analysis those who never lose sight of the larger picture linking leadership to human development. For this to happen, leadership needs to be freed from the domination of the business model, liberalised and related to human development, and ultimately democratised to be made accessible to leaders in all fields.

In his discussion of Leadership for Peace and Dialogue, Dr. Oscar Arias distinguishes five qualities, which he deems indispensable for successful leadership in this area: Patience, perseverance, humility, commitment, and compromise. He asks rhetorically: Wouldnít we all like these qualities to be more prominent in our elected representatives? For these qualities are not only personal virtues, but also necessary job qualifications. They are, Dr. Arias says, what allow progress to be made in the face of ordinary, everyday conflict and disagreement. He advises aspiring politicians and public policy leaders to do everything they can to cultivate and defend these values, in themselves and in their colleagues.

The same qualities, Dr. Arias says, are also crucial for those whose leadership will be in the areas of business, education, civil society, or any other field. In any of lifeís endeavours, he affirms, very little is ever achieved by clinging to a single point of view or way of doing things. We must hold to our principles, Dr. Arias advices, but be also prepared to compromise. If we want a world at peace, he argues, we cannot allow ourselves to fall prey to extremism of any sort. We should begin, he advises, by examining our own hearts and minds and eradicating the seeds of exclusion, intolerance, and violence that exist within each one of us. We must, he says, weed our internal gardens to make room for the healthy plants of respect, compassion, integrity, and trustworthiness. With these qualities, Oscar Arias concludes, we will be able to provide capable leadership in the most difficult of situations.

Erg‚n Olgun is Under-Secretary to the President of the TRNC. In his discussion of the Ripeness in the Resolution of International Conflicts and the Significance of Leadership, he argues that conflicts are usually protracted because of asymmetry of hurt by the parties, in which case the stronger party insists on a zero-sum outcome. It is possible, however, argues Mr. Olgun, to have a win-win negotiating outcome to major conflicts, if the parties and especially the leadership accepted the notion that their respective interests would be better served by such an approach than by the unilateral pursuits of zero-sum outcome.

Mr. Olgun points out that proactive and progressive leadership plays a significant role in the transformation of conflict from a confrontational zero-sum mindset to a win-win problem solving mindset. Transformation in the mindset of conflicting parties is by far the most critical turning point in the process of negotiation, he says, and it is this turning point, he argues, which opens the door for meaningful negotiation and for resolution. It is however, Mr. Olgun points out, a dramatic turning point for political leaders because it involves a departure from accustomed and safe popular positions to ones that are risky and necessitate the payment of attention to the concerns and interests of traditional enemiesí.

Such transformation, Mr. Olgun concludes, requires strong leadership, foresight and the realization that by working together and addressing the legitimate concerns of each other all parties would have realized their interests far better than they would have done unilaterally. This requires hard choices, which only strong leaders can make.

Harriet Mayor Fulbright is former Executive Director of the Presidentís Committee for the Arts and Humanities in the Clinton Administration and of the Fulbright Commission. In her discussion of Leadership and Peace, she focuses on the great changes that have occurred in the past century and argues that visionary leadership is urgently needed more than ever. Great leaders, she says, must have a vision of how to bring about and maintain peace, prosperity and the well being whether they are leaders of a company, a community or a country. To do this successfully, Mrs. Fulbright argues, it is essential that leaders learn to increase their capacity of foresight. They must also learn, she says, to create teams to translate complicated issues into understandable language. Leaders, especially political leaders, Mrs. Fulbrigth argues, must work hard to put in place policies that benefit humanity rather than the special interest that might have enabled their election.

Mrs. Fulbrigth cites the example of her late husband Senator William Fulbright as a leader who had a vision, to serve humanity not just his country, and who worked hard to make his dream a reality. His vision of peace in the world led him, in 1943, to initiate a Congressional resolution to create a multi-national organization for the purpose of promoting peace among nations, the United Nations. It was peace in the world that led him to create the international education exchange program that bears his name. He believed, says Mrs.Fulbright, that if potential future leaders learned how to exchange ideas and realized that we are all human beings with the same underlying aspirations, perhaps they would not be so quick to exchange bullets.

The late Prof. Howard Berry was the co-founder and President of the International Partnership for Service Learning in New York. In his discussion of Reconstructing the World Anew: Education and Leadership, he argues that yes leadership is indeed ultimately about human development, but it is also about about character, virtues, and inner democracy. Professor Berry points out some of the contradictions in the phenomenon of globalisation. He says that economic globalism is self-contradictory. It is driven by a consumer economic structure, yet this very structure leaves out large segments of society who cannot buy the goods produced. He raises an important moral issue when he asks: Where is the countervailing voice to economic globalism and worldwide consumerism? Where is the leavening institution speaking for and attending to the alienated, those unable to speak or act for themselves?

Professor Berry then develops his long-held and cherished vision of service linked to learning in universities around the world. He rhetorically asks: Is it too much to think of the idea, through service connected to education, of a social apprenticeship, or an apprenticeship in civic virtue? This is a vision, he says, but it is not chimerical. It is not limited to the poets, the novelists, the philosophers, or the idealists and radical activists. Professor Berry argues that the businessperson who understands this is a better businessperson; the engineer is a better engineer; the lawyer is a better lawyer. He urges everyone to dare to begin the journey of realising his or her dreams. As many from philosophy and religion have told us, he points out, the value is in the striving, not merely in the achieving else whatís a heaven for. Professor Berry summons Goethe to his aid: Whatever you can do or dream you can, begin it. Boldness has a genius, power and magic in it.

Dr. Mansour Yousef Elaagab is former elected Member of Parliament of Sudan and currently chairperson of the Organisation of Sudan Human Rights. In his discussion of Leadership for Human Rights, he argues the need for leaders who are committed to democratic practices, human rights and democratic institutions, to economic self-reliance, equitable distribution of wealth, full employment, and balanced development with a human face. He places particular emphasis on the need for leaders committed to real popular participation in economic, political, and social decisions. This means that we badly need leaders who have integrity, accept accountability, display authority, and who have positive mental attitudes. Leaders who hold the principles of consideration and respect, and constancy of purpose, and who are committed to team building and consensus decision-making. Such leaders, argues Dr. Elaagab, are leaders who believe in serving people and are ready to make sacrifices and take risks. Such leaders are learned, enlightened people who are open to new ideas. Only such leaders can seriously claim to be committed to leadership for human development.

Dr. Bernard M. Bass is distinguished Professor and Director of the Centre for Leadership Studies at Binghamton University, Binghamton, New York, in the United States. In his discussion of transformational and transactional leadership styles, Professor Bass explains that *Transformational* leaders raise the awareness of their followers about what is important and increase followersí concerns for achievement, self-actualisation and ideals. They motivate followers to go beyond the followersí self-interests for the good of the group, organization and /or society. *Transactional* leaders cater to the self-interests of their followers by means of contingent reinforcement. If the followers carry out their assignments, as agreed, they are rewarded, promised rewards and praised.

Professor Bass argues that the leadership and management can be conceived, as transformational and transactional leadership respectively. Furthermore, he points out that the rapid changes in the environment have required much more need for leaders and followers to be more flexible and imaginative. Leaders are faced with a rapidly changing workforce, technology, markets, societies and communities. Globalisation, whatever one thinks of it, is a fact of life.

To deal effectively with this rapidity of change, Dr. Bass advises that, the good supervisor, the good official and the good executive have to be both good managers and good leaders. In this new environment of the late 20th and early 21st centuries, they have to be good managers who plan, organize and control as well as good leaders who envision, enable and empower.

Dr. Bruce Lloyd is Professor of Leadership and Management at South Bank University, London, England. In his discussion of Leadership and the New Economy, he places the emphasis on the need to place the issue of values at the heart of any approach to leadership. He believes that the whole issue of leadership begins and ends with the need to combine that greater concern for 'others', with a more insightful and relevant balance between Power and Responsibility issues.

Professor Lloyd argues that leadership should not, in any way, be preoccupied with Power and the 'self'. He strongly believes that it is crucial for the sanity and success of individuals engaged in leadership and management activities, and therefore for the success of the organisation, to get the relationship between the self and others, between Power and Responsibility, right. Dr. Lloyd says that this balance that we must all seek is the key issue to leadership and it is one that we can have an impact on. Only when we strive to get this broader balance right, will we be able to focus on the theme advocated by Dr. Safty, namely the relationship between leadership and human development.

Dr. Carol Allais is chairperson of the Department of Sociology at the University of South Africa. In her discussion of Globalisation and the Challenges of Leadership in South Africa, Dr. Allais reviews leadership as a critical factor in the transformation of South Africa and examines the most effective leadership style for addressing democratic nation-building in South Africa. In the wake of the transition from authoritarian rule to democracy, leadership gaps are being experienced at all levels. Leaders, as change agents and holders of values, in interaction with their followers, can play an important role in the process of transition and the achievement of national social and economic goals. Leaders, or their masses, cannot go it alone.

The leadership style of the most effective leaders, Dr. Allais argues, may be identified as interactive. This is leadership that is in constant interaction with its constituencies/followers, co-leaders and adversarial elites/leaders. It strives to maintain bottom-top and top-bottom communication. Dr. Allais looks at the Truth and Reconciliation Commission under the chairmanship of

Archbishop Desmond Tutu as a post apartheid civil society initiative in democratic nation building.

Dr. Mahy Abdel Latif is Counsellor in the Egyptian Foreign Ministry. She was also a political analyst at the Organisation of African Unity. In her discussion of Leadership and the Changing Nature of Conflicts in Africa, she argues that intra-state conflicts do not represent the only challenge that Africa is facing, but that it is impossible to reflect on intra-state conflicts without considering the dimensions that could trigger inter-state conflicts as well.

Conflicts, Dr. Abdel Latif writes, of whichever nature or kind, have adverse and negative ramifications on peace, security and stability in the African continent as well as on its prospects of socio-economic and human development. Africa finds itself in a vicious circle of causes of conflicts, argues Dr. Abel Latif, their negative repercussions on socio-economic development, the impact of poor economic performance on the society and on the state's capacity to respond to internal tensions, demands and pressures, and the eruption of conflicts in Africa.

If Africa is to avoid political and economic marginalisation, concludes Dr. Abdel Latif, difficult decisions must be made and serious national commitments undertaken. There is urgent need for a leadership committed to promoting durable peace and sustainable development in Africa.

Mrs. Anjelika Baravikova is a Political Analyst at the International Agency for Atomic Energy in Vienna. She discusses the leadership style of President Putin of Russia and says he is no ordinary politician because he skipped several steps on the way to the presidency. The first election he ever fought was for the office of President. In analysing his leadership style, Mrs. Baravikova finds that Mr. Putin is a statesman, for whom Russian interests are most important. He has a sharp sense of state interests and is most determined to strengthen the role of the state. Mrs. Baravikova wonders how much the process of strengthening the state will affect social reforms. She cautions against the widespread fear that the strengthening of the Russian state would be at the expense of civil liberties and the civil society. She argues that much will depend on the circumstances and foreign factors. Mr. Putin wishes to modernise Russia, she says, but it is the same familiar modernisation from above, in a different way, as those of Peter the Great, Lenin or Stalin.

Mrs. Baravikova says that Mr. Putin is not an anti-Western politician. He is prepared to promote political and economic integration in the globalisation process, but while firmly keeping in mind specific Russian interests, not American interests. Mrs. Baravikova argues that Mr Putin is trying to modernise the Russian economy but without blinding following imported prescriptions from the West. The West is very cautious about Putin, says Mrs. Baravikova, as Western observers think that such an independent policy as that followed by Putin could lead to less democracy in Russia and more authoritative/authoritarian style of leadership in Russia.

Mr. Jiang Xuewen is an award-winning radio broadcaster in China. In his discussion of Leadership in China: Social Stability and Freedom of Expression, he says that in the eyes of Western society, the leaders of China emphasize social stability at the expense of freedom of expression. In the Chinese wisdom of administering a country, however, Mr. Xuewen argues, social stability and freedom of expression complement one other. This is because freedom of expression requires effective guarantees of an economic development, which in turns requires social stability. Never in the history of humanity, writes Mr. Xuewen, have we witnessed absolute freedom of expression, because freedom is a relative and dynamic process of evolution.

Mr. Xuewen argues that on the one hand, the maintenance of definite social stability and the promotion of economic development will give further impetus to the achievement of freedom of expression; and, on the other hand, freedom of expression may also advance the development of the economy, and in turn enable the society to maintain economic prosperity and social stability. The practice in China, he says, reveals that only under the prerequisite of social stability and economic prosperity will freedom of expression be able to expand continuously. Mr. Xuewen concludes that the Chinese leadershipís determination to give priority to the maintenance of social stability and the development of national economy are based on some historical, cultural, realistic, and understandable reasons.

Professor Hafiza Golandaz is Professor at The International Leadership and Management Alliance (ILMA) Mubai, India. In her discussion of Leadership for Creativity: The Case of Mughal Emperor Akbar, she says that in a group, leadership roles are people-centered and task-centred and can be performed theoretically by one person. This is common knowledge, she says, but what are less commonly known is the nature and the importance of the role of the leader in encouraging the emergence of creativity in a group. Professor Golandaz uses the example of Emperor Akbar who identified, brought together, encouraged and rewarded not one but nine creative persons who effectively became nine Jewels in the Kingís Crown.

In examining Akbarís leadership style, Professor Golandaz finds support and fresh vindication for the basic axiom of synergy that the whole is greater than the sum of its parts. Indeed, Akbar himself often suggested that the genius of a great leader consisted in the constant harmony of holding variety of great purposes in mind all at once.

Professor Golandaz credits Akbarís imagination for his extraordinary ability to range across the large mass of details that confronted a war leader. Among Akbarís many other qualities, Professor Golandaz singles out candour, plain speaking, decisiveness, imagination and vision. She also discusses the Kingís ability to balance a view of the whole scene with attention to details, ability to take bold new initiatives, ability to delegate, flexibility in problem solving approach and tolerance for heterogeneity. Emperor Akbar was also remarkable for his ability to accept dissent and to surround himself with people who knew more than him.

Ambassador Fathi El Shazly is Egyptís ambassador to Turkey. In his discussion of Clash of Civilisations: A Muslim Perspective, he argues that Trans-Civilization cultural interaction has always existed with differing intensity and different directions. Long before the post cold war attempts of theorization, London hosted in 1936 a joint session of dialogue between Al-Azhar and the Vatican. Al-Azhar hosted another session in Cairo in 1978.

The Barcelona Process, writes Ambassador El Shazly, for building a comprehensive partnership between the EU and twelve Mediterranean countries made a valuable contribution to the debate about the future relationships between cultures around the Mediterranean. The United Nations declared the year 2001 as the year of dialogue between civilizations. What added a sense of urgency to the subject, Ambassador

El Shazly points out, was obviously the terrorist attacks of September 11, 2001 on New York and Washington.

Ambassador El Shazly points out those civilizational dimensions are now being politicised in order to promote national interests and serve strategic objectives. He argues that most of the 20th century combating parties to the two World Wars that left tens of millions of victims and caused devastation and terrible sufferings, belonged to the same civilization. The driving force behind the conflicts, he points out, was conflicting interests. When an alliance was formed in the 2nd World War between the two European axis powers and Japan, that alliance was not founded on a common civilization but simply on shared interests.

In the age of globalisation, Ambassador El Shazly warns, any attempt to impose universal cultural uniformity is against the thrust of history. A uniform global outfit, he says, cut and trimmed according to the measurements dictated by the World Information Order will result in repulsion, resistance and withdrawal.

In the era of Information Technology, he concludes, what could and should be done is to deploy technological innovations for the propagation of a multifaceted plural culture knitted around the moral system common to all civilizations.

Ambassador Ingmar Karlsson is Consul General of Sweden and Director of the Istanbul Centre for Turkish-Swedish Cooperation. In his discussion of Clash of Civilisations: A European Perspective, he argues that Huntintonís argumentation has seemingly been justified by the tragic events of September 11. Ambassador Karlsson argues, however, that the Clash of Civilisation thesis contains a number of weak points: Huntington divides the world into seven or eight major civilizations : Western, containing Western Europe and North America, Confucian, Japanese, Islamic, Hindu, Slav-Orthodox, Latin American and possibly an African civilization.

This division, says Ambassador Karlsson, is rather inconsistent. Some civilizations seems to be defined according to religious and cultural criteria while in other cases the key factor seems to be geography. Ambassador Karlsson asks: What distinguishes the Western civilization from the Latin American? Both North and South America are inhabited by European immigrants who brought along values that they have retained ever since. In fact, both South and North America can be characterized as Western civilizations but with different degrees of other cultural elements.

Ambassador Karlsson writes that Huntington seems to be on a firmer ground when he claims that conflicts at the micro level will run along the fault lines between cultural spheres. The civil war in Tajikistan and the conflicts in the Caucasus seem to support this thesis and even more so the civil wars in the former Yugoslavia where the front lines largely followed the traditional frontier between the Eastern and the Western Roman Empires and between the Ottoman and Hapsburg empires.

Even these arguments, Ambassador Karlsson points out, do not bear closer examination. Not a single war during the last century was provoked by a clash between civilizations. In 1914, he points out, the Protestant Berlin got allied with the Catholic Vienna and Muslim Istanbul against the Orthodox Moscow, the Catholic Paris, and the Protestant London. The aggressors in the Second World War, Italy, Germany, the

Soviet Union and Japan were able to co-operate in spite of their belonging to different cultural spheres and when Hitler attacked Stalin, Churchill and Roosevelt did not ask their new ally whether he was an Orthodox Christian or a communist.

The majority of the wars that took place after 1945, Ambassador Karlsson points out, have been fights within civilizations : Korea, Vietnam, Cambodia, Somalia, Iraq, Iran, and Kuwait. The longest and most blood-filled conflict in the Middle East in the eighties did not take place between the Arabs and the Jews but between Muslims in the war between Iran and Iraq.

If we regard Huntingtonís reference to Islam s bloody borders as an indisputable fact, the Swedish Ambassador concludes, we shall never be able to integrate our growing Muslim population. In that case Huntingtonís prophecies of a clash of civilizations might become a reality but not in the form of a military measuring of strength between the West and the rest and a new siege of Vienna but as a permanent guerrilla warfare in the suburbs of the big European cities turned into ghettos.

This, says Ambassador Karlsson, is the real risk of a clash of civilizations. To prevent this from happening is the greatest challenge for the European politicians today.

Prof. Halil G‚ven is President of Bahcesehir University in Istanbul, Turkey. In his discussion Civilisations and Natural Law: A Positive Sciences Perspective, he discusses civilizational disharmony in the world, in light of Huntingtonís (1993) claims of clash of civilizations. He then argues that civilizations have both social and material components, and that these two equally important aspects of civilizations should be kept in balance. A civilization with enormous material basis (rules, regulations, laws, order, and efficiency at all levels) without a balanced social component would make the end-users of that civilization (i.e., human beings) unhappy. Similarly, an enormous social civilization (social ties, family ties, warmth of individuals, spiritual capital, etc.) without a balanced material component would create the same effect on its constituents: unhappiness. Professor G̦ven therefore suggests the need for a better balance between social and material components of civilizations.

He then argues that the industrialized western civilizations had developed advanced material civilizations, amassing enormous amount of wealth and with it the potential to dominate other civilizations. It would be wrong, he points out, to assume that civilizations could be rank ordered, that is, to consider one to be superior to the other. This would create accumulated civilizational disharmony, leading to a clash. To avoid this clash of civilizations, Dr. G̦ven suggests a better diagnosis of the problems at hand (e.g., impact of globalization on civilizations and cultures); a better dialogue among civilizations on an equal footing, as opposed to monologue and dictation from one to another; and especially more sharing, understanding, respect, goodwill and tolerance among civilizations.

In his second discussion, Dialogue of Civilizations: Paradigms on Economic Development and Social Advancement, Dr. G̦ven argues the need for a common language between civilizations. He believes that the establishment of a common language, common values, and common goals among countries and/or civilizations, will do away with the notion of the Otherí and create an understanding of *civilizations on equal footing* . Education,

Professor Güven argues, has a role to play in preparing the future generations for this task. As somebody who set up a new university with such a philosophy in mind, he feels confident that higher education has a valuable contribution to make in this area.

Dr. Güven suggests therefore that students be offered an inter-civilizational educational curriculum that by the time they graduate will have implanted the idea of an inter-civilizational dialogue in their minds as a crucial agenda item for common actions. It is through education that the potential leaders of the future, writes Professor Güven, can reach a level of mutual understanding whereby using a common language with the members of different civilizations, and basing their ideas and opinions on common values and, in fact, cherishing common goals become the norm.

This *inter-civilizational education* should also become instrumental in facilitating *economic development* and *social advancement* simultaneously, eventually resulting in integrated *human development*.

In his third contribution, Leadership in Education: An Intercultural Model in Progress, Dr. Güven discusses the leadership challenges involved in setting up a new university and describes his vision. The goal is to create pragmatic inter-civilizational educational models by means of which students shall graduate speaking a common language that would be instrumental in establishing an inter-civilizational dialogue between the South/East and the North/West.

Dr. Güvenís vision is to promote inter-civilizational education and produce graduates who can speak a language common to both, Eastern and Western civilizations, and who can thus efficiently work on economic development and social advancement in this part of world, and who will, he is hopeful, contribute to human development in their society and in the world at large.

I trust the thoughts and ideas contained in this book will help the reader think about the journey of leadership, a life-long journey, and about helping ourselves to help others, about doing the right thing for the benefit of all, because ultimately all leadership activities are and ought to be about human development.

Adel Safty
Istanbul, July 2002

Leadership for Human Development

Adel Safty

Introduction

Leadership is rapidly emerging as a field of study at universities and research and training centres, mainly in North America, but increasingly in Western Europe too. The field is largely dominated by a unique conception of leadership equating leadership with effective management of private sector corporations, albeit with occasional references to the political and military fields for inspirational models. Lagging far behind is a much smaller number of institutions and writers concerned with leadership as it relates to public policy and national, and occasionally, global governance. Leadership by international institutions is reflected upon only in the most peripheral way.[1] Leadership as effective corporate management is ultimately concerned with corporate profitability. Leadership in public policy and national governance is ultimately concerned with a certain definition of the national interests.

---

[1] See Adel Safty, edit. *Leadership and the United Nations*; *Leadership and Global Governance*; and *Leadership and Conflict Resolution*. Eastern Mediterranean University Press, 2000.

It is my contention that in the age of globalisation and emerging global civil society, both conceptions, though useful for their own purposes, are inadequate as a model of what may be termed international leadership in the age of globalisation.

It is my argument that because of the phenomenal growth of trans-national activities, the seemingly unstoppable drive of globalisation, the emergence of global civil society, the multiplicity of challenges- economic, political, social, and environmental- facing the international community, there is a growing need to learn from the experiences of corporate and institutional leadership models. This can help us produce a synthesis that could provide the underpinnings of a multicultural and multidimensional definition of global leadership. In addition, the growing recognition of the need for leadership to promote peace, democracy, and development within states and between states, makes it possible for us to postulate that leadership is ultimately about human development. In his/her concern for the professional and personal development of the companyís staff, in the national leaderís responsibility to serve his people, in the United Nationsí and global civil societyís efforts to promote peace and development worldwide, the effective leaders are in the final analysis those who never lose sight of the larger picture linking leadership to human development. For this to happen, leadership needs to be freed from the domination of the business model, liberalised and related to human development, and ultimately democratised to be made accessible to leaders in all fields.

Corporate Management as Leadership

Leadership conceived of as effective corporate management almost exclusively dominates the field of leadership and leadership studies.

There is no reason why the leadership skills and attitudes associated with effective management of corporations and large institutions cannot be transferable to other environments and activities. For instance, the literature on leadership as effective management describes the effective manager/leader in the following terms. Such a leader is able to think proactively, and to be a situational leader (one who is more interested in finding solutions which flow from the needs of the situations rather than from the authority of the office). Such a leader is able to strike a balance between task-orientation and people-orientation, to have a vision, to inspire commitment to work, to invest in trust, and to be an effective communicator. These are valuable leadership skills and attitudes in any institution.

Peter Drucker, arguably the leading figure in this dominant prescriptive literature on leadership as effective management, readily accepts the view that leadership skills can be transferred and made valuable in any environment and in any institution. He sums up his experiences in, and thinking about leadership activities by saying that all real leaders knew four things: The only definition of a leader is someone who has followers; popularity is not leadership, results are; leaders are visible and, therefore, they are role-models; and that leadership is not rank or title, it is responsibility. In his book, *The Leader of the Future* Drucker rightly reminds us that whether we work in private or public organizations, we will always find opportunities to learn about leadership.[2]

A successful author of leadership books and recipes, Stephen Covey is a typical representative of this school of leadership as effective management. In his book, *The Seven Habits of Highly Effective People*, he urges managers to be proactive, to manage their own lives in order to better renew their energies, and to seek to understand first in order to be better understood. He asks managers to try to focus on the positive, and on the win/win situations as a prerequisite for creating synergy in the work environment. Again, these are useful skills and attitudes in any environment.[3]

At the same time, there is an emerging sub-field of leadership that tends to focus more on public policy and public issues. The literature on leadership as it relates to public policy is relatively small, but growing. Let me briefly refer to the work of four or five professors, all American, who are active in this field: Cleveland, Gardner, Bennis, Heifetz, and Burns. Harlan Cleveland, a veteran diplomat and a distinguished professor, emphasizes the relationship between leadership and the information revolution, and argues that modern leaders should learn to become knowledge executives, able to transform information into knowledge, and knowledge into useful tools of decisions.

A veteran in the field, Howard Gardner is author of, in particular, *The Leading Mind* in which he adopts a cognitive approach to the study of leadership. In his book, Gardner

---

[2] See Peter Drucker (editor).. The Leader of the Future. Jossy-Bass Publishers, San Francisco. 1996

[3] Stephen Covey. The 7 Habits of Highly Effective People. Simon & Schuster. New York. 1989

identified common characteristics shared by the great leaders of the 20th century. These included excellent communication skills, interest in understanding other people and in expanding one's own view points by travelling outside one's homeland, and a concern for moral issues.

A former University President and a scholar of leadership, Warren Bennis has had a variety of professional experiences during which he thought about leadership. He sums up his experience as a leader of a public institution (the University of Cincinnati) and a scholar of leadership, with a conviction and a felicitously constructed conclusion. Bennis became convinced that most of the academic theory on leadership was useless. That is because theory often had little relation to the reality of the leadership challenges he faced. His conclusion is that we must distinguish between managers and leaders: "Leaders are people who do the right thing; managers are people who do things right. Both roles are crucial, but they differ profoundly. I often observe people in top positions doing the wrong thing well."[4]

I have personally benefited from the distinctive approach and views of my friend and colleague Prof. Ronald Heifetz of Harvard University. His approach to leadership has been organized around two fundamental distinctions: the first between technical challenges (which require routine solutions) and adaptive problems (which require innovative solutions); the second distinction is between leadership and authority. He argues that modern society requires adaptive leaders: That is, leaders willing to take responsibility without

---

[4] See Warren Bennis. Why Leaders Canít Lead. Jossy-Bass Publishers. San Francisco. Oxford. 1991

waiting for a vision or a request, or a bureaucratic permission.[5]

I have also learned from a scholar who may arguably be considered as the leading scholar in this sub-field of leadership in public policy: James McGregore Burns.[6] His long-standing interest in American Presidents and American democracy informs his approach to leadership challenges, which he views in terms of ability to reconcile conflicting interests. After a talk I gave to leadership scholars gathered, in late 1997, at the Library of Congress in Washington to celebrate the inauguration of the James Burns Academy of Leadership, Prof. Burns came to me and said: "O.K, this United Nations Leadership Conference you organized in Amman was interesting, but what did the participants argue about?" And by way of clarification, he added: "What was the leadership conflict?" For Burns leadership is about transactions designed to reconcile differences.

Bernard Bass viewed leadership from the perspective of social psychology. He describes Burnsís transactional political leader as one who motivates followers by exchanging with them rewards for services rendered. This is in contrast with a leadership approach, which motivates followers to work for higher goals transcending material rewards, and focussing on self-actualisation rather than self-interests. The transactional leader is engaged in economic-exchange transactions designed to meet subordinatesí material needs in return for specific performances. Bass argues that the transformational leader also recognises these

---

[5] See Ronald Heifetz. Leadership Without Easy Answers. The Belkanap Press of Harvard University Press. Boston. USA. 1995.
[6] See James MacGregor Burns. Leadership. Harper and Row. New York. 1979.

existing needs in potential followers but goes further by arousing and satisfying the higher needs (of the Maslow hierarchy of needs) of self-actualisation in the followers.[7]

Institutional Global Leadership

It may be inevitable that a leader will always be faced with the challenge of reconciling conflicting interests, whether in a private corporation, a public institution, or in global governance. Certainly, the UN throughout its history has been striving to provide leadership through reconciliation of conflicting interests. It may not have always succeeded in reconciling differences in the crucial areas of peace and security, but it certainly has rendered enormous public service in the areas of development and humanitarian assistance. The lessons to be learned from the experiences of institutional leadership will thus include two essential leadership skills: reconciling differences, and sustaining a commitment to public service.

In thinking philosophically about leadership and especially about global leadership, an argument can be made that global leadership, intellectually speaking in the sense of competing powerful intellectual paradigms, is fundamentally about the power of universal values. Much of our social and political history can be seen as the history of ideas and values competing for global acceptance and dominance: Polytheism versus monotheism; one religion versus another, political power versus religious power, revolutionary order versus established conservative order; protectionism versus free

---

[7] See Bernard Bass. Leadership and Performance Beyond Expectations. The Free Press: New York. 1985.

trade; colonialism versus self-determination; democracy versus fascism, and capitalism versus communism. Although each claimed universal relevance and appeal, few were universally accepted. Recently, some people have argued that the end of the Cold War heralded the end of history in the sense that the end of the competition between capitalism and communism has seen the triumph of liberal democracy and capitalism that are now destined to spread to the rest of the world.

In the 20th century, two organizations were founded to provide global leadership: that is to mobilize universal support behind some dominant values: The League of Nations and the United Nations. At the end of World War I, the League of Nations held the promise of global leadership based on universal values such as the value of self-determination and the principle of collective security to preserve the peace and banish war from international relations. The Leagueís mandates were supposed to be a sacred trust of civilization, a triumph of universal values over parochial values, the triumph of President Wilsonís principle of self-determination over the imperial interests and colonial designs of the imperial powers. But The League and the mandates turned out to be little different from the political balance of power system of the Congress of Vienna which restored and defended the conservative monarchical order shattered by the Napoleonic wars. The League became a congress of European powers determined to tenaciously defend colonialism against the rising tide of self-determination, and to fight communism while turning a blind eye to the danger of fascism in their own backyard. The result was a collective failure of leadership. World War II attested to the magnitude of that leadership failure.

The United Nations came into existence in1945, again with the promise of global leadership based on universally shared human values and ideals. However, the reservation clause to the statute of the International Court of Justice allowing countries to opt out of its compulsory jurisdiction, the veto power in the Security Council, and the Cold War, meant that the UN would reflect the *realpolitik* balance of power brought about by the military realities of the results of World War II.

The end of the Cold War gave rise to hopes that the UN, freed from the paralysis of ideological conflict, would be able to provide effective global leadership, especially in its core values of keeping the peace, and peaceful resolution of disputes.

The challenge of keeping the peace in the post Cold-War era has proven to be formidable. Between 1945 and 1987, the UN established 13 peacekeeping operations. Between 1988 and January 1995, it has had to establish another twenty-one. The end of the Cold War era was followed by a period of intense ethnic conflicts, border disputes and disintegration of states. This resulted in a massive increase in the number of displaced persons (those of concern to the UNHCR have gone from 17 million in 1991, to 23 million in 1993, and to more than 27 million in 1995, with a growing number of states increasingly obstructing the arrival of asylum seekers and returning refugees to their country of origin).

Realizing that the end of the Cold War created unique opportunities for institutional global leadership, former UN secretary general Boutros Boutros-Ghali strove to strengthen the international organization by asserting its leadership responsibilities. For instance, he emphasized the very useful role of preventive diplomacy, and introduced the concept of peace-building. Resolving a military conflict, he said, is only the first step. Peace building goes beyond the cessation of hostilities and addresses the underlying root causes of the conflict. To build peace, leadership efforts should be directed at improving educational and economic opportunities, building the infrastructures of good governance, and helping to empower the less privileged elements in the society. In other words, building peace requires leadership commitment to human development.

Boutros-Ghaliís Agendas (Agenda for Peace (92), Agenda for Development (94), and Agenda for Democratisation (96)) must figure among his many leadership achievements as UN Secretary General. He maintained that peace, development, and democracy are inextricably linked. At the 1998 United Nations Leadership Conference I organized in Amman, Jordan, he reminded us that peace is a prerequisite for development; that democracy is essential for development to succeed over the long term. He argued that democracy was needed not only inside a state but also among states in the international community.[8]

In June 1997, the UN General Assembly adopted the Agenda for Development. UN Secretary General Kofi Annan hailed the achievement as "one of the most far-reaching agreements on the central issue of development ever attained by the international community." This is because the agenda went beyond the usual areas of economic growth and poverty eradication, and covered such fundamental issues to development as human rights, good governance, and the

---

[8] See Boutros Boutros-Ghali. Agenda for Peace. The United Nations. New York. 1992; and Agenda for Development. The United Nations. New York. 1994; and Agenda for Democratisation. The United Nations. New York. 1996.

empowerment of women. "The Agenda" said Mr. Annan, "represents a major step in articulating an international consensus on the diversity of views concerning the fundamental goals of and requirements for economic and social development."[9]

These are praiseworthy contributions to global leadership. At the same time, we must recognize that the ability of the UN to provide global leadership is necessarily restricted. That is because while the demands and expectations on the UN and its overstretched resources have increased tremendously, the UN is still able to do only what its members, and especially its permanent Security Council members, will allow it to do. The inability of all 14 members of the Security Council to renew, in December 1996, the mandate for then secretary general Boutros Boutros-Ghali against the opposition of the US is a reminder of that reality.

The UN Conferences on Leadership

The growing interest in leadership and leadership activities in all fields was evidenced from the overwhelming response we received for participation at the United Nations International Leadership Conferences, which I convened and over which I presided in 1997 and in 1998 in Amman, Jordan. Further, the commitment in time to, and in active participation in the leadership conferences by distinguished and emerging leaders from all over the world, demonstrated the consensus shared by all who came to the conferences that leadership in public policy was of immediate and meaningful relevance to our lives.

---

[9] See Kofi Annan. The United Nations. The Agenda for Development. Department of Public Information. New York. 1997.

At the United Nations International Leadership conferences in 1997 and in 1998, I invited some distinguished leaders from around the world to interact directly with emerging leaders from over 100 countries and to share thoughts and experiences about leadership and leadership activities. At the risk of oversimplification, I wish to share one or two thoughts, which may characterize the leadership views and or the attitude of some of these distinguished leaders. The late King Hussein of Jordan argued that leadership was about building rapports with followers. Queen Noor of Jordan believed that leadership meant active involvement for social justice. Prince Hassan bin Tallal said that political leadership in the final analysis must be concerned with human welfare and human security. Jordanian Prime Minister Abdel Salam Majali pointed out that leadership in any field is the art and the ability to see the larger picture and separate it from details. Israeli leader Shimon Peres argued that leadership meant among other things, having the courage to change your previously held convictions. Then Egyptian Foreign Minister Amre Moussa (currently Secretary-General of the Arab League) pointed out that leadership in the new international environment must include the ability to adapt to oneís environment. President Yasser Arafat thought, appropriately enough, that leadership was first and foremost about perseverance. In an elegant expose of his enormous erudition, Pakistani former Minister of Foreign Affairs Sahabzada Yaqub Khan gently reminded his audience that leadership was a continuing quest for multidisciplinary knowledge and wisdom for better decision-making.

Former President of the European Parliament and French Minister Simone Veil cited the leadership roles of Jean Monet and Maurice Schumann in the history of the European Economic Community to conclude that leadership in the modern age must be about coalition building. Former Kennedy Administration Assistant-Secretary of State Harlan Cleveland, a leadership scholar in his own right, analysed some of the implications of the information and communication revolution to conclude that modern leaders must be knowledge executives. That is, they must have the ability to transform information into useful knowledge, and knowledge into wisdom. US congressman Paul Findley, famous for his account of American leaders who defied the Zionist lobby in his best-selling book *They Dare to Speak*, pointed out that leadership was about the courage of standing behind your personal convictions. US Congressman Paul McClosekey, famous for being the first Republican to challenge the presidency of Richard Nixon in 1972 and to call for his resignation, also believed that leadership meant having a passion for your own convictions. President Andrea Pastrana of Colombia, preparing for the election in his civil-war torn country, suggested that political leadership, nationally and internationally, means the ability to build partnerships for peace and development. Chinese Minister HUI Hongzengh suggested that leadership in the new era was about having an open mind and a vision for the future. Former Minister of Defence in the Thatcher government Lord Gilmour suggested that critical thinking was a crucial intellectual tool for effective leadership in any field.

Former UK labour Minister of Development Lord Judd argued that leadership was about how to advance human development in every field. President of the Liberal International Lord Steel thought that hard work, and initiative and risk taking were crucial features of any effective leadership. Indian UN ambassador Arundhati Ghose pointed out that leadership required courage to defend oneís convictions. Former Norwegian Secretary of State Jan Egeland recalled his experience in facilitating the Oslo meetings that led to the mutual recognition and the Oslo Accords between Palestinians and Israelis in 1993, and argued that the effective leader is a facilitator and organiser of opportunities for peace. President Oscar Arias of Costa Rica made a strong case for leadership as a responsibility for educating people and followers. Mrs. Harriet Fulbright gently explained how the arts and humanities served to humanise leadership activities and sensitise leaders to our commonalities. For Dr. Boutros Boutros Ghali, former UN Secretary General, global leadership requires linking peace, democracy, and development.

Many of our emerging leaders repeatedly asked our distinguished leaders if they could describe how they became leaders. Almost without exception, none was able to do so. Real leaders do not set out to become leaders by following a prescription. But they do become leaders through learning, application of lessons learned, hard work, and a combination of other factors. The most common characteristic of the responses of our distinguished leaders was that they did not know how they became leaders, but that they knew that they had always been open to learning, and that they had always been committed to hard work.

To these crucial factors, former President Mikhail Gorbachev, whom I brought to Amman, Jordan, in April 1998, for a series of roundtable discussions on the topics of The Responsibilities of the Intellectual and on Leadership Challenges in the post Cold-War Era, added two important leadership traits. These were the ability to learn from one's failures -and many people pointed out to Mr. Gorbachev what they thought was his own failure to keep the communist block together- and the importance of positive thinking. The latter is crucial not only for the leaders' ability to understand and effectively learn from failures, but also for their ability to motivate the people around them.

The desire to find a commonly accepted definition of leadership proved to be another recurrent preoccupation for many of our emerging leaders. Many of the distinguished leaders often hesitated to offer the participants a clear definition of leadership. This is not surprising. First, because there are as many definitions of leadership as there are leadership activities, as is clear from what these political leaders had to say about their conceptions of leadership. Second, leadership may involve making controversial decisions and hard choices, which are not reducible to theoretical definitions. The late Egyptian President Anwar Sadat and former President Mikhail Gorbachev are cogent examples of leaders whose perceptions of leadership, vision, and hard choices were viewed by some as evidence of leadership at its best, by others as proof of failed leadership[10]. Third, most of our distinguished speakers were leaders who were much more preoccupied with the activity of leadership than with theoretical reflections about leadership. They spend more time actively pursuing leadership goals than wondering about an appropriate theoretical definition for leadership.

Globalisation and Leadership

If leadership as management dominates the field of leadership, the global field of ideas, notwithstanding the UNís valiant efforts, is dominated by the idea of

---

[10] See Adel Safty. From Camp David to the Gulf. Black Rose Books. Montreal and New York. 1993 and 1997.

globalisation - a logical global expression of the leadership as management idea. Perhaps there is no better illustration of this than the annual gathering of CEOs and political leaders at the World Economic Forum at Davos, Switzerland.

Although globalisation may mean different things to different people, its most commonly conjured-up meaning is that of the globalisation of trade, finance, and investment opportunities for and by multinational corporations.

However, whatever its other merits, globalisation cannot lay claim to global leadership based on universally-shared human ideals. It is axiomatic that the effective management of a corporation is first and foremost measured by the economic interests of the corporation. If and when there are other economic and social benefits to the society at large, they come as a by-product, not as the principal goal of effective corporate management.

For instance, the economic benefits of globalisation, if measured by direct foreign investments, have gone largely to East Asia (70%, with China alone accounting for 40%), while Africa, suffering already from falling official development assistance, is receiving only 4% of direct foreign investments. One would be hard pressed to find unconditional supporters of globalisation in Africa.

At the same time, according to the latest UNDP Poverty Report 2000, rich countries continue to protect their farmers, for example, while developing countries are being asked to open up their own agricultural sectors a measure that threatens to undermine their food security and spread povertyÖ If trade expansion is to benefit the poor, the international rules of the game must be made fairer. A high priority is to eliminate the protectionism that is biased against developing countries. [11]

Ignacio Ramonet reminded us in the November 1998 issue of *Le Monde Diplomatique* of some UN statistics which rarely come up when the benefits of globalisation are being enumerated. For instance, in 1960, the income of the 20 % of the world's population living in the richest countries was 30 times greater than that of the 20 % in the poorest countries. In, 1995 it was 82 times greater. In over 70 countries, per capita income is lower today than it was 20 years ago. Almost half of the world population live on less than two dollars a day. Almost a third of the 4 billion people living in the developing countries have no drinking water. Every year, almost thirty million people die of hunger. This, at a time when the total wealth of the world's three richest individuals is greater than the combined gross domestic product of the 48 poorest countries. [12]

According to UN calculations, the basic needs for food, drinking water, education and medical care for the entire population of the whole world could be covered by a levy of less than 4 % on the accumulated wealth of the 225 largest fortunes. To meet world's sanitation and food requirements would cost only $13 billion, less than what the people of the United States and the European Union spend every year on personal perfume.

According to the UNDP Poverty Report 2000, based on commitments made at the 1995 World Summit for Social Development, developing countries are being encouraged to launch full-scale campaigns against poverty. Yet despite

---

[11] See The UNDP Poverty Report 2000. Overcoming Poverty. P. 10
[12] See Le Monde Diplomatique. November, 1998.

having net ambitious global targets for poverty reduction, donor countries are cutting back on aid and failing to focus what remains on poverty. [13]

Globalisation did not cause this dismal state of affairs; but it created the environment in which failure of national leadership was exacerbated by the absence of democracy and by market-driven social Darwinism. This is both a failure of institutional leadership at the global level and a failure of national leadership. A failure to understand that leadership is ultimately connected to human development. As the UNDP Poverty Report 2000 put it, effective governance is often the missing link , we might add, between leadership and human development.

A Certain Conception of Global Leadership

There is a real need for a new conception of leadership, one that transcends the limitations of the separate fields of leadership studies and leadership models, while encompassing and reflecting their commonality.

Such a conception must first of all be multicultural and multidimensional to reflect the cultural diversities of our world, notwithstanding the homogenizing effects of globalisation, and to reflect the lessons learned from the experiences of the different leadership fields. There is no reason why leadership studies, still confined to North America and Western Europe, should continue to reflect only Western cultures and Western managerial and public policy

---

[13] See Overcoming Human Poverty. UNDP Poverty Report 2000. UNDP. New York. p.8.

experiences. There is no reason why corporate managers as leaders should only have a peripheral knowledge of the world of governance and public policy leadership, or conversely that public policy leaders should remain indifferent to the lessons of leadership as effective management of corporations and institutions.

Such a new conception must also take into account the growing international consensus on the relationship between democratic governance and human development, on the one hand, and between effective management, in the public as well as in the private sectors, and human productivity in all fields, on the other hand. Finally, the new conception of leadership must take account of the fact that in the age of globalisation, trade and political regional associations, alliance-formation and multilateral cooperation have become a necessary leadership challenge.

Thus, the new multicultural and multidimensional conception of leadership would be one that is related to good governance, good management, and multilateral cooperation. Whether it is at the local, national, regional, or international level, whether it is in the political arena, in the market place, in civil society institutions, in the academy, in the public or private sector, we need leaders motivated by moral convictions, and sustained by commitment to human development. Leadership will thus have been democratised.

Political Governance and Human Development

It was the United Nations Development Programme that first systematically promoted a relationship between democratic governance and human development. The United Nations

Development Programme, originally created in 1965 as a funding agency, became by 1990 more of a development agency with specific development priorities. These included: (1) poverty alleviation; (2) environmental sustainability; (3) management development; (4) women in development; (5) technical co-operation among developing countries; and (6) private sector development.

As this shift of focus was taking place, a new understanding of development was emerging. The UNDP first Human Development Report, in 1990, suggested that human development was more than economic growth and increase in personal income. Any measurement of human development, the report said, must also include such indicators as income distribution, levels of education, life expectancy, access to clean water and sanitation, access to medical services, and population growth. The report also stated that despite the resources that had been directed to developing countries, the most vulnerable groups in these countries were still unable to satisfy their basic human needs.

The 1991 UNDP Human Development Report openly attributed this failure to the lack of political commitment, not of financial resources. In 1992, the UNDP was formally using the term governance and good governance to describe the actions and environment required for turning economic growth into sustainable human development.

In a 1994 document entitled Initiatives for Change, the UNDP stated that "the goal of governance initiatives should be to develop capacities that are needed to realise development that gives priority to the poor, advances women, sustains the environment, and creates needed opportunities for employment and other livelihoods."

In January 1997, the UNDP published a policy document entitled Governance for Sustainable Human Development, in which it stated that sustainable human development and governance are indivisible. It also made a commitment to supporting national efforts for good governance for sustainable human development.

The policy document defined governance as the exercise of economic, political, and administrative authority to manage a countryís affairs, and the means by which states ensure and promote the well being of their populations. An environment of good governance is one in which there is broad public participation in decision-making, especially with respect to the allocation of development resources and the protection of the poorest and most vulnerable groups in the society. An environment of good governance is also one that promotes the rule of law and the accountability of institutions and officials.

Technical assistance to strengthen democratic governing institutions is driven by the conviction, contained in the final Declaration of the World Social Summit, that "democracy and transparent and accountable governance and administration in all sectors of society are indispensable foundations for the realisation of social and people-centred sustainable development."

The 1999 Human Development Report reiterates the relationship between good governance and democratic institutions and practices. It points out that good governance stems from a humane organisation of society in which the ultimate power over decision-making lies with the people through participation and devolution. In short, that there is a relationship between democratic governance and human development.

Leadership as Agent for Human Development

There is thus general agreement that democratic governance is the most effective way for promoting human development and welfare. It is my contention that democratic governance is not the monopoly, nor the privilege of any single culture. Democratic governance understood as diffusing the sources of power, encouraging accountability, promoting collective and individual freedoms, and building human capacity, requires leadership.

But, why the growing preoccupation with leadership in the first place? Because, as Jordanian Prime Minister Abdel Salam Majali argued at the United Nations Leadership Conference in 1997, in a world of emerging global civil society, the world needed leaders committed to bringing peoples and cultures together. In its 1995 report entitled *Our Global Neighbourhood* The Commission on Global Governance had said the same thing: "The world needs leaders made strong by vision, sustained by ethics, and revealed by political courage."[14]

In short, leadership is needed to bring about change and reform, and to articulate and mobilise support for the interconnectedness of democratic governance and human development.

Leadership is the sine qua non agent of change and empowerment necessary to bring about the emergence and consolidation of democracy in the new democracies and the democratising countries. It is also the sine qua non agent of

---

[14] See The Commission on Global Governance. Our Global Neighbourhood. Oxford University Press.UK. 1995.

restraint and protection against the excess of democracy in the established liberal democracies.

We know that philosophers and democratic leaders agree on the importance of education and participation. Madison insisted that only participation in the political process could preserve and enhance individual liberties. Mill maintained that education and participation were essential for representative governments to succeed. Jefferson showed a similar inclination.

The 1999 Human Development Report: South Asia points out that whatever the specific characteristics of a countryís change strategy, success in advancing policy and institutional reforms toward humane governance and securing human development ultimately depends on leadershipÖleadership for humane governance is leadership with a clear and long-term vision.

The Commission on Global Governance concluded its study by stating: As the world faces the need for enlightened responses to the challenges that arise on the eve of the new century, we are concerned at the lack of leadership over a wide spectrum of human affairs. At national, regional, and international levels, within communities and in international organisations, in governments and in non- governmental bodies, the world needs credible and sustained leadership.

The UNDP has learned from its experience that in all its five focus areas of governance, that the most effective approach to increasing human development through good governance lies in an integrated approach that addresses leadership development, skills training, and organizational structures.

An Opportunity for Leadership Initiatives

The strong consensus on the need for leadership at all levels in the society, the paucity of any coherent approach to leadership in public affairs, and the crucial need for multilateral co-operation, especially among the countries of the South, have converged to present unique opportunities for leadership initiatives and leadership training.

I have suggested at the UN Leadership Conferences in 1997 and 1998, and elsewhere, the urgent need for leadership training centres, institutes, and leadership training programmes. I have also suggested that the international community needed to convene an annual forum to be called the global leadership forum to which emerging leaders from around the world and from all walks of life would meet for a series of interactive seminars focussing on leadership development. The forum would be divided in three series of seminars on leadership as good governance, leadership as good management, and leadership in fostering multilateral co-operation. The forum would be under the general theme of leadership for human development, cast within a context of dialogue of civilisations.

Such a forum would provide the participants with opportunities to learn from distinguished leaders from public and private sectors, scholars, and from each other. The learning would focus on leadership as good governance with specific emphasis on democracy, peaceful resolution of disputes, human rights, civil society, and human development. Leadership as good management seminars will place the emphasis on learning from the experiences of successful administrators of public and private enterprises, and should focus on such areas as self-knowledge, assessment, values and vision, situational leadership challenges, negotiations, and communication. The third component of the global leadership forum should be devoted to developing skills and techniques for networking, pooling material and human resources, use of technology, collective problem solving, and fostering multilateral co-operation between countries of the South.

The leadership task at the new leadership training programs and institutes is to provide interactive learning opportunities about leadership skills and attitudes and to help construct a new discourse and intellectual leadership capital: a leadership discourse anchored in democracy, peace, and development- one that promotes the globalisation of common human concerns and the imperative of human security. Such a leadership should help bring about a rapprochement, not a clash, of civilizations, facilitate the trans-border movement, not only of goods, but also of people and ideas, sensitise future leaders to the imperative, not only of conflict resolution, but also of reconciliation and peace-building.

The UNDP in New York, for which I worked, has taken up the challenge of setting up their Leadership Development Program in the early part of 2001. They should be congratulated. Similarly, Dr. Halil G,ven and Mr. Enver Y,cel, respectively, the president and Chairman of the Board of Trustees of Bah esehir university in Istanbul, Turkey, should be congratulated for taking up the challenge of leadership. Their university now house the International Institute of Leadership and Public Affairs, the first of its kind in Europe, devoted to leadership education and leadership training in the areas of good governance, good management, and multilateral cooperation for human development in a context of dialogue of civilisations. The efforts and the initiatives of such people, such leaders, are helping bring about a paradigm change in how we all think about leadership. Their efforts and initiative should be supported and emulated.

In the final analysis, such a global conception of leadership for human development will be enriched by the various experiences of the past. We can draw on what has been learned by our institutional experience, namely that it is crucial for any global leadership to be based on truly universal human values. We can draw on the lessons of leadership as corporate management, namely that any effective leadership must be based on a proactive approach to problem solving, and driven by an ability to communicate, inspire, and empower. We can also draw on the lessons learned from leadership as politics and governance, namely that there can be no effective leadership unless it strongly represents the aspirations of the people. This completes and illustrates the link between leadership, democratic governance, and human development.

The September 11 events are not about how the world became globalized or interconnected. It had been so for quite some time. They are about how America lost its invulnerability. The lessons would be lost if we delude ourselves into believing that a stricter projection of military power would solve problems that have to do with moral issues. American foreign policy is right to insist on respect for human rights and high moral standards around the world. But it is wrong to apply double standards, especially in the case of Palestine. Double standards diminish the moral authority of American leadership. And no amount of power, however afar and intensely projected, can repair that damage.

September 11 and the loss of American invulnerability ultimately and poignantly pose a leadership challenge to American policy makers. Can they cast their gaze beyond political expediency and rise to the higher call of moral leadership? Or will we soon return to business as usual?

Finally, at the Forty-Six Session of the International Conference on Education organised by the UNESCO in Geneva, in September 2001, the Congress pointed out that the economic empires that control markets, including that o f information, are widening the breach between the countries of the North and the South, promoting the brain drain and sometimes hastening a decline in the quality of education through the agency of global financial institutions. These are not the models that we wish to emulate. The participants engaged in frank discussions about the relationship between citizenship education, democratic government and sustainable development. The participants called for more profound exploration of the following questions: What is the definition of citizenship education? How can it be implemented? In addition, how can we meet the challenge of an open civic education at the local, regional, and global levels?

This makes the relationship of power and morality an indispensable element of any leadership paradigm. It also illustrates the crucial role that education has and must play in the mental and social development of the future leaders of tomorrow. Leadership, in whatever field, must, then, ultimately be about human development.

Leadership for Peace and Dialogue

Oscar Arias

Dr. Oscar Arias is a former President of Costa Rica and Nobel Peace Laureate

All we have to do is pick up a newspaper or look at the television news to see how desperately the world today needs leadership for dialogue, negotiation, and peace. The ongoing conflicts in Israel/Palestine, Chechnya, Congo, Colombia, and Sudan pose tremendous challenges to leaders in those countries and around the world. The residents of these war zones are traumatized and exhausted, attending funeral after funeral, sinking ever deeper into hopelessness and helplessness. Well-meaning onlookers from around the world sympathize with those suffering, but have no idea how to help. In some cases, leaders are hard at work, desperately trying to stem the tide of violence and restore calm. In other cases, no leadership has yet emerged.

Leadership in these times is fraught with risks and difficulties, and yet I also believe that there is reason to hope. Twenty years ago, Central America was mired in a morass of conflict, and few believed that an end was in sight. During the seventies and eighties, the stark inequalities that prevailed in the region exploded into a series of bloody wars that claimed the lives of more than two hundred thousand people. Teachers, labour organizers, priests, and human rights workers became targets of repression. We lost a generation of students. As Ezra Pound wrote in the wake of another terrible conflict, There died a myriad, and of the best among them.

When I became President of Costa Rica in 1986, I was determined to give voice to the millions of Central Americans who knew that, somehow, the killing had to end, and that it was up to us to act. All around there was a steady chorus of voices saying that peace would be impossible. And yet our people persevered in demanding a peace with justice. Indeed, it was this popular resolve that allowed me to bring the Central American presidents to the negotiating table.

Perhaps we were just lucky in the end. But we, the children of Cervantes, Neruda, and Garc a Marquez followed our passion and fantasy. We lowered our lance, charged every windmill in sight and after a long, hard struggle, the guns were silent.

The change is deep. Ballots have replaced bullets. Government agencies commit themselves to human rights. Murder and torture are no longer leading causes of death. Our young people study agriculture, engineering, medicine, and law, rather than infantry tactics, sabotage techniques, and fields of fire. We are no longer exiles in our own hearts and homes.

Today, we do not live in a paradise in Central America, but we do not suffer the utter devastation of only a few years ago. Panama, for decades a military dictatorship, now has a democratic government and has joined Costa Rica in constitutionally abolishing its armed forces. El Salvador has worked to purge its army of human rights violators, built a civilian police force, and created a political system in which former guerrilla leaders are now leaders in the National Assembly. Nicaragua has emerged from the horrors of its civil war, and the process of reconstruction is underway. And Guatemala is now building a new political system, and is beginning to reckon with the long-repressed memory of genocide. A recent conviction of political assassins in that country has opened the way for an end to impunity for the horrible crimes of war.

I do not profess to have any magical solutions for all the challenges to diversity and community that we now face. But my experience tells me that we must persevere in non-violence despite the difficulties. Throughout the world, people are calling out for peace and justice. I believe that these voices can prevail. A commitment to diplomacy and reconciliation in the face of conflict and tension is a first step in establishing the peaceful world we all long for.

Given a commitment to work at resolving conflicts peacefully, what kind of leadership is needed to be successful in this extremely challenging arena? Yesterdayís topic was leadership and values, and I must say that it is a topic, which I believe will continue to come up throughout the days of this conference. For in my view, values are a part of the fundamental core of leadership, and touch on every context in which leadership is exercised, including situations of conflict. In fact, it is in times of tension and discord that a leaderís values are most strongly put to the test.

I would like to mention five qualities I believe to be necessary for successful leadership in conflict resolution situations. They are patience, perseverance, humility, commitment, and compromise. For some people, these qualities are inherent in their personalities, and from an early age they function as mediators in disputes between friends or family members. For others, these qualities are not instinctive, but must be cultivated. We should not be ashamed to recognize our shortfalls in these areas and work to overcome them. For who among us has not at times been impatient, quick to give up on something, prone to overvalue our own importance, forgetful of a past agreement, or unwilling to give an inch? Shakespeare wrote that some are born great, some achieve greatness, and some have greatness thrust upon them. I suspect, though, that anyone who finds himself in a position of leadership will acknowledge a combination of these three circumstances. As leaders we must use what we were born with, work to achieve more, and deal with the circumstances, which are, at times, thrust upon us.

Why these particular five attributes? Let us take a look at them one by one. Patience is the first quality on the list, and is absolutely essential to successful conflict resolution. By the time most conflicts reach the negotiating table, they have already been going on for some time, and may even be so deeply entrenched that people have a hard time remembering why they began in the first place. If a confrontation has been building for years, decades, or even centuries in some cases, it is simply not possible to put it to rest in a day, a week, or a fortnight. Patience is vital to keeping hope alive, and it is only with hope that peace can be achieved.

But patience does not imply simply waiting for something to happen. To patience we must add perseverance, the active pursuit of what we are patiently hoping for. Perseverance implies the willingness to return to the negotiating table again and again and again, until a final agreement can be arrived at that is acceptable to all. Perseverance also includes flexibility. The most common saying in English to illustrate the value of perseverance is, If at first you donít succeed, try, try again. I would add, however, that if your first attempt did not succeed, instead of trying the same thing again, ·it would be prudent to search for a different alternative. Do not be like the fly that, seeing the sunlight through a closed window, crashes into the window again and again in a futile attempt to get out, never seeing the open door just a few centimetres away. To find workable solutions to difficult conflicts, persevere with flexibility.

Humility is also a vital quality for anyone looking for a just solution to a conflict. It is a virtue, which comes more naturally to some of us than others, but in situations of tension and disagreement, humility often tends to disappear altogether, as all parties feel the need to justify their positions. To be sure, we must speak our point of view clearly and not allow ourselves to be intimidated. However, we must never step over the line and attempt to intimidate others by inflating ourselves. Cultivating humility helps us to recognize when that line is being crossed. Humility, without sacrificing self-respect, respects the points of view of others. Conflict resolution cannot happen without it.

Commitment is the fourth necessary quality. We have all known of peace agreements that failed because one or more of the parties signed and promptly violated their commitment to the agreement. And here I would insert a caution regarding, once again, humility. For when we attempt to use our power to impose an agreement on an unwilling party, when we forget about humility and resort instead to intimidation, then the signature we get from the other party is not likely to be accompanied by a strong degree of commitment. At the same time, each of us must be responsible for making commitments in good faith, and adhering to the commitments we do make.

The fifth necessary quality for participants in successful negotiations is willingness to compromise. Given that conflict resolution is always between two or more parties with at least some opposing views, it is perhaps obvious that compromise will be necessary to solve the conflict. Despite the obvious need to compromise, however, we repeatedly witness parties going into negotiations determined to give up nothing, and to get everything they demand. Obviously, if both or all parties behave this way, there will be no solution. But even if one side is willing to compromise and the other is not, any solution agreed will not be a real resolution of the conflict, but only the imposition of the will of the more stubborn party. This type of agreement seldom holds, as the party, who has compromised in good faith, while the other has not, will leave the negotiations feeling bullied and taken advantage of. These resentments grow and eventually rekindle the conflict.

For all parties to a conflict to be willing and able to compromise, it will be necessary to trust. Building trust is perhaps the most difficult but also most essential job of the peacemaker. Our peace process in Central America faced dogged opposition from the Reagan administration in Washington, who tried to convince all the other Central American leaders that the government of Nicaragua could not be trusted to keep the agreement it had signed. Of course, we all know that the U.S. during those Cold War years had its own agenda and interest in maintaining support for the armed Contra rebels in Nicaragua at that time. And so, in the face of an agreement that, among other things, stipulated an end to outside intervention in the Central American conflicts, the government of the United States resorted to sowing the seeds of distrust in order to retain their position in our region. In the end, Mr. Reagan was wrong. The Sandinista government did hold democratic elections, and did abide by the results, even though they lost. Despite strong pressure and great obstacles, our efforts at negotiating with each other in good faith, and trusting even when it wasnít easy, were rewarded by the establishment of a real peace based on democracy. And although there are still problems, I believe we can say that democracy in Central America is irreversible now.

I have been speaking about conflict resolution in the context of wars and armed confrontations. However, the skills and attributes I have been talking about are just as necessary in the more mundane worlds of everyday politics, business, and organizational life. For conflict is a natural part of life in all spheres, and if handled well, it can be quite healthy. We all know that a sign of a strong democracy is the freedom people have to disagree with each other, and especially to disagree with the State. Political parties with differing views on how to meet the challenges of the day, or even on what the main challenges are, are as vital to democracy as food and water are to human survival. But what happens when such disagreements and differences of opinion turn into political standoffs and strong-arming?

I believe that many of todayís well-established democracies are in trouble because they lack leadership for the resolution of conflicts. People lose confidence in their governments when they see legislators, month after month, accomplishing nothing for the country because they are so entrenched in their political positions that they refuse to collaborate or compromise. A few years ago, the government of the United States of America, the most prominent democracy in the world, was actually shut down because legislators could not or would not come to an agreement over the budget for that fiscal year. I mention this example only because it is probably the most well known. I am sure that each of you can think of others, in your own or neighbouring countries. In my own country, Costa Rica, a democracy for more than one hundred years, the important position of Ombudsman recently went vacant for nearly three months while legislators politicised the selection of someone who is supposed to be a non-political defender of all the Costa Rican people.

Patience, perseverance, humility, commitment, and compromise. Wouldnít we all like these qualities to be more prominent in our elected representatives? For these qualities are not only personal virtues, but also necessary job qualifications. They are what allow progress to be made in the face of ordinary, everyday conflict and disagreement. To those of you who aspire to a political future, or who are already in positions of public service, my advice is to do everything you can to cultivate and defend these values, in yourselves especially, and through your example, in your colleagues also.

The same can obviously be said for those whose leadership will be in the areas of business, education, civil society, or any other field. In any of lifeís endeavours, very little is ever achieved by digging in your heels and clinging to a single point of view or way of doing things. I am not, on the other hand, advocating floating on the wind and going along with whatever is popular at the moment. As leaders we certainly must stand for something, and must hold firm to our principles. But when our way of acting on our principles clashes with someone elseís way of acting on theirs, let us remain calm and open, and negotiate a just middle ground. To return to the example of armed conflict, both sides in any given war may claim to be fighting for principles, but these principles mean very little to the families who lose their loved ones in violence that seems senseless. In light of the fact that civilians make up 90% of the casualties of todayís conflicts, how can the principles of armies, rebels, or paramilitaries justify such obscene destruction? I can assure you that the vast majority of the people in any of the conflict zones I mentioned earlier would rather have compromise and negotiation to end the violence, than continued bloodshed in defence of someoneís principles.

If youíll indulge me for a few minutes more, Iíd like to take a look at some current events on the world political scene in light of the necessary qualities for effective leadership in the resolution of conflicts. Unfortunately, when we read or watch the news the type of leadership that most often stands out is that which embodies the opposite of peaceful conflict resolution. In Myanmar, we see a military junta, which for eleven years has refused to recognize the democratically elected government, and instead hold its leaders under house arrest. One of those leaders, Aung San Suu Kyi, has repeatedly called for dialogue with the military and a peaceful and non-violent transition to democracy. So far, her pleas have not been heeded, and the people of Myanmar continue to suffer distressing levels of poverty while military officials live a life of luxury and repress the basic freedoms of their people.

In Afghanistan, we know that the ruling Taliban wants nothing to do with dialogue or compromise. Instead, they base the oppression of women and the labelling of religious minorities on a fundamental interpretation of Islam that is rejected by nearly all of the other Islamic countries. It is important in this situation that we not demonise Islam itself, for we know that Hitler committed many atrocities in the name of his own version of Christianity, and we have seen Hindu nationalists in India inflame crowds by disparaging the Muslim and Christian minorities in that country. The common denominator among these leaders is not their religiosity, but rather their desire to exert absolute control and their willingness to use violence to achieve their means. If we want a world at peace, we cannot allow ourselves to fall prey to extremism of any sort. We should begin by examining our own hearts and minds and eradicating the seeds of exclusion, intolerance, and violence that exist within each one of us. We must weed our internal gardens to make room for the healthy plants of respect, compassion, integrity, and trustworthiness. With these qualities, we will be able to provide capable leadership in the most difficult of situations.

Leadership, which refuses to compromise, is not limited to Asia and the Middle East. The American continent also has its share of stubbornness and intransigence on the part of some of its leaders. One example is the determination of the United States government to build a National Missile Defence system, in direct violation of the 1972 Antiballistic Missile Treaty with Russia. President Bush and his advisors have been travelling the world in attempts to win over governments who object to the plan, and yet this really seems to be more of a song-and-dance than a real attempt at dialogue. For all along, the message has been, We will consult with our allies, but we are going to go ahead and do what we want to do, no matter what. It is widely acknowledged that the implementation of an NMD system would lead to increased arms build-up in China, Russia, South Asia and potentially the Middle East, and that it would actually decrease rather than increase global security. For now, the hopes of leaders around the world are pinned on the fact that the system is still years away from functionality and therefore implementation. But technical failures are a very poor basis for a sense of safety. Rather, safety and global security ought to be born of dialogue, diplomacy, and cooperation. Until the Bush team recognizes that the U.S. is just one of one hundred eighty-nine world governments, the other one hundred eighty-eight have good reason to be apprehensive.

We could list many more examples of dangerous and frightening leadership in the world, but I believe you get my point. And let me add that not all the news is bad. We also bear witness today to many governments whose leaders do work tirelessly to reach fair compromises among opposing parties. The creation of the European Union and its ongoing struggles to integrate while preserving national cultures and law is a fascinating example that one could devote years to studying. After many months of horrendous violence, negotiations are again showing some promise in the conflict between Israelis and Palestinians. There is much to be done there still, but it seems that there may be reason to hope. We also see peace negotiations happening now in earnest in the Democratic Republic of Congo, whose conflict had sucked in the armies of six different countries along with various rebel groups. For all the intransigence and violence that we see in the world, we are also beginning to hear the voices of a new leadership, one that values peace over war, and dialogue over intimidation. You are members of this generation, and it will be your responsibility to uphold the values of genuine leadership in future times of crisis.

My friends, you may or may not have an opportunity in your life to be involved in high-level negotiations to end entrenched armed conflict, but each and every one of us will have many opportunities to act as peacemakers in our daily lives. Let us enter into every human interaction bearing the standard of leadership for peace and dialogue, and in this way, we shall each be contributing to a world with more friendliness, more solidarity, and more hope. And if we all do this, perhaps one day, high-level negotiations, along with the conflicts that require them, will be a thing of the past.

Ripeness in the Resolution of International Conflicts And the Significance of Leadership

Erg,n Olgun

Mr. Erg,n Olgun is Under-Secretary to the President of the TRNC

Negotiation

The only peaceful means of resolving international conflicts is through negotiation. Negotiation involves give and take in order to enable conflicting parties to achieve a satisfactory outcome. Negotiation happens in situations where the negotiating parties have some interests that are shared and some that are opposed.

Negotiators use powerí as the means to influence or induce others to achieve their goals. The main source of power in our day are information and expertise, the ability to develop arguments that will influence others, control over resources, the capacity to influence international public opinion, the capacity to build alliance, domestic solidarity and morale, effective lobbying, legitimacy, and the ability to develop a BATNA (Best Next Alternative To a Negotiated Agreement).

Because of its complexity and interdisciplinary character negotiation requires teamwork. The composition of teams depends n the specific topics under discussion. All teams naturally include a leader and usually a lawyer and an economist.

Ripeness

One of the topics that is occupying negotiator and conflict resolution experts most is the point of transformation in the process of resolution where the parties to conflict simultaneously move from positional zero-sum approaches to the win-win problem solving approach.

Professor Joseph Montville has conceptualised this as the point of ripeness for resolutioní. Others have tried to understand the forces behind transformation. On the basis of his extensive research and experience Professor William Zartman has concluded that the point of transformation comes when there is a mutually hurting stalemate, where all the involved parties are equally and simultaneously hurt from the existing status quo. His argument is that so long as one of the parties is relatively less hurt, then that party will prefer to continue with zero-sum approaches with the expectation that the other side will eventually be forced to lower its demands.

I prefer to explain transformation as the point of powerlessnessí where no party is any more capable of hurting the other without significantly hurting his or her own interests. It is at this point that conflicting parties are likely to realize the mess they are in, put an end to unilateral action, and start the process of meaningful negotiation involving give and take.

Experience in the field also points out the need for approaches of symmetry in conflict resolution. Professor William Zartman stresses that Structural equality frees parties from efforts to equalize positions and allows them to turn to the creation of larger benefits for equalized outcomes. The alternative to structural equality in negotiation is the situation where the strongest side wins. But negotiation is about all sides winning and not about surrender. Professor Lewicki, Saunders and Minton point out that there has to be a situation of mutual dependency or independence for negotiation and resolution to be possible. It is in situations that parties need each other that negotiation takes place. Long standing conflicts, which are often called protracted conflicts, are long standing because of hurt, need and power asymmetry and because of the strong forces that prevent moves toward structural equality and a win-win-resolution.

I could give as an example the Cyprus question where the Greek Cypriot side, one of the two equal constituents of the 1960 partnership Republic, is only preoccupied with the maintenance of the monopoly of power it has violently acquired in 1963. The international community has since been paying lip service to the plight of the Turkish Cypriot people while the UN is on the one had pointing out to the need for structural equality (the UN Secretary-Generalís statement of 12 September 2000) while on the other trying to codify the injustice of 1963 (the UN Secretary-Generalís Oral Remarks of 8 November 2000). The Cyprus question has become protracted because after 37 years of conflict-habituated positioning Greek Cypriots are unable to put aside their obsession that Cyprus is Hellenic, while Turkish

Cypriots cannot accept to give up their sovereign equality and be subordinated to a Greek Cypriot dominated government.

In terms of the degree of hurt the Greek Cypriots have a significant advantage because they can continue under the pretence that they are the legitimate government of the whole island and integrate with the rest of the world while imposing isolation on the Turkish Cypriot people. This is perpetually preventing conditions of a mutually hurting stalrmateí and thus a win-win resolution.

Leadership

Negotiating teams in major international conflicts are usually led by Heads of Government or Head of State. Proactive and progressive leadership plays a significant role in the transformation of conflict from a confrontational zero-sum mindset to a win-win problem solving mindset. Transformation in the mindset of conflicting parties is by far the most critical turning point in the process of negotiation and it is this turning point, which opens the door for meaningful negotiation and for resolution. It is however, a dramatic turning point for political leaders because it involves a departure from accustomed and safe popular positions to ones that are risky and necessitate the payment of attention to the concerns and interests of traditional enemiesí. Such tansformation requires strong leadership, foresight and the realization that by working together and addressing the legitimate concerns of each other all parties would have realized their interests far better than they would have done unilaterally. This may sound simple in conferences like this one but in real life it is a hard choice, which only strong leaders can make. The late Turkish President Kemal Attat‚rk, the late Egyptian President Anwar Sadat and the former Soviet President Mikhail Gorbachev were among such strong leaders.

At this point I would like to return to the case of Cyprus where the Greek Cypriot side has been stubbornly pursuing zero-sum approaches since 1963. In spite of the International Treaties of 1960, which endorse and reflect the equal political status of the Turkish Cypriot people, and in spite of the realities on the ground, the Greek Cypriot position is that Cyprus is a Hellenic island, and that the Greek-Cypriot usurped Government of Cyprusí represents the whole island, and that the Turkish Cypriot people are a political minority in Cyprus. Greek Cypriot political leaders have failed to show foresight and to realize that self sustaining peace and stability in the island and in the region can best come about through the equal partnership of the two peoples and states of the island. Such a partnership would also finally disprove Huntingtonís theory of the Clash of Civilisations and boost Turkish-Greek and Turkish-EU relations.

One final point is that leaders engage in the negotiation of major international conflicts have many layers of responsibility. The first layer of responsibility is towards the negotiating team where the leader is responsible for encouraging and securing teamwork, the generation of ideas, the motivation of the people around him, the securing of proactive and adaptive strategies and the balancing of task and people orientation.

Leadership and Human Progress

Harriet Mayor Fulbright

Harriet Mayor Fulbright is former Executive Director of the Presidentís Committee for the Arts and Humanities in the Clintonís Administration, and of the Fulbright Commission.

It is a real pleasure to be here at another international leadership conference remarkably organised by Adel Safty, though it is a bit daunting. The subject Dr. Safty suggested is indeed fascinating but would be better treated in a full year-long seminar course. I can only outline subjects for further thought, but I felt that it might be worthwhile to encourage discussion of the key issues affecting us   issues of profound influence on us humans and by us, since we do not often give adequate consideration of the consequences of our actions.

Science and technology, mass communication and medicine, the environment and education are all areas of endeavour where our impact has become so great that what we decide and do now is creating a chain of events that will affect the planet and the lives of our descendents for generations to come. This makes the question of leadership of critical importance. I will therefore outline the issues in these areas and end with a few thoughts about the leadership needed to deal with them.

Science and Technology

Human-invention and discovery in the 20th century has been remarkable. In 1902 the Wright brothers made their miraculous flight of 120 feet, in a double winged plane capable of carrying only the pilot, and it started a revolution in transportation. Since that time many have flown faster than the speed of sound, across oceans and to all parts of the planet. Several have even made it to the moon and back. On the ground within this century people now travel a mile a minute or much faster on wheels instead of on foot or animal, revolutionizing daily life everywhere.

Discoveries in the field of physics have been equally extraordinary and have transformed our understanding of man, matter and the universe. Shortly after the turn of the century Einstein announced the development of his theory of relativity, which totally changed the way we look at the world. Scientists have since studied our planetary system and the universe beyond, using not only powerful telescopes but also space satellites with the capacity to travel millions of miles out of our atmosphere. They have at the same time performed extraordinary studies on particles so small we can know them only by the trails they leave, and this research has led to discoveries of power at once more destructive and at the same time more magically beneficial than anyone could have imagined a century ago.

And just a few years after the Wright brothers and Einstein made the news - the year my father, who is still alive, was born - the first national radio program was broadcast in the United States, marking the beginning of mass communication. High technology now delivers not only sound but images worldwide; a news event is communicated via satellite within minutes of its happening to radios and television sets on every continent. And big governments and businesses are not alone in their ability to gather news and spread information. Millions of individuals can turn on their computers or pick up their telephones and interact with those they have never met face to face, to conduct research, join together in campaigns, or just enjoy conversations.

Modern medicine is now close to making the bionic human a reality. Transplants of hearts, livers, kidneys and other vital organs are now commonplace, and miracle drugs are bringing people with life threatening diseases back from the brink of death. This means that not only are men, women and children recovering from diseases and accidents that would have killed them a century ago, but they are living longer thanks also to better nutrition, which significantly affects our numbers on earth. In less than 150 years we have gone from a global population of 1 billion souls to one that is about 6 billion, and more than   of the people live in developing countries. In the year 2001 there are more people living who cannot read or write *at all* than there were people alive in 1900. Now for the first time in human history, one half of the worldís population lives in cities. That means that we are no longer surrounded by nature; we *surround* it. And there are more powerful facts that cannot be ignored:

- We are the first generation of humans to become a force of geological proportions;

- We no longer affect just weather, we affect climate as well;

- We no longer just affect crop yield on a regional basis, we affect the very process of photosynthesis.

- We have synthesized endocrine disruptors - copycat hormones - that invade the bodies of animals, including humans, and disrupt the endocrine system, changing lifeís basic processes in ways we cannot imagine or anticipate;

- We can no longer avoid genetically engineered food, and we are not certain of its long-term effects;

- We will continue to lose habitat; and we lose biodiversity daily. With the loss of both, we reduce our capacity to respond to the stresses of everyday life, not to mention the extraordinary events that happen from time to time.

- Finally, the unequal distribution of resources - human, natural, educational, technological, and financial - amount to an unequal distribution of the ability to respond to these stresses.

Again, the issues we must untangle are far too numerous and complicated to cover adequately in this short paper, but let me touch upon some of the most important.

The Environment

Clearly the effects just listed and many more describe the deep and lasting impact that people and their activities have had and continue to have on the environment. Humans have for hundreds in fact thousands - of years changed the nature of their surroundings by planting and raising livestock and by building shelter. Four thousand years ago the Sahara Desert, for instance, was a fertile region until nomadic tribes began to settle and establish herds that overgrazed the land. This caused plant life to disappear, and the lack of moisture from those plants, which used to rise into the atmosphere, seriously diminished the subsequent amount of rainfall, slowly creating the landscape of the sand dunes we now see. The same type of overuse of land caused the terrible dustbowl of the 1930ís in the American southwest.

Overcrowding of all kinds and its outcome is now understood, but we are all struggling with and arguing about the implementation of the changes necessary to correct the situation. The mere tinkering with techniques can no longer help us. Now we must make basic changes in human values or ideas of morality.

Even if we deal with trends we can identify, there are even more events and changes with unforeseen consequences. An example of this occurred in the U.S. in the 19th century. As the country became more urbanized and sophisticated, the male population gave up beaver caps in favour of the more elegant high silk top hat. As a result, the number of beavers increased considerably, which in turn caused a significant increase in the dams they constructed along streams and rivers, and the number of marshlands multiplied. In todayís world, unintended consequences could be a great deal more significant. The airplane, for instance, which was designed for human and cargo transportation has also carried the AIDs virus around the world with equal speed. Just think what devastation a terrorist could create with a deadly genetically engineered disease for which there is no cure.

Another environmental issue is pollution. There is now, for instance, a spirited debate about the current impact of human activity in general and fossil fuel use in particular on the entire planet. Clearly global warming is now a fact. Also indisputable is that auto and industrial emissions are an influence on the climate. So far we have continued to increase our output of the very substance that causes a rise in temperature, all the while arguing about how significant its effect is and whether we can afford to correct the problem.

What is clear is that energy expended in any one country affects at the very least the neighbouring nations and eventually the whole globe. Chernobyl is certainly one of the most dramatic but by no means the only example of the far-reaching effects of air pollution. In the American hemisphere another slower acting but equally destructive pollutant is acid rain, which laid waste whole forests in the U.S. and Canada. There are alternative clean energy sources, such as sun, wind and hydrogen fuel cells. All these methods are already in use but cost, power and storage are all issues that have not been adequately solved, and they will not be solved without more research. Conservation methods also need far more visibility and implementation.

Mass Communication

The influence of mass communication goes far beyond instant worldwide news and the ease of emailing friends around the world. Let me give you one example. In our small and largely rural state of Vermont, one young woman by the name of Jody Williams decided that the use of land mines was killing and maiming civilians, including women and children, in unacceptable numbers, and long after the troops they were supposed to deter had left. She therefore bought for her modest home in the village of Putney a fax machine and a computer to begin an international campaign to stop using them. Within five short years she succeeded in convincing eighty countries to ban the use of land mines, despite her own country's opposition, and she won the Nobel Peace Prize for her efforts.

Jody is not an isolated example of the recent power of an individual. Jessica Tuchman Matthews pointed out in a fascinating article called Power Shift that mass communication has brought about a redistribution of power among governing bodies, businesses and societies.

The most powerful engine of change in the relative decline of states and the rise of non-state actors is the computer and telecommunications revolutions, whose deep political and social consequences have been almost completely ignored. Widely accessible and affordable technology has broken governments' monopoly on the collection and management of large amounts of information and deprived governments of the deference they enjoyed because of it. In every sphere of activity, instantaneous access to information and the ability to put it to use multiplies the number of players who matter and reduces the number who command great authority. The effect on the loudest voice which has been the governments has been the greatest…

Above all, the information technologies disrupt hierarchies, spreading power among more people and groups. In drastically lowering the costs of communication, consultation and coordination, they favour decentralized networks over other modes of organization…
In a network, individuals or groups link for joint action without building a physical or formal institutional presence. Instead they have multiple nodes where collections of individuals or groups interact for different purposes. Businesses, citizens' organizations, ethnic groups and crime

cartels have all readily adopted the network model. Governments, on the other hand, are quintessential hierarchies, wedded to an organizational form incompatible with all that the new technologies make possible.

Education

Communication, and the exponential growth of available information, has also transformed education. There was a time when societies around the world felt that there was a manageable body of knowledge that, when mastered, gave people the confidence to function in their chosen profession and instilled in them a method of study when confronted with the unknown. But the times are so different now. Today, the Sunday New York Times newspaper provides more information than any 4th century early Greek citizen saw in a lifetime. Today, the Internet contains a web site for the Olympics - a two-week sports event which if put on regular paper and stacked, would rise to a height of 8 miles. This is more information than in all of President Thomas Jeffersonís libraries combined, and his library was one of the best in the world in the early 19th century. Clearly, this information, coming at us not only in print but also through sound and visual images, requires a radically different approach to learning and understanding.

What makes the change all the more powerful is the access children now have to information and ideas. Gone are the days when parents had control over what their children could see and read and who could associate with them. Both parenting and schooling have been turned upside down: children need and respond to authority figures who guide rather than dictate, who teach them methods of inquiry suitable for life-long learning. The new discoveries now surfacing every week so change long held beliefs that experience no longer retains its former exalted position; precedents are no longer as valid, and authority is therefore undermined.

Essential elements to be nurtured in education today are good communication skills, critical thinking and creativity, and the majority of schools have not changed accordingly. Leading Western thinkers concerned with education have been expressing a deep disquiet. In the words of George Macaulay Trevelyan, "Education has produced a vast population able to read but unable to distinguish what is worth reading." Critical thinking, judgment and a focus on the common good are found wanting.

In the United States education is considered one of the nation's top priorities, but the path to excellence is still not clear. Unfortunately a depressing amount of money is spent on boring mediocre rote education. One student was heard to remark that he was so glad that his school did not have any sex education courses because then he would be bored with that as well.

The challenge to both parents and teachers is to find the best methods of encouraging and developing children's curiosity, imagination and creativity something each human being has 1,000 times more of than is put to use. This is best done by those who know how to inspire their students and channel their extraordinary energy in positive directions, and the arts can be particularly helpful in this regard. It is especially important because the paths we now follow into the future are so critical. Never before have the consequences of our actions been so far-reaching, long-lasting or powerful.

Leadership

The challenge in the area of leadership is similar to that in education. Leadership has also been turned on its head by human inventions and the indomitable human urge to use them. Leaders in the 19th century and earlier could and did successfully control whole nations by combining military muscle with a blanket of secrecy. In todayís world even the latest weapons whose accuracy and destructive powers are awesome are not enough to maintain a corrupt and greedy autocrat.

As Tom Friedman describes in The Lexus and the Olive Tree, Indonesia was essentially brought down by international financial leaders, who could see, thanks to the computer and Internet that the government was economically inefficient and wasteful, and so they withdrew their support. Earlier when the Russian military tried to launch a coup against Gorbachev, it was blocked by the rapid and unstoppable communication stream through the newly developed fax machine as well as the ever-present television crews.

This being the case, what qualities are needed in a leader to further progress; in other words, what qualities can lead to the development of a society in a direction considered superior to the previous level. It is obvious that just as in education, the information needed to make informed decisions is more than any one man can digest. A leader of today must therefore enable those around him to help in the decision making process. True progress will come only through teamwork guided by someone unafraid of giving others real responsibility, of recognizing the leadership of those in the team in their areas of specialty, and of guiding the whole group through a vision.

By vision I am not talking about a determination to institute a specific policy such a tax reform or military preparedness. I am talking about broader ideas such as peace, environmental sustainability, or equality. My husband Senator Fulbright, for instance, set his sights on one main idea throughout his whole 30-year tenure in the United States Senate, and that was peace. It was the idea of peace that inspired him to initiate a resolution to create a multi-national organization for the furtherance of peace the United Nations - and that was in 1943, at the height of World War II. It was peace he had in mind when he created the international education exchange program that bears his name; he felt that if potential future leaders learned how to exchange ideas and realized that we are all human beings with the same underlying aspirations, perhaps they would not be so quick to exchange bullets.

Thus, great leaders must now have a vision of how to bring about and maintain peace, prosperity and well-being of a company, community or a country. To do this successfully, it is essential that leaders learn to increase their capacity of foresight to become more aware of trends with significance for the future. They must learn to create teams to translate complicated issues into understandable language and work to put in place policies of benefit to the planet rather than to the special interest that might have enabled their election. This is especially important at a time of radical change when it is difficult to see clearly what needs to be done.

The changes now before us can mean the greatest threat to living organisms and natural systems in recorded history, or they can help bring about a period of unprecedented well-being for the planet and all its inhabitants. Whatever the outcome, they will require leadership with a greater ability to listen and analyse, and all of us need better consensus building and communication skills than ever before.

The frontiers we face are now vertical. Conquest of land is, or should be, a thing of the past. What we now need to explore are those vast unknown territories which have nothing to do with land. We need to reach beyond the current findings in technology, communication, and science. We need to conquer starvation and deadly diseases such as AIDs. We need to wage war on starvation and discrimination. If we can focus on aims such as these, we can honestly say that human progress has really begun.

Constructing the World Anew: Education, Leadership and Global Realities

Howard A. Berry

The late Prof. Howard Berry was the co-founder and President of the International Partnership for Service-Learning, New York. USA.

My title is Constructing the World Anew. Jane Adams, the American reformer, from whom the term is cited, had a foundational vision for human development and learning. I believe this Forum is exploring a similar foundational vision.

My sub-title is Education, Leadership and Global Realities. I believe these are keys to constructing the world anew. They are what we have been about for the past twenty years.

A brief word about The International Partnership. Founded in 1982, The International Partnership has been an advocate for, and a practitioner of, the importance of the union of academic study and community service in higher education. We believe, and have much evidence for, that the pedagogy of service-learning enlivens and reforms education, and that it equally develops habits of civic concern and responsibility in the emerging generation. We currently work closely with well over one hundred universities around the world. The

Ford Foundation, the Henry Luce Foundation, the Hitachi Foundation, and others have funded us.

The timing of this Forum is entirely appropriate. The world is changing in ways that make such discussions urgent, and even imperative. As the writer and poet Paul Valery put it some years ago, The future is no longer what it used to be.

I would suggest we keep in our thoughts that putting new wine into old bottles improves neither the wine nor the bottles. New structures may be needed to carry the new content.

Its theme, Leadership, is equally important. Even without yet knowing what the full scope and the consequences of globalisation are, it is apparent that new leaders with broadened perceptions are called for. Adel Safty is, I think, correct in his premise that we need a multicultural and multidimensional definition of global leadership. He is equally, and importantly, correct in his summation that leadership ...is ultimately about human development. I would add that it is also about character, virtues, and inner democracy.

But while discussions, reflection and definitions are needed to form a persuasive conceptual basis, ways of generating the needed new leadership will not come from workshops or seminars. The conceptual basis must also be accompanied by strategies for institutionally encouraging and implementing broad-based leadership education ultimately concerned with human development. In our estimation, and experience, one social structure, existing in all countries and historically the training ground for this, could be higher education.

The emerging global world is the subject of much popular rhetoric. But it has, I think, complexities to it that send an urgent message to education.

That globalism on an unprecedented scale exists is true. Money, goods, technology and products move around the world virtually unhindered. Rapid transportation and instant communication have changed our lives.
Some, including educators, have seen in this a brave new, and desirable, world. In many ways it is but not for everyone.

Two levels of this globalism have been little noted. It is almost entirely economic and it is largely consumer-good based. Now, by itself this is neither new nor necessarily negative. In three periods over the past 600 years it has been economics and trade that have led the way to internationalism and trans-national integration. [1]

However, a point of note today: Of the worldís 100 largest economies, 51 are not nations but corporations. The 500 largest corporations account for 70 percent of world trade. [2] Couple that with the second level of this globalism, its heavy consumer goods thrust, seen easily by simply watching TV ads. A crucial fault appears.

This vaunted globalism, and its accompanying benefits, is occurring among a very narrow stratum of society. Large numbers are not participating in this globalism. Large numbers are not part of its prosperity. [3]

Cheap labor particularly among women and children is fueling the economic engine. The gap between what are called the haves and the have-nots is widening within nations and between nations. Parallel to that, some other phenomena are also global: environmental issues; diseases; human and social problems; migration of peoples. If we are wired closely together economically, we are equally closely wired humanly. The issues are both practical and moral.

On a practical level, this economic globalism is self-contradictory. A consumer economic structure, which leaves out large segments of society who cannot buy the goods produced eventually, is self-defeating.

But the even deeper issue is the moral one. One of values. Where is the countervailing voice to economic globalism and world-wide consumerism? Where is the leavening institution speaking for and attending to the alienated, those unable to speak or act for themselves? The question speaks to the very nature and purpose of civilization and the functioning of civil society.

The classic view of society is an organic one. [4] This holds that there are four major social institutions the magistrates, the ministers, the merchants, and the masters: Government, Religion, Trade, and Education.

They all have their role, traditions and identity. But they do not exist alone or in isolation. They form ecology. They are the DNA strands of society, entwined in an interactive helix. Like DNA, when they work properly in tandem, each with its proper role, social health ensues. When one is missing or broken the social fabric is torn.

Education is one of those strands. One of its historic roles has always been to transmit knowledge and prepare the next generation. To prepare it for careers and leadership in the life of the society. To that end, the link of education to economic structures is neither new nor wrong.

But education has another, and deeper, role. To provide the young with a rite of passage and a journey to maturity. A rite of passage which sets challenges and experiences that help imbue them with values and standards. Values that allow them a proper sense of themselves   a sense of self-worth, not self-esteem. Values that also allow them a proper sense of, and sensitivity to, the human needs and human condition of other levels in the society. To prepare leaders who have this knowledge and these concerns as life-long habits.

And what of education within our new globalism? As corporations create structures that transcend borders, as governments create geographic free-trade regions, as laws create global applicability, where is the DNA strand of educational creativity?

The record is mixed, but not entirely cause for optimism. Universities respond by the rush to develop curricula to prepare students for international economic careers. International MBAís flourish. Corporations shape and influence the creation of whole colleges in state university systems to produce future managers. Think. Of the 283 endowed academic chairs at M.I.T. 80 [almost a third] have been set up by corporations. Donations from corporations in 1996 accounted for $2.8 billion, 20%, of all voluntary support to US higher education. [5] There is a risk of the educational DNA strand being absorbed.

But what of the other role of education? That of generational development. The countervailing voice. Where is the global dimension to that?

If our students are to enter the producing and consuming sector as they will and should let us at least help them do it with the habits of the heart that keep them aware of human needs and the human condition. Help them be leaders who are also servants. Not by fragmenting education from economic developments, but instead enhancing both by the value-added character of our graduates.

Apprenticeship in the arts, the law, politics, technology, is an old and venerable concept. Is it too much to think of the idea, through service connected to education, of a social apprenticeship, or an apprenticeship in civic virtue? This is a vision, but it is not chimerical. It is not limited to the poets, the novelists, the philosophers, or the idealists and radical activists. The businessperson who understands this is a better businessperson; the engineer is a better engineer; the lawyer is a better lawyer. It truly spans the curriculum.

It is in this vein that we at The International Partnership have been advocates for service-learning the union of academic studies with substantive community service. Service-learning is academically sound. It enlivens the disciplines across the curriculum, creates new partnerships between faculty and students, and helps put academic institutions into a right relationship with their communities local, national and global.

Beyond that, service-learning, especially when conducted in international/intercultural settings, addresses the need to develop habits of civic virtue through experience. Civic involvement and multicultural appreciation will not be accomplished in the classroom or lecture hall.

Aristotle pointed this out two thousand years ago. As he wrote in the Nichomachean Ethics: For we learn a craft by making the products which we must make once we have learned the craft. For example, by building we become builders, by playing the lyre, lyre players. And so too we become just by doing just actions, and temperate by doing temperate actions...in a word, states of character are formed by corresponding acts. [6.]

Aristotle equally recognized that experience alone is not enough. The same causes and means that produce each virtue also destroy it. For playing the lyre produces both good and bad lyre players. Proper instruction from a reliable mentor is essential. Thus the union of academic education and civic experiences.

But individual and fragmented efforts are not enough. If we are to create a critical mass capable of having its voice heard and its influence felt we need a structure which itself is global. A structure that can be the educational counterpart to the international and trans-national corporations. As these corporations move goods and money through porous borders, so the world needs a humanistic counterpart. An organization that links the worthwhile but individual and fragmented efforts into a larger and coherent whole.

Suppose we took the term university literally. Suppose such an international coalition were to think about a shared, recognized curriculum, based on the linking of studies and service. Suppose students, and faculty could move from country to country a year here, a year there engaging in studies based firmly in disciplines, but accompanied by the experience of service in each case.

Suppose such an international coalition were to think of itself not as a series of isolated institutions fragmented fiefdoms jealously guarding their supposed territory but instead were to see itself as campuses which happened to be located in Europe, Asia, Latin America, the US, the Caribbean?

Suppose such a coalition thought of itself as a world-wide university? Such an educational organization could take its institutional place alongside the economic and political globalism, which, for good or otherwise, is creating an international society. It could add a crucial and needed voice to the shaping of values and spiritual life of that new society. It could help our students see their journey into maturity and leadership in global as well as in personal terms.

The odds are in favor of trying. If we do not try we will never know. If we do try we may fail, but equally we may just succeed, or even if not, in trying we may open other possibilities not yet imagined. As many from philosophy and religion have told us, the value is in the striving, not merely in the achieving   else whatís a heaven for.

Goethe has put it succinctly: Whatever you can do or dream you can, begin it. Boldness has a genius, power and magic in it. [6] I commend you, Adel Safty, for your boldness here.

We will try to continue to move forward with the same boldness, and would welcome a continuing relationship with the developments and coalitions we fully expect will emerge.

References

1. Landes, David S. *The Wealth and Poverty of Nations.* New York: W. W. Norton & Company, 1998. Landes discusses this throughout his study.

2. Kaplan, Robert D. Was Democracy Just a Moment? *The Atlantic Monthly,* Vol. 280, No. 6, December, 1997, pp. 55-80.

3. *Ibid.*

4. The organic view of society is an old and traditional one. The terminology used here is from categories used by Edmund Burke. The addition of the Masters (education) is the authorís.

5. Basinger, Julianne. Increase in Number of Chairs Endowed by Corporations Prompts New Concerns. *The Chronicle of Higher Education,* Vol. XLIV, Nr. 33, April 24, 1998, pp. 51-52.

6. Hunter, James Davison. *The Death of Character.* New York: Basic Books, 2000, pp. 109-110. Hunterís concern is with the decline of moral education and concepts of leadership and character.

7. Anster, John, trans. *Faustus: A Dramatic Mystery,* Part I, line 303. 1835.

Leadership and Human Rights for Development

Mansour Yousif Elaagab

Dr. Mansour Yousif Elaagab is chairperson of Sudan Human Rights Organisation

This discussion will focus, first, on our understanding of development as against growth. Secondly, on certain aspects that relate to basic rights, which have great economic implications for the people. Thirdly, institutional factors and democratic leadership needed for the realisation of these rights. Fourthly, the consequences of deviating from basic rights. Fifthly, the impediments that render the realisation of these difficult will be broadly highlighted. Finally some basic elements of an alternative reforms path necessary for their liquidation will be suggested.

How we see the main objective:

In my view, the main purpose of our exercise here is to deliberate and agree on issues and guidelines of direct and practical relevance to constructive dialogue among people and positive, inclusive, socio-economic and political transformations in our countries. These two represent the main prerequisites of peaceful coexistence within and among nations. For these to be realised certain tools need to be discovered and used. Among these are development with a human face and broad-minded democratic leadership.

Holistic Development with a Human Face as an alternative:

Today, however, while not losing track of the need for adopting an inter-disciplinary approach for addressing the above mentioned broad issues, one will concentrate mainly on matters that have direct impact on the economic well being of the people, as little attention has been given to this previously.

The development model based on the hegemony of growth centric economic development that had been followed after the Second World War had two main drawbacks. In certain situations, it took place within the context of racial discrimination and in countries terrorised by violent dictatorships excluding the majority and resulting in unheard of sufferings, greater inequalities, poverty and discrimination. To be sure, that model failed dramatically in resolving the dual realities of plenty and famine, health and disease, technological advancements and growing illiteracy, the agony of child labour, as well as the bleak prospects of the poor and in particular women. (Rao and Kumar, 2000, p.p. 111-112).

Witnessing the failure of that model that ignored the human dimensions of development, many started advocating an alternative development path that puts the human being at its centre. A common understanding is now developing that increasingly perceives development in non-economic human terms. Further there is also a shift from blind adherence to develop blue prints designed by experts for the poor. Development according to this view is a process to unleash the initiatives, ideas, and enthusiasm of the poor. Malaga (1982:1) asserts that what is needed is organising people for power. Perhaps the most significant word in the vast amount of jargon invented by development economists is the word empowerment. This essentially means helping the poor to help themselves. Hence, countries, prominent leaders, economists and international agencies increasingly advocate participatory development that involves, caters and cares for the poor.

Development, the way we see it, is qualitative compared to growth that is quantitative. It is holistic as it has economic, political, social and environmental dimensions and entails a spill over into all of these important spheres of life. It encompasses both growth and change. However, change does not only mean change in the volume of production, but in the composition of output, the conditions under which it takes place and the distribution of its benefits. The basic argument is that the pursuit of growth oriented economic policies has resulted in serious structural drawbacks, income inequalities and detrimental humanitarian implications. These policies do not emphasise the necessary elements for the development of the human resource, the need for empowering the people and the inclusion of the large numbers of small-scale producers, the poor and women in the decision-making processes and. The inclusion of these groups offers the basis for more sustainable long-term development as they have a vast unutilised potential for expansion.

Nowhere is the need for empowerment more crucial than in the role of women in the LDCs. What is needed here is a reappraisal of the role of women and the poor in economic development and a major transformation of their miserable conditions. This calls according to Professor Paul Baran, for a national scheme that not only targets the mobilisation of the actual economic surplus but most importantly the potential economic one. This by necessity raises the urgent need for an institutional framework that ensures delivery of investment resources and public goods and services to the poor and women in particular who are to a very great extent live under conditions of absolute poverty.

In many LDCs the disregard of the human dimension of development seriously undermines women. Women in these countries usually undertake tasks, which are the last to benefit from labour-saving devices. Their tasks of fetching water and rearing children are arduous and time consuming. 'Economic development often displaces womenÖ. The process of economic development often ignores women and bypasses them; it can even worsen their position. If women are to participate in the fruits of development then they must be freed from the tyranny of large families and a hand-to-mouth existence ". (Charles Smith, Economic growth and welfare, 1994, pp.60-62). Women are concentrated in low paid jobs and work for long hours producing according to the UN Children's Fund (UNICEF) about half the world's food. Men make most development programmes policy and take decisions without any gender perspective.

Furthermore, most of the women living in the LDCs live in rural areas where subsistence economy is dominant and facilities to empower them are found in distant cities. In addition, the majority of the illiterates in the LDCs are women with few ownership rights. Multinationals, too, target women with inappropriate products such as dried milk for babies in countries with unreliable water supplies. Similarly, their advertisement to market tobacco in LDCs encourage husbands to divert highly needed family resources on an unnecessary smoking habit that can lead to loosing a bread winner through a smoking related disease.

In contrast to orthodox economic and multinationals thinking, one is of the opinion that income inequality, a characteristic of many LDCs, is not a purely economic phenomenon. As Charles Smith argues it is created by society's general attitudes towards the divisions between wealth and labour and the value it places on different kinds of labour: what might be termed differences in 'social class'. Michael Towsey and Dhanlou Ghista go further than Smith does in their interpretation of inequalities. They consider "the accumulation of wealth above and beyond the need for health and reasonable self-expression is in fact the attempt to appease a psychic hunger. Where an individual accumulates extra ordinary wealth regardless of rationality and the suffering caused to others, this should be understood as a mental disease, an addiction not dissimilar to bulimia or alcoholism". (Paper entitled: economic democracy and development policy, Franklin Vivekananda and Olayiwola Abegunrin edit. the political economy of South-South Co-operation, 1998,p.213).

The need for a new approach along the lines explained earlier has long been felt. In India, for example, the new approach to development took in the fifties, the form of Community Based Development as opposed to central planning that excludes those outside the government's official circles.

Prime Minister Nehru of India in criticising top down central planning that excludes the people, wrote the following: " It does infinite harm in the sense that it provides few opportunities for the people to learn to do things for their themselves, to develop a spirit of self-reliance, self-dependence, and even to make mistakes if they want to make mistakes. Such an approach comes in the way of the very development of the spirit of self-dependence, self-reliance, of co-operating with one another, and will encourage something which, I believe, is completely wrong and which is so prevalent in this country: looking up to Government for everything". Quoted by Myrdal, 1968,p.877.

Prominent economists such as Myrdal point also to the importance of people's involvement in development policies and decisions. He wrote in a section entitled 'the quest for popular support and participation' that 'in India, the ideal has always been that the plan should come from the people, meet their needs, and have their support in thought as well as deed'. Myrdal (1968, chapter 18,p.850).

Statesmen like Robert McNamara, the President of the World Bank, in his famous speech at Nairobi in 1973 ' Redistribution with growth and the emphasis on Basic Needs' drew world attention to the importance of poverty eradication as an overreaching objective of development.

The UNDP in 1990 launched a holistic humanitarian approach to development by introducing a new Human Development Index (HDI), which is published each year in the Human Development Report (HDR) with information about each of the 160 countries. Human Development according to the UNDP is a 'process of enlarging people's choices'.

Three choices are considered to be critical by the UNDP

These are:

- Access to resources (purchasing power, which is calculated from GNP per capita and a calculation of the cost of living).

- A long and healthy life (as reflected by figures for life expectancy).

- Education (measured by the adult literacy rate).

The emphasis here is not only on the accumulation of physical capital but equally important is on intellectual, spiritual and human capital.

Capital in this sense means intellectual, spiritual and human as much as physical capital. The importance of intellectual property was recognised by the victors of World War Two when the allies systematically took every available technical, trade and industrial idea they could find. On the other hand spiritual capital till recently has not enjoyed the attention of economists' as intellectual capital, which they treat as a catalyst for building physical capital. However, while the faculty of human intellect has helped in generating much physical wealth, it has not guaranteed its equitable distribution. Intellectual capital alone as the recent history shows has not been able to secure freedom from starvation or the access to a livelihood.

This failure in the view of some can be attributed to lack of development of spiritual capital that directs intellectual capital towards human welfare. To develop spiritual capital means to develop open-mindedness, heartily considerations, intuition subtleties, universal outlook, avoiding narrow sentiments, based on race or social status that discriminate against people and set them apart. In the meantime it recognises differences among individuals without which individual welfare ca not be realised. In brief, spiritual capital refers to the development of benevolent intellect which objective is the promotion of social, economic and social harmony.

Human capital to use the words of Charles Smith " is the accumulated knowledge, skills and attitudes of the working population. It also encompasses the physical mental and social health of a nation. Education, health and training are often wrongly regarded as part of a country's social welfare system, rather than as economic issues with implications for growth and development. Countries which neglect human investments are unlikely to develop as rapidly as they otherwise could." (Charles Smith, 1994, p.23.)

Furthermore, several international conferences have treated holistic humanitarian development as their key issue. The fate of children was linked for the first time to the state of development at the World Summit for Children in 1990. The Rio Earth Summit, 1992, in particular its Agenda 21 address humanitarian issues directly by linking environment and development to the survival of human beings. The World Conference of Human rights, 1993, the International Conference on Population and Development, 1994, The World Social Development Summit, 1995, also addressed development issues. A number of international women conferences, Mexico, 1975, Copenhagen, 1980, Nairobi, 1985, and Beijing, 1995, specifically addressed necessary actions for the advancement of women.

It is our contention that development with a human face can not take place in situations where basic human rights of people are violated. The respect of these basic rights represent the prime mover and decisive factor necessary for the empowerment of the impoverished broad masses and the ending of the direct, structural, identity, cultural, and institutional forms of violence that characterise a number of countries today.

Rights as basis for entitlement

A. People's natural rights are basic and indivisible:

Our main concern here is with the people and their natural rights that are inherent in them as human beings. Natural rights, it must be emphasised, are the source of all other human rights, be they legal, conventional, or contractual. History has shown that disregard for the people and their natural rights can produce conditions that are fraught with many dangers.

In the meantime, all human rights are indivisible as the violation of one right often affects the respect of several other rights. For instance, access to the right of education affects employment opportunities as well as use of information, voice in decision making processes, vulnerability to violence and access to judicial systems. Similarly, it is meaningless that an individual is granted the right to life without granting him or her the right to subsistence and reproduction. To be more specific, the right to material goods must be granted to all human beings if the right to life is to have any meaning.

Thus, in this sense, the realisation of civil and political rights becomes a function of the achievement of economic, social and cultural rights.

B. Economic rights are the basis for empowerment:

Our understanding of human rights transcends the limited perception of human rights as legal rights alone to engulf other rights, in particular the economic rights that empower and entitle all people to claim their rights to opportunities and services that are available in their country.

An important concept that relates to this issue and which needs to be properly understood by any future policy maker is the concept called marginalisation. Many political leaders commonly use this concept, though ambiguously.

Simply speaking, the term marginalisation or lack of equality usually refers to non-access to, or non-availability of key resources. For the purpose of our discussion we can identify two forms of marginalisation. Generally, people are marginalised when they are deprived of the material, social and cultural goods that they need to live a worthwhile life. We can further distinguish between the marginalisation that occurs when people are deprived of access to the means of production and the marginalisation that takes place when key goods are not distributed between people. The cause of the first type of marginalisation lies in the realm of production, while the cause of the second form lies in the realm of distribution.

The consequent inequalities in education, health, employment, income, access to resources and services and political representations that are associated with marginalisation, perpetuate the powerlessness of the excluded. Individuals can be granted equality of life conditions, only if they have access to the goods that meet their basic needs.

C. Democracy is more than a form:

Most people agree that any representative and accountable government must have five important elements to qualify as a democratic polity. The first is periodic free and fair elections in which all parties and candidates enjoy relatively equal access to, and protection by the rules. The second is the existence of a plural civil and political culture. The third is the separation of powers. The fourth is the constitutional guarantee of the fundamental rights of expression, assembly and organisation. The fifth is the alteration of power.

However, while these five elements deal essentially with the forms of democratic polity, they do not address distribution issues i.e. how power is allocated among groups in society. Formal democratic governance may indeed reproduce or even create, social and economic inequalities- in class, ethnic, racial, or gender terms, for instance; and it may not produce the best leaders. The policies and programmes of political representatives may better reflect the interests of a ruling elite or powerful business oligarchies- who have more resources, networks and capacities to influence public policies- than those of workers, petty traders, artisans or small holder farmers who occupy the lower rungs of society. Similarly, the situations where a single ethnic or racial group enjoys an absolute demographic majority, it is very possible for formal democracy to produce all, or a disproportionate number, of its political representatives from the dominant ethnic or racial group. In such situations, the votes of the minority groups may not carry the same weight as those of the majority. In other words, formal democratic systems of government, like markets, though non-discriminatory in the judicial sense, are not necessarily just or equitable.

A number of economists have convincingly argued from an economic point of view against inequality. Inequality, they say, is harmful to growth. Some attributes income inequality to the adoption of the structural adjustment programmes, SAP. In Africa, fore example, the percentage of the labour working in formal sector jobs has declined while the economic and social system is incapable of generating sufficient jobs in other sectors to accommodate the retrenched workers from the public sector. ILO, 1996, indicates that in most of the countries adopting SAP in the 1980s, wage dispersion increased with falling real wages. They also experienced weak linkages between large businesses and small ones. The liberalisation of the economies associated with SAP actually accentuates the disadvantage of small producers as well as shifting incomes from labour to capital. This has led to changes in consumption patterns and lifestyles adding to inequity. It has also resulted in the decline of trade union membership weakening the bargaining powers of workers.

With respect to changes in human capital formation, liberalisation of the economies has put social expenditure in LDCS under strong pressures. In consequence, education, health and infant mortality that is relevant to the poor has deteriorated immensely. The resultant inequity in income distribution is harmful to growth as it negatively affects the composition of demand as well as factor endowment affecting the supply of human capital. It is the contention of the writer that a more equal income distribution leads to an increased demand for industrial goods, which triggers off innovation and growth. Growth is further enhanced by increased investment in education by low-income groups, as a consequence of increased equality in income and capital, allowing them to build up stocks of human capital more rapidly.

In contrast, inequality causes political instability and prevents governments from effective management. In addition non-equity outcomes may affect the cohesion and stability of formal democracies and discourage investors from investing in countries with looming conflicts causing further deterioration in living conditions. Democracy has to be liveable if it is to be sustainable.

In Africa, according to Adebayo O. Olukoshi, 1999, SAP has tended to reinforce crisis in several respects in spite of the grafting of a social dimension to the programmes. They failed to make a major difference on the problem of social decline, widening inequality, and growing poverty in Africa. Hence, accelerating the erosion of the basis for the social citizenship that had been integral to the post-colonial social contract. The anti-statism embodied in SAP has practically emptied citizenship of its social content as the state abdicated its most basic responsibilities to the citizenry. Key elements of the social basis of state-society relations have been eroded and increasingly citizens perceive the state as predatory, coercive and corrupt.

At another level the anti-statism orientation of SAP, had negative implications for those whose fortunes are tied to the public sector. Those are many since the public sector, and in spite of its retreat, is the biggest employer of labour in Africa. The biggest losers are labour, students, and various categories of professionals who have historically been the bearers and defenders of the national-territorial and secular state project. The weakening of these social forces had adverse consequences for the nation- state project. It opened the way for the revival of ethnic, regional and religious fanaticism that not only favoured their members, but also challenged the entire nation-state project in the process. In addition, the exodus of many skilled personnel from the public sector where remuneration and moral had collapsed and the immersion of those remained in parallel modes of livelihood seriously reduced the state capacity (Mustapha, 1992).

Furthermore, the stripping of the state of its assets and cutting it down to size had serious implications for national identity.

SAP and their related reform efforts also tended to reinforce the top down, centralising administrative mode of rule that was in place in most African countries as the implementation of these programmes depended solely on the central government.

Similarly, the adjusting countries abandoned policy efforts aimed at reducing uneven regional development. The neglect of the problem of uneven regional development during the adjustment years has widened the gap between regions and ethnic groups in such social services as access to education, health, safe water, electricity and roads.

Saying this, one does not mean to absolve the post colonial unity project from its discernible class, ethnic, religious and regional base. But to draw attention to the seriousness of the negative implications of SAP related expansion of a market - generated structure of domination, exclusion and neglect for national cohesion. For many communities in Africa the retreat of the state in favour of the market, meant the collapse of the only non-coercive evidence of state presence and the symbol of inclusion in a political and economic community to use the words of Olukoshi, 1999.

D. Institutional relations affect entitlement:
It is necessary to understand the relationship between institutions and those they serve to understand how different social groups and actors secure different capabilities and entitlements. In other words, the issue here relates to the role of institutions whether formal or informal in determining endowment and entitlement. Endowment refers to the individual owned assets and personal capacities that he or she can use to establish entitlement to resources. Entitlement relates to relationships, established by trade, direct production or sale of labour, through which an individual or household gains access to resources. (Amartya Sen, The political Economy of Hunger, 1990 p.36). Rights, opportunities, and power which institutions can sanction or restrict, play an important role in the extent to which people can successfully use institutions for accessing resources.

The objective of distributing resources in favour of the poorest depends on the composition and orientation of these institutions and the appropriateness of delivery mechanisms adopted by them. Institutions that are long oriented to the non-poor tend to develop operating procedures and structures that reflect the nature of their de facto clientele and which hinder them from serving a new target group. Insistence, for example, upon collateral in the form of land for credit may be an absolute obstacle to participation by the poor. Similarly, a limited banking network may result in an obstacle to delivery to the poor for whom the costs of communicating with a bank at considerable distance might add significantly to the real cost of credit. Adding to this are the hindrances imposed by the subtle control of these institutions by the elite acting as gate keepers, particularly in the area of co-operative societies.

In our opinion an effective way of channelling resources to the poor, therefore, means the elaboration of institutional means of delivery consistent with their circumstances. This requires a system of government where the economic plurality of society is recognised and necessary measures are taken that moderates between the different economic interests.

The place of civil society institutions and organisations in this is very important. Both at the macro and micro levels, civil society institutions connect people in collective efforts and may keep governments accountable. When states are weak or are considered by particular social group to be illegitimate, civil society institutions may step in as people's primary points of access to social, material, and natural resources.

The appreciation of all this calls for democratic leaders and not patrons. Leaders who are democratic in behaviour and deed and who accept democracy as a culture of tolerance that accommodates differences. Most importantly leaders who are in the service of their people and not the other way round.

Democratic Leadership

Democracy according to Abraham Lincoln is the government of the people, for the people, by the people. Of the people relates to substitutability through periodical elections; for the people denotes accountability through the separation of powers, independence of the judiciary, the rule of law and respect of basic rights; and by the people stresses participation in the decision making processes at all levels.

The commitment of leaders to these principles is more than necessary. Experience has shown that when adhering simply to the substitutability condition alone and disregarding the other two important conditions of accountability and participation as under formal forms of democracy in a number of Third World countries, many persistent social and economic problems have become the norm. These include mismanagement of the state apparatus, inefficiencies, high economic and social costs, bureaucratic corruption, inequalities, ethnic problems, civil wars, and violation of human rights, economic dependence, poverty and famines. Professor Sen argues that famines rarely occur under democratic regimes as access to resources is secured and as pressure groups of civil society draw the attention of governments before crisis take place. Fukuyama, 1993, also argues in favour of democracy when writing "of the different types of regimes that have emerged in the course of human historyÖthe only form of gover nment that has survived intact to the end of the twentieth century has been liberal democracy". (Quoted by T.N. Srinivasan, Economic Policy and State Intervention, 2001,p.532).

Nnoli argues convincingly that the persistence of the ethnic problems in Africa is linked to weak or absence of democracy. He wrote, " there is a democratic side to the ethnic question in Africa. It concerns the right of each ethnic group to be treated equally with all the others, for their members to be secure in their lives and property, from arbitrary arrest and punishment, and for them to enjoy equal opportunity in trade, business, employment, schooling and enjoyment of social amenities". (1989:206).

History has also shown that the so-called benevolent dictators and the one party system have resulted in unheard of abuses, excesses, corruption, deprivation and destruction of social cohesion.

Furthermore, incompetent and undemocratic leaders who favour nepotism and fall back on ethnicity have created conditions of discontent with the state resulting in civil wars; causing death, severe destruction of social, human capital and physical infrastructure.

Here is a list of some negative consequences the result of deviation from human rights and development with a human face in some Third World countries:

While countries are differentiated, they also share common features with respect to this issue and which we can summarise in the following:
- Repressive laws that violate human rights.
- Repression of free speech and thought.
- The inefficient or unfair administration of justice.
- Sexual, religious, racial, linguistic, economic or aged-based discrimination.
- The retreat of the national state.
- State failure and decay.
- Asymmetrical power relations
- Severe inequity in wealth and income.
- Stagnation and protracted decline in people's real incomes.
- High inflation rates.
- Abject poverty, the vast majority of the populations' lives beneath the poverty line.
- Serious food insecurity where large numbers are chronically food insecure due inaccessibility.

- Severe food shortages and man made famines.
- Spread of diseases such as malnutrition, gastro-enteritis causing infant mortality; AIDs, tuberculosis, malaria, night blindness, guinea worm, kala-azar, goitre, and breathing etc.
- Resource based conflicts, ideological conflicts and identity conflicts.
- Direct violence, structural violence and cultural violence.
- Very huge cost of armed conflicts and civil wars, in addition to their high social costs.
- Heavy taxation. Indirect taxation, which falls disproportionately on low-income groups, represents very high proportion of the total tax revenue.
- Severe social disparities.
- Regional disparities where large proportions of the national income and basic social services are usually concentrated in certain areas close to the capital cities
- High rates of internal migration, urban drift and exodus of skilled labour that are reaching alarming proportions.
- Severely deteriorating social services. Most of these counties are experiencing serious deterioration in the medical, educational and other social services.
- In some countries politicised and fanatic educational system oriented towards **'jihad'** has instilled a culture of violence and discrimination.
- High levels of unemployment.
- Continuing severe deficits in their budgets.
- Continuing deterioration in the balance of trade and payments. .
- Huge national debt, the size of which has reached alarming magnitudes. This is increasing annually in a number of countries as a result of the accumulated debt service that absorbs most of the returns from export.
- Contraction of foreign aid in countries with alarming human rights record. .

- Destruction of fixed capital stocks.
- Damage to the environment and the ecological balance.

Causes of the social and economic plights:

- The negative effect of economic decline on state capacity.
- Globalisation increased marginalisation and intensified dependence.
- Weak predatory illusory state.
- Absence of democratic institutions.
- Organisations of civil society absent or weak, with limited prospects for stability.
- Dictatorial regimes and monolithic partisan political systems that have catered only for the elite, and marginalised the rest of society and provided basis for alarming human rights violations.
- Rural democracy has never been adopted as a basic principle. Rural democracy is the foundation of effective national democracy. It is more than a form. When there have been some gestures towards local democracy, they have been little more than slogans.
- Concepts of leadership have centred on patronage and the abuse of the state power, accentuating disparities.
- Leaders are self-opinionated, lack vision, enlightenment and scientific insight.
- Popular participation has been vulgarised. It lacks genuine institutions catering for the poor. Instead, those in positions of authority in 'popular' institutions have acted as gatekeepers and in fact barred real active participation.
- Most LDCs have been maintained in dependent economic relations with industrial and oil producing countries, perpetuating under-development.

- The legacy of colonial rule included major socio-economic and regional distortions, notably a concentration of resources in the centre at the expense of the peripheries, which have impeded equitable growth and development. The perpetuation of uneven development and unequal distribution of resources has contributed to extreme deprivations, tensions and conflict.
- Structural inequalities, monolithic and hegemonic oppressive institutions, cultural and religious segregation, resulting in structural, institutional and cultural violence.
- The effects of drought in some countries and above all war have exacerbated the poor performance of the economy and protracted decline in income per capita, in turn contributing to social dislocation and disturbance. There is increased competition for scarce resources, jobs and other opportunities heightening conflict and vulnerability.
- The dual nature of the economy, in which the traditional sector is kept under highly, disadvantaged conditions, which have impeded capital formation, expansion of the local market, and development of labour skills.
- The way in which a dominant economic class, parasitic on the national economy, has controlled the commanding heights of the economy, impeding equitable development and increasing social and regional disparities.
- The poor quality of planning in government, which is uncoordinated and inefficient. The basic requirements for effective planning, which are that it should be decentralised and co-ordinated, have been absent. The purging of qualified personnel for political reasons has robbed many governments of their greatest human resources.
- Weak and deteriorating physical and social infrastructure. This is related to the blind way in which governments have adopted a free market economy, without the required regulatory frameworks that can ensure that the

economy is free from corruption, favouritism and misallocation of resources. In the absence of any effective government regulations and with the weakness of civil society organisations to play a counter-balancing role to expose the realities of the situation, and to represent the interests of the people, high private sector profits have been made at the expense of the public.
• Structural adjustment programmes, including austerity programmes and the privatisation of national assets, have been implemented in a manner that favours special interest groups and the dominant social stratum. An oligarchic capitalism has been created that impoverishes low-income groups, undermines social services, and does not promote the public good.
• Productive sectors have suffered from low levels of investment and misallocation of investment to ill-conceived grandiose schemes. This has contributed to low and declining levels of productivity in both the agricultural and industrial sectors.
• Agricultural sectors characterised by low productivity, unbalanced patterns of investment, marketing imperfections including distorted credit markets, and a tendency for horizontal expansion instead of intensification of production. This has led to strip-mining tendency of the mechanised agricultural sector in some African countries, with serious adverse consequences for sustainability, the environment, and the livelihoods of rural people. Overall this has also contributed to chronic food insecurity.
• Depletion of national resources across many countries, due to mismanagement, lack of regulation and poor economic policies.
• Waste of economic potential and depletion of national reserves due to bad management, conspicuous consumption by the dominant groups, smuggling, corruption, expatriation

of money and assets, and the high costs of armed conflicts and security services.
- Wrong approach to industrial development resulting in weak industrial sectors plagued by many problems, including lack of forward and backward linkages with other sectors and in particular the agricultural sector as well as being characterised by limited absorptive capacity for surplus labour from the rural areas.
- The economic and human costs of famines, including the waste of human potential, the setbacks to the rural economy, high levels of displacement, economic distortions due to international relief programmes, not to mention the cost of those relief programmes themselves, which displace more important long-term development assistance.
- The degrading position of women, and the presence of obsolete attitudes and traditions towards women.
- Last but not least, the extreme heavy human, social and economic costs of wars. There can be few places in the world where social and economic conditions today, at the dawn of the 21st century, are no better and often worse than they were fifty years ago. The war-affected regions of Africa sadly number among those parts of the world.

Broad elements of an alternative reforms path

- Leaders committed to democratic practices, human rights and democratic institutions, economic self-reliance, equitable distribution of wealth, full employment, balanced development with a human face, conservation and management of resources, and real popular participation in economic, political, and social decisions. Leaders who have integrity, effective communication, responsibility, accountability and authority, and who have positive mental attitude. Leaders who hold the principles of consideration and respect, constancy of purpose and team work. Leaders who believe in serving people and are ready to make sacrifices and take risks. Leaders, who are learned, enlightened and open to new ideas. Leaders committed to people's centred democratic institutions and capacity building.

- Resolution of conflicts through dialogue and interaction.
- Lasting and just peace and stability is an absolute essential precondition for the achievement of human rights and social and economic development. Related to this, we need appropriate conflict management and resolution systems, through increased participation in decision-making at all levels, and the raising of human rights awareness.
- Socio-economic rehabilitation and development programmes are absolutely necessary. Among these are the transformation of both the agricultural and industrial sectors, balance between the production of consumer and capital goods, primary health care, poverty alleviation, democratic forms of civic education, rural development, food security programmes, land utilisation plans for the equitable distribution of land and preservation of environment.
- Pluralism as a culture of tolerance, of human equality, of respect for different including opposing views. Collective, parliamentary democracy and a federal system of government are most relevant to many African countries.
- Civil society organisations provide the cultural institutional basis for democracy. These can ensure that government is open, responsive and accountable. They can ensure that the agenda of basic social and economic rights remains on the table at all times.
- Participatory development is the foundation of sustainable development and the achievement of basic rights for all. This requires more than good planning, more than

parliamentary democracy. It requires the active engagement of all citizens as full participants in a national project, based upon respect for their human rights. A new constitutional dispensation is needed for this, which will reach into many aspects of the political order including the relation between religion and the state.

- Government has essential regulatory roles, both with respect to its own workings and with regard to the operation of the private sector. Accountability and transparency are essential to combat corruption, inefficiency and misallocation of resources.
- The minimisation of socio-economic distortions and external dependency relations, especially with regard to the productive and service sectors. The number one issue here is the integration of the national economy, so that the traditional sector and the modern sector each play their part. Creating an integrated national economy will in turn reduce the external dependency of most of these countries. This does not mean an end to integration with the global economy: on the contrary it is the foundation for a more effective integration that can serve the interests of the African people. This will require an effective intervention by the government.
- There is urgent need for sound fiscal, monetary and investment policies at all levels. This will require the adoption of a joint national integrated plan with Africa's international creditors and donors. Measures such as debt swapping for essential development and rehabilitation activities are needed.
- The domestic banking sector needs reform so that it can cater for the demands of rural development. Special measures are also needed to attract back to Africa the funds held by African expatriates abroad.

- Adopt measures to mobilise both actual and potential economic surpluses.
- African countries need to look at their neighbours, and develop plans and policies for regional integration.
- A special trust fund for the rehabilitation of the war-affected areas is needed. There will be an urgent need for the most basic social and economic rehabilitation of these areas, including the return and resettlement of refugees and internally displaced persons, and the reintegration into civilian life for ex-combatants. These essential programmes should proceed without any conditions attached, based on local needs.
- The question of the equal distribution of revenues from resources needs to be addressed. Revenues such as oil revenues can either be a blessing or a curse. The cases of Angola and Nigeria demonstrate how oil can enrich elite and impoverish a country. Countries need to consider how the income from exhaustible resources can be best used for national development, overcoming regional inequalities and tackling poverty and food insecurity.
- Advancing the role of women.
- Illiteracy campaigns and campaigns against obsolete traditions and believe.
- Propagation of human rights principles among the population, particularly women and the youth.

Conclusion

In conclusion, our human rights approach calls for the realisation of three principles:

1. Participation.
2. Inclusion.
3. Obligation.

On the basis of these, it should be possible to build our countries along lines that can achieve basic rights for all their citizens. The Istanbul conference that opens today can be an important opportunity for building an international consensus on these issues. This, we believe is the way forward. In fact, it is the only way forward if we are to avoid disasters and tragedies of the past, and achieve progress in our countries in which every one can achieve his or her potential, and be proud to be called a citizen of their country.

References

1. Basta, Lidija R., Ibrahim, Jibrin,(eds.), 1999 : Federalism and Decentralisation in Africa, the Multicultural Challenge, Institut de Federalisme, fribuourg, Suisse,
2. FAO: 1999, Implications of economic policy for food security, a training manual.
3. Frigon, Normand, 1996, The leader.
4. Van der Hoeven, R., 2000, Poverty and structural adjustment.
5. Myrdal, Gunnar, 1968, Asian Drama: an Inquiry into the Poverty of Nations, II.
6. Narayana, N.S.S, ed., 2001, Economic policy and State Intervention.
7. Narayan, S., 2000, Anthropology of Disaster Management.
8. Rao, D.V., 2000, Development with Human Touch.
9. Rupesinghe, K., 1998, Civil Wars, Civil Peace.
10. Sen, Amartya, 1993, The Political Economy of Hunger.
11. Smith, C., 1994, Economic Development, Growth and Welfare.
12. Vivenkananda, F., 1998, The political economy of South-south Cooperation.

The New Paradigm And The Ethics Of Authentic And Pseudotransformational Leadership

Bernard M. Bass

Dr. Bernard M. Bass is distinguished Professor and Director of the Center for Leadership Studies at Binghamton University. Binghamton, N.Y. 13902-6015

According to U.S. Secretary of State General Colin Powell, LeadershipÖis accomplishing more Öthan management says is possible. The leadership and management be can conceived as transformational and transactional leadership respectively.

In a recent landmark essay in 1999, J.G. Hunt, editor of the Leadership Quarterly, found that the study of leadership had been moribund in the 1970ís. It was filled with doom and gloom arguments that the study was in its death-throes. In 1975, one leadership scholar quipped:

Once I was active in the leadership field. Then I left it for about 10 years. When I returned, it was as if I had been gone 10 minutes.

Also in 1975, John B. Minor declared, The heresy that I propose is that the concept of leadership has outlived its usefulness. Hence, I suggest we abandon leadership in favor of some more fruitful way of cutting up the theoretical pie.

The New Paradigm

Instead, a new paradigm emerged of transformational/ transactional leadership. In 1999, Hunt argued that the book Leadership and Performance Beyond Exp ectations (Bass, 1985) turned the field towards new directions by providing models, theory, experiments and surveys about the concepts and measurements of transformational and transactional leadership.

The treatise was based on the seminal work of Robert House, 1977) chapter The 1976 Theory of Charismatic Leadership and James Macgregor Burnsí publication in 1978 of his book simply entitled Leadership . Hunt presented 5 reasons why transformational/transactional leadership was a new paradigm.

The Basque National leader, Jose Antonio Aguirre, illustrated transformational leadership at its best. At 17, he joined the Basque Nationalist party and became its youth director. He was a star football player for the Athletic Club of Bilbao. His good looks and charisma made him a popular, natural leader. He was an impressive orator who could hold the attention of the Basque crowds, He preached a gentler Basque Nationalism. He declared that Our nationalism should be universalÖit should not be turned into a source of discord between peoples (Kurlansky, 1999).

President Franklin Delano Roosevelt was being transformational in his inaugural address of 1933 in the midst of the Great Depression when he proposed, The only thing we have to fear is fear itself. Likewise, President John F. Kennedy in his inaugural address in 1960 was transformational when he said My friends, ask not what your country can do for you; ask what you can do for your country. But both could be transactional as well. In their election campaigns Roosevelt and Kennedy made many promises to the voters in exchange for their votes.

Need for the New Leadership

The rapid discontinuous changes in the environment have required much more need for leaders and followers to be more flexible and imaginative. They are faced with a rapidly changing workforce, technology, markets, societies and communities. Globalization is a fact of life.

To deal effectively with this rapidity of change, the good supervisor, the good official and the good executive have to be both good managers and good leaders. In this new environment of the late 20th and early 21st centuries, they have to be good managers who plan, organize and control as well as good leaders who envision, enable and empower.

Components of Transformational and Transactional Leadership

Transformational leaders raise the awareness of their followers about what is important and increase followersí concerns for achievement, self-actualization and ideals.

They motivate followers to go beyond the followersí self-interests for the good of the group, organization and /or society. The leader with idealized influence, inspirational leadership and charisma envisions a valued future, articulates how to reach it and sets an example with which followers identify and want to emulate. The intellectually stimulating leader encourages followers to question assumption, and to look at old problems in new ways to enable the followers to be more creative and innovative. The leader with individualized consideration treats each of the followers according to their different needs for support and development.

Transactional leaders cater to the self-interests of their followers by means of contingent reinforcement. If the followers carry out their assignments, as agreed, they are rewarded, promised rewards and praised. Leaders manage-by- exception if the followers fail in assignments. When leaders actively manage-by-exception, they monitor the followersí performance and correct or discipline them. If the leaderís passively manage-by-exception, they wait for problems in the followerís performance to arise, then make corrections or discipline the followers.

Laissez-faire leaders remain unconcerned about their followers, procrastinate, avoid making decisions and are absent when needed.

Since 1980, several hundred published and unpublished studies of transformational and transactional leadership have been completed using to a considerable degree the Multifactor Leadership Questionnaire in at least 40 countries in over 10 languages.

Studies have been carried out in business firms, NGOís, the military, police, churches, health clinics, hospitals and government agencies as well as university laboratories and classrooms, high schools and professional schools. They have been used for assessing individuals, providing 360 degree feedback to leaders from superiors, colleagues, and subordinates.

Many of the different studies have looked at the effects of transformational and transactional leadership on follower performance and outcomes of the leadership. Positive correlations were found with inspiring commitments to exceeding market share and meeting quotas.

Meta-analyses pool the results of multiple studies. The highest positive correlations were found in 3 meta-analyses for transformational leadership, next highest and positive was contingent reward. In the military, active management-by- exception was low positive; elsewhere it was low negative. Passive management-by-exception was slightly negative and laissez-faire leadership was most negative. The effects were similar in investigations of directors of health clinics, school principals, and church ministers among others. (Bass, 1998).

The correlative effects run high when the same subordinates rate both the effectiveness of their leaders and the extent their leaders are more transformational. Charisma has the highest relationship with leadership followed by individualized consideration and intellectual stimulation. The values are lower for contingent reward and close to zero for management-by-exception. The blue bars show the correlations between the same transformational and transactional factors and objective measures of the organizations or units led by the leaders. The measures include productivity records, profitability, and the like. They reveal a similar pattern except that management-by-exception is slightly negative in its impact on effectiveness.

The Full Range of Leadership

Every leader has a profile of the transformational and transactional MLQ factors. The effective or optimal leader is high in transformational leadership and low in laissez faire leadership. As just noted, the individual leaders are rated using the Multifactor Leadership Questionnaire (MLQ) by those above, below and at the same level in their organization. The vertical axis of the model is based on the hierarchy found empirically. Field studies find that transformational factor scores correlate more highly with the independently-based effectiveness of leadership than do the contingent reward scores, which in most circumstances are positively associated with effectiveness, but to a lesser extent. In turn, contingent reward correlates more highly with effectiveness than does management-by-exception. Active management-by-exception varies from low positive to low negative correlation with effectiveness. Passive leadership is almost always negatively correlated with effectiveness.

The horizontal axis is a matter of definition. By definition, there is a hierarchy in activity of leadership from active to passive. (Avolio & Bass, 1991). Transformational leadership is more active than transactional leadership. Least active is laissez-faire leadership. Interactive data processing, automatic scoring and confidential feedback are available at the website <www.collaboratevirtually.com >.

Every leader exhibits some frequency measured on a scale from 1 to 4 on each of the components and on each of the items contributing to the components. Ordinarily, improving leadership performance depends on reducing passive leadership and managing-by-exception and increasing the frequencies of transformational leader behaviors.

The Full Range of Leadership, showing an ineffective inactive leader low in transformational leadership and high in management, does not change in pattern as we move from country to country. Everywhere there is a universal tendency for transformational leaders to be seen as generally more effective. Nonetheless, the behaviours displayed may be more specific to the country. For instance, charismatic CEOs in Japan remain modest about their abilities; In Indonesia, they stress them. In Japan, there is an adage that the rice shoot that lifts its head above the others, gets its head chopped off. In Indonesia, followers feel more secure when their leaders emphasize their own abilities.

Studies of the impact of transformational and transactional leaders were reported from countries on every inhabited continent. Context was of importance, but the fundamental phenomena transcended countries and organizations (Bass, 1997).

For instance, in Spain, Molero Alonso (1994) reported a study carried out in 40 primary health care centers. The study focused on the transformational leadership of the centre coordinators and their effects. Each coordinator was a leader of a team of family doctors, paediatricians, nurses, and clerks. The leadership was seen as significantly more legitimate in the eyes of team members in those centres in which coordinators earned higher MLQ scores in the transformational components. Team members found it more acceptable for the coordinators to organize, manage, control and evaluate their performance. There was less role conflict, better interpersonal relations and more feelings of autonomy when the coordinators were seen as transformational on the MLQ according to the schools' teachers.

In Canada, Howell and Avolio (1993) demonstrated that the transformational, but not the transactional scores of department supervisors in a large Canadian financial institution predicted consolidated departmental performance a year later. Findings of greater effectiveness and satisfaction of subordinates under transformational leaders ranged from a Chinese state enterprise (Davis, Guan, et al, 1996) to Polish and Dutch firms (den Hartog, 1997). Garcia (1995) obtained similar results with American sales personnel. . Bass & Avolio (2000) obtained the same for U.S. Army infantry platoon leaders and sergeants in near-combat military exercises. Dvir (1998) showed in a controlled field experiment in the Israeli Defense Force that training in transformational leadership made for more effective military officers when their units were followed up.

Many studies in the developed world have found that the women leaders are a little more transformational than their male counterparts Men are more likely to practice passive managing-by- exception and laissez-faire leadership. Women are slightly more effective. This fits with findings elsewhere that woman seek fairness while men favour justice; women form networks; men are more hierarchical.

Both transactional and transformational leadership can contribute to effectiveness.
Transactional leadership, especially contingent reward, meets the material needs of followers. Transformational leadership increases in followers their feelings of self-worth,

and their identification with the leader. They become more aligned with their group, organization and/or society in norms, values and goals. But transformational leadership does not replace transactional leadership; transformational leadership augments transactional leadership. When combined, they predict effectiveness more than they do alone. This augmentation has been confirmed in several investigations (Bass, 1998).

Towards a Theory Transformational Leadership

Theoretical explanations are available to explain why transformational leadership usually works to arouse follower motivation.. One such theory focuses on the self-concept of the follower and the followerís sense of self-worth. The transformational leader encourages the follower to build a self-concept that identifies with the leader's self-concept and mission. Striving for consistency, the follower is motivated to exert extra effort to match the follower's own self-concept and mission with the perceived expectations of the leader and thereby raises his or her own sense of self-worth as a consequence. (Shamir, House & Arthur (1993).

These effects increase as we move up the organizational ladder. Feedback about the self rather than about the task increases in importance as we rise in the corporate hierarchy according to a meta-analysis of 607 individual analyses (Kluger & DeNisi, 1996) Furthermore, the quality of the relations between the leader with an individual follower depends on the leader supporting the self-worth of the follower by showing confidence in the follower's integrity, ability and motivation, and attending to the follower's feelings and needs. This support for the follower's self-worth is more important to the quality of the relations with the leader than the expertise and leadership style of the leader (Dansereau (1995). This is consistent with Greenleaf s (1977) servant leadership and Block's (1993) leader as steward; the view that leadership exists to serve those led and the fulfilment of the needs of those served. In an organizational hierarchy, those served include supervisors, peers and subordinates. And so, 360-degree appraisals of a leader's performance are justified. The leader's generally positive mood appears to be inspiring. George (1995) observed that job involvement were greater for sales managers if they saw their own boss as positive in mood but transactional contingent rewards were also important for their performance.

Summary

In sum, we began with the rapid and discontinuous changes in social, political and economic societal trends that provided the context for the new paradigm of transformational/transactional leadership. Next, we examined their components, their measurement, and their impact on effective performance. We considered the paradigm model of the Full Range Model of leadership to describe the relationships. We also looked at the different but parallel functions of the good manager who makes use of transactional leadership and the good leader who is likely to be more transformational. We considered whether the transformational leadership concept was universal or country and organization-specific, the small but significant differences between the sexes, and why transformational leadership works. We turned next to the ethics of authentic or truly transformational leadership and false or pseudotransformational leadership.

Ethics, Authentic and Pseudotransformational Leadership.

Criticisms of Transformational Leadership

Critics have offered at least four criticisms of transformational leadership. First, transformational leadership may rely on impression management. Here the good points about the leader are emphasized. My rebuttal is that the transformational leaders must be trustworthy and although they may engage in enhancing their image, they must avoid losing credit with their followers by promoting impressions that fail to stand up under close inspection.

Second, transformational leaders may use emotional appeals to override more rational arguments. My rebuttal is that institutions have to build in checks and balances in their governance. The majority in the legislature created at the U.S.Constitutional Convention could pass unsound legislation that might, for instance, trample the rights of the minority. James Madison, one of Americaís Founding Fathers, made sure that the U.S.Constitution contained enough checks and balances so no leaderís or factionís emotional appeals could trample the minority. The President could veto the legislation or the Supreme Court could find the legislation unconstitutional. Similarly, the legislature could vote to overturn Presidential Executive Orders and offset Supreme Court decisions. The President recommended the appointment of the justices, but a majority of the Senate had to approve the appointments.

Third, the practice of Organizational Development pushes for consensual decision-making and other democratic principles. In rebuttal, I suggest that transformational leaders work to align the interests of the organizational members and the organization. The leaders may be directive or democratic depending on the circumstances. They may be persuasive as when national leaders speak out on issues in order to sway public and legislative opinion.

Fourth, a criticism that points to unethical behaviour is when transformational leaders raise expectations then violate them. Woodrow Wilson and Franklin Delano Roosevelt in their campaigns for re-election in 1916 and 1940 ran on the slogan that they kept the U.S. from entering the World Wars. My rebuttal is if they knew that the U.S. would have to enter the war as Roosevelt surely did, they were being pseudotransformational.

Authentic Vs. Inauthentic Leadership

Transformational leadership is moral if it deals with the authentic needs of followers who can make informed choices, if it spells out real problems followers face, and if it provides real solutions to the real problems. Naturally, all of this is in the framework of universal moral principles and values.

Many scholars have commented on the dark side of charismatic and transformational leadership, charismatic and transformational leadership that is destructive rather than constructive, that invents crises, use provocateurs to arouse mob violence, distort the news, hides information important to followers and so on. I say this is pseudotransformational not transformational leadership

But first, we need to introduce the concept of authenticity. Authentic transformational leaders are true to themselves and to others. Inauthentic leaders deceive themselves and others.

Authentic transformational leaders align their own interests with the public good and may even sacrifice their own interests for the public well. They articulate their followers' real unmet needs and envision attainable futures. They practice what they preach as role models. They sound the alarm when real threats arise. Their communications can be trusted. The authentic transformational leaders are ethically mature and they set examples that uplift the moral values of their followers. Eleanor Roosevelt comes to mind as the epitome of such a world-class leader.

Inauthentic transformational leaders appear to support the public good but their own self-interests take precedence. They create artificial needs in followers. They arouse fantasies and delusions in their followers. They declare, Donít do as I do, do as I say. They manufacture threats and crises when there are none and stretch the truth. For them, the ends justify the means. They are less morally mature. Destructive dictators from Benito Mussolini to Seke Mobuto are illustrative.

Authentic transactional leaders keep promises, treat failures as learning experiences, take corrective action according to follower needs; and criticize follower behavior not the follower as a person. On the other hand, pseudotransactional leaders overreact to follower failure, take corrective actions arbitrarily and follower failure personally,

The differences can also be seen in the each of the components of transformational leadership behavior, cognitions, values, beliefs and perceptions.

Idealized influence, charismatic, inspirational leadership

Authentic charismatic and inspirational leaders focus on universal values such as the brotherhood of humanity; the inauthentic charismatic and inspirational leaders highlight us against them, their values and motives. The authentic charismatic and inspirational leaders focus on the best in people, tell followers what the need to hear, not what they want to hear, and truly empower followers. The inauthentic charismatic focus on the worst in people, mislead, prevaricate, and demonize opponents, seem to empower followers but actually create dependencies. The true charismatic leaders can be trusted; the false charismatic leaders ask to be trusted, but cannot be. The true charismatic espouse integrity and honesty; the inauthentic charismatic and inspirational leaders assign blame to others and treat opposition as disloyalty. Contrast Desmond Tutu and Idi Amin.

Intellectual Stimulation
A particularly important component of transformational leadership that has been ignored too often in evaluating senior executives is intellectual stimulation. Authentic intellectual stimulation involves among other things transformational leaders emphasizing the merit of issues; in their intellectual stimulation, inauthentic pseudotransformational leaders overweight authority and underweight reason. Authentic transformational leaders provide logical reasoning when they are intellectually stimulating. Authentic transformational leaders stimulate full examinations; contrarily, pseudotransformational leaders oversimplify arguments. Authentic transformational leaders

build arguments on truth and evidence. Pseudotransformationals intellectually stimulate by building arguments on ignorance, prejudice and half-truths. The true transformational leader intellectually stimulates using relevant metaphors and valid analogies; the pseudotransformational leader uses irrelevant ones. Compare Pope John XXIII with some of his predecessors.

Individualized Consideration

This component is last but not least. For some followers and leaders, it is the most important component and easiest for pseudotransformational leaders to simulate as true individualized consideration. President George W. Bushís compassionate conservatism is seen by many as inauthentic. Authentic transformational leaders are concerned about developing their followers; pseudotransformationals encourage unrealistic development goals. Authentic aim to develop followers into leaders; inauthentic, to develop submissive disciples. Authentic transformational leaders are empathetic; pseudotransformational leaders shed crocodile tears. While the truly considerate leaders are supportive and espouse fairness and human rights, pseudotransformational leaders are ingratiating, patronizing and condescending. Authentic transformational leaders are concerned for society and the environment; pseudotransformational leaders are focused on exploitation of society and the environment.

Conclusion

My purpose has been to shed some light on the dark side of transformational leadership by introducing to its study the need to distinguish between authentic and inauthentic leadership and between transformational and pseudotransformational leadership. I think we can add to authenticity, conscientiousness and trustworthiness, to further discriminate between true transformational leadership and pseudotransformational leadership. Much empirical research will be needed to test and confirm the validity of these concepts to contribute to the growing literature on the ethics of leadership. Some of this has begun by the Research Group of the Gallup Organization and at Victoria University in Melbourne.

References

Avolio, B.J. & Bass, B.M. (1990). Training and development of transformational leadership: Looking to 1992 and beyond. *European Journal of Industrial Training, 14,* 21-27

Bass, B.M. (1985*) Leadership and performance beyond expectations.* New York: Free Press.

Bass, B.M. (1997) Does the transactional-transformational leadership paradigm transcend organizational and national boundaries? *American Psychologist, 52,* 130-139.

Bass, B.M. (1998) Transformational Leadership: Industrial, Military and Educational Impact. Mahwah, N.J. Lawrence Erlbaum & Associates.

Bass, B.M. & Avolio, B.J. (2000, May 31) Platoon readiness as a function of leadership, platoon and company cultures. Final Report. U.S. Army Research Institute for the Behavioral and Social Sciences, Arlington, VA.

Block (1993) Stewardship. San Francisco, CA : Barrett-Koehler.

Burns, J. B. (1978*) Leadership.* New York: Harper & Row.

Dansereau, F. (1996) A dyadic approach to leadership: Creating and motivating it under fire. *Leadership Quarterly, 6,* 479-490.

Davis, D.D, Guan, P.L., Luo, J.J., & Maahs, C.J. (1996) Need *for continuous improvement, organizational citizenship, transformational leadership, and service climate in a Chinese enterprise.* Unpublished manuscript.

Den Hartog (1997*) Inspirational leadership.* Academisch Proefschrift: Free University of Amsterdam.

Dvir, T. (1998) *The impact of transformational leadership training on follower development and performance: A field experiment.* Doctoral Dissertation. Tel Aviv University, Ramat Aviv, Israel.

Garcia (1995*) Transformational leadership processes and salesperson effectiveness: A theoretical model and partial empirical examination.* Doctoral Dissertation Fielding Institute, Santa Barbara, CA.

George (1995) Leader positive morale and group performance: The case of customer service. *Journal of Applied Psychology, 80,* 778-794.

Greenleaf (1977) *Servant leadership.* New York: Paulist Press.

Kluger, A.N. & DiNisi (1996) The effects of feedback interventions on performance: An historical review, a meta-analysis, and a preliminary intervention theory. *Psychological Bulletin, 119,* 254-284.

House, R. (1977) *A 1977 theory of leadership.* In J.G. Hunt & L.L. Larson (Eds.) *Leadership: The cutting edge.* Carbondale, IL: Southern University Press.

Howell, J. & Avolio, B.J. (1993) Transformational leadership, transactional leadership, locus of control and support for innovation: Key predictors of consolidated business-unit performance. *Journal of Applied Psychology, 78,* 891-902.

Hunt, J.B. (1999) Transformational/charismatic leadershipís transformation of the field: An historical essay. *Leadership Quarterly, 10,* 129-144.

Kurlansky (1999) *The Basque history of the world.* New York Praeger.

Minor, J.B, (1975) The uncertain future of the leadership concept. Paper, Southern Illinois Leadership Conference. Carbondale.IL.

Molero, Alonzo, F. (1994) Charisma y liderazgo carismatico: Una zproximacion empirica desde las perspectivas de Bass y Friedman. Doctoral Dissertation, Universidad Nacional de Educacional a Distancia, Madrid, Spain..

Shamir, B; House, R.; & Arthur, M.B. (1993) the motivational effects of charismatic leadership: A self-concept based theory. *Organizational Science, 4,* 577-594.

Leadership, Globalisation and the New Economy: What is different and what is not?

Bruce Lloyd

Dr.Bruce Lloyd is Professor of Leadership and Management at South Bank University. London.

I would like to take this opportunity to congratulate Professor Safty on his initiative to establish The International Institute of Leadership and Public Affairs. Leaders dare to pursue their dreams and I commend you for daring Dr. Safty.

To start with a few words on my background, which I am sure has had some influence on where I am coming from on these issues. I originally did a Degree in Chemical Engineering; then a Business Degree, before spending 20 years working in industry and finance, including sometime with BP and ICI, as well as the Commonwealth Development Finance Company, who invested in small companies in various parts of the world. In 1989 I joined the academic world and have ended up writing, researching and lecturing strategic issues. My focus is on 'what makes organisations work' -- preferably work better, whether in the public or private sector. At the base of this work is the exploration of the essential links between individuals, organisations and society as a whole.

One theme I will argue strongly is that values are critical to organisational success in the long term but that does not mean that I have any formal religious agenda. In the end you might feel that I am being a little evangelical but I would like to emphasise that I approach the religious dimension from the viewpoint of a positive agnostic. I consider that to mean that I don't know all the answers to the big questions but I am very interested in exploring the questions and answers, particularly those concerned with values; this means using phrases like 'the soul of the organisation' without it having any specific religious overtones.

Of course, in the end, just focusing on what works begs questions such as how do you define what works, and that depends on what we are trying to do, and then how we define that to be a 'good thing'.

Before I get into the core of my remarks I would like to briefly making two points.

First on the Leadership vs. Management debate. Warren Bennis is quoted (by Professor Safty among others) as saying 'Leaders are people who do the right thing; managers are people who do things right'. It is interesting to note that decades ago people argued that division was used to distinguish between the approach taken by managers and administrators. I do not consider the manager/leader division is helpful to either understanding these issues in theory, or in operation in practice. I believe all good management activity has important leadership elements to it, and virtually all good leadership has a management element. I believe it is much more useful to consider the two words as interchangeable.

In the UK at least, I believe the separation of leadership and management has its roots in the 19th century class divisions when there appeared to be a widespread believe that some people 'were born to lead'. A core theme of my remarks is that leadership is a matter for us all; it occurs at all levels of an organisation or society and every time people interact with each other. Perhaps I can also add that is useful to include the word 'entrepreneur' in any analysis and, if we wanted to use glib phrases, we could define an entrepreneur as 'a person who just does things and then, later, tries to make them right'. Note, even here the word 'right' has a strong 'values' overtone.

The second lingering debate is over the question of whether leaders are born or made; the nature or nurture debate. This is a point I will return to later but I would like to emphasise at this point that I have not come across a leadership gene and my assumption is the vast majority, but I would not necessarily argue all, leadership behaviours are learned. However, I do not thing it is helpful to have the, usually academic, debate about the extremes Ö answers are invariably somewhere between the extremes and we need to focus on what can be done, and what needs to be done, to make a small shift in the right direction.

(For those of you who are interested in the more detailed academic arguments I would draw your attention to a paper I originally published a few years ago on 'Power, Responsibility, Leadership and Learning: The Need for an Integrated Approach' Leadership and Organisational Development Journal, Vol 17, No4, p52-56.)

Leadership and Power

Power and Responsibility

To move onto the main theme of my remarks which are focused on the link between 'leadership and power'. This discussion will start with some basic comments, which I am sure you are familiar with and they overlap with points already made by other speakers. I will start by raising the question: "What do we mean by power?" The word 'Power' is probably one of the most important word in any language; if not *the* most important word. In essence, power is the ability to make things happen. There are an enormous number of books on power, whether from a sociological or management perspective. These books tend to focus on power from the perspective of how to get it and how to keep it. It is surprisingly rare to find that the literature effectively discusses the inter-relationship between power and responsibility.

But why do I consider it is important for the two concepts to be considered together. Essentially the answer is simple. I consider responsibility to be the way in which we answer the question, in whose interests is the power being exercised? Yet it appears to be surprisingly rare for the relevant literature to discuss the issues of power and responsibility together.

Power has traditionally been associated with a mechanism through which we are able to get our own way; whereas being driven by a sense of responsibility means that we are primarily driven by wider interests. Of course, few people are at one extreme or the other, but 80/20 splits one way, or the other can produce a significantly different pattern of outcomes.

Power and Stress

The word empowerment is widely used in an organisational context today. Yet, in practice, it is the source of considerable misunderstanding, even stress. Empowerment is usually concerned with the idea of giving people more responsibility, although there does not appear to be such as a word 'emresponsibilityment' - at least in English! In one way thank goodness! But, unfortunately, empowerment is often more concerned with responsibility than power, or authority. And if we encourage more responsibility without the necessary authority, it can easily be a classic recipe for stress. In fact stress related illnesses are now reaching epidemic proportions in many industrialised countries and this is largely a reflection of the fact that there is a widespread perception that no-one cares and that there is almost a complete lack of appreciation, which some believe to be an inherently damaging side effect of an over-emphasise on competition. One recent research project showed that a desire to be appreciated was the number one need of an individual in work context (out of a list of nearly 20 characteristics) and that factor was at the bottom of the list in terms of what people perceive to happen in practice.

It can be useful to see these issues in terms of a two-by-two box, with power (P) (+/-) on one axis and responsibility (R) (+/-) on the other axis. Where we have P+/R+ everything is reasonably OK; but if we have P+/R- there are strong tendencies to megalomania; where there is P-/R+ you have the classical recipe for stress, whereas P-/R- is where we find most drop outs. This is a very general and sweeping division but I believe it does help us understand the issues and the critical relationship between power and responsibility.

When we look at most of the articles and books on stress these issues do not seem to be addressed and, certainly, the vital role played by the *quality* of our relationships is virtually ignored. Stress has much more to do with the *quality* of our relationships than with the *quantity* of work itself.

Abuse of Power

Many issues, such as bullying, sexism, and racism, whether individually or institutionalised, are much more usefully seen in the overall context of the existence of an abuse of power culture, than most of the other approaches taken. We need to begin, and end, with a genuine respect, and concern, for others. If we try to solve these problems with more and more rules and regulations we are likely to be doomed to failure, unless we appreciate the key role of values, and the link between power and responsibility, in the overall process.

Knowledge and Power

In considering these issues in a management context, one critical point is to recognise that virtually all the management techniques that we try to use, whether it is Total Quality Management, Re-engineering or Learning Organisation concepts, all depend on sharing knowledge if we want them to be effective. Yet, if we did a survey of the perception of people within our organisations, the all too frequent answer is that there is a perception of a 'knowledge is power', rather than a 'sharing knowledge', culture. If there is a 'Knowledge is Power' culture, it is not surprising that we find that most of these management techniques don't produce the results expected.

Change and Power

There is a general assumption that people resist change. But that begs the question of who is in charge of the process. If we are in control of the process then we usually welcome change; it is only when change is imposed on us that problems start. The key factor is 'in whose interests is it perceived that the change being made.' In an organisational context it is usually the case that the more change the less empowerment, with more resistance and greater stress. Overall, there is a widespread belief that there can be no assumption that change can be equated with progress. If we perceive change to be in our interests we have little or no problem with it.

Language of Power

I have some reservations, as I am sure most of you do too, about Political Correctness. But the way we use language, formally and informally, does change culture and cultural change also changes the way we use language.

The law is obviously important in helping to change culture and behaviour, but the role of values in society is more than just arguing about the interpretation of the law. Only lawyers might believe that we should leave everything to the lawyers. And I expect that most of them would have reservations over such an approach.

However, if I could pass one law, or enforce on form of Political Correctness, it would be to require substitution of the word responsibility every time we use the word power. We talk about the 'corridors of power' - Why not 'corridors of responsibility'? We talk about people 'lusting after power' - Why don't people 'lust after responsibility'? Power is considered to be an aphrodisiac. We don't seem to consider responsibility in quite the same way. Why not?

It is a great pity that there is not a greater emphasis on considering Rights and Responsibilities together. It was mentioned earlier today that the UN Declaration of Human Rights did emphasise the importance of Responsibilities in the final paragraph. But it is a pity that the connection was not made in the title. I know that there are people who are trying to rewrite the document as the 'Declaration of Human Rights and Responsibilities'. The key point here is that it is essential that those with power see it used within the wider context of 'in whose interests is it being used'. Power and responsibility need to be seen as two sides of the same coin. The more power we have the greater should be our sense of responsibility. The fact that this doesn't happen as often as it should is partly due to the fact that we are not encouraged, or we have not learned, to think that way in the first place.

Learning about Leadership

This is not the place to go into details about the characteristics associated with effective leadership, which have been considered by others at this meeting. While it is probably impossible to teach leadership, it is nevertheless learned somehow. If we look at the detailed list of the characteristics of an effective leader, some are basic competencies that are likely to be relatively easy to learn. But other issues are more difficult and these relate to characteristics such as integrity, energy, persistence, and responsibility, which together influence commitment, rather than competence. Commitment is what really makes things happen, and this reflects an individuals values and deeper sense of meaning. These areas are virtually impossible to teach, but they are critically dependent on what, and how, we learn about values.

One point that always needs to be clearly recognised is that people do not take much notice of what anyone says - unless they are forced to - but they do take a lot of notice about what they do. This reflects the importance of setting an example, of 'walking the talk', particularly in such 'soft' cultural areas as the use of power, sharing knowledge, or being really customer driven. All these points emphasise the importance of reflecting a genuine concern for the long-term interests of the organisation as a whole. If those at the top of an organisation are not perceived to be working in the interests of the organisation then there is little chance that those is the middle, or further down, will be working on that assumption. Effective communicators must be doing things that are consistent with what they are saying, and through that showing that they really believe in what they are saying and doing. Any effort in this direction must not be perceived as a new level of manipulation. Hence the importance of establishing credibility through the effective use of integrity, with integrity being, in essence, an assessment of 'in whose interests power is being used.' Unless leadership is seen to operate within a culture of integrity, it is almost inevitably, likely to lead to even greater hypocrisy and cynicism. Which brings us back to the starting point of any discussion of what we mean by effective leadership.

Leadership and 'The New Economy'

So what, if anything, is different about the so-called 'New Economy'. Compared with a 'traditional' organisation, we usually find that there is:

- A higher focus on people development.

- A higher focus on innovation and change.

- Greater emphasis on the integration of all the talents in the organisation to be used in the long-term interest of the organisation as a whole.

In the knowledge economy, more than ever, people are your greatest asset; that means they need to be appreciated and they need to be developed in a positive and supportive environment. All this is much easier to say than do, as many dot.com companies have found to their cost.

There has been a considerable discussion around the importance of 'trust' - another word that could be researched by the multi-cultural socio-linguists. But rarely do we find the discussion of trust linked to a discussion on openness and the fact that trust is basically a function of 'a perceived sense of fairness'. This point about fairness creates many actual and potential problems within organisations, as well as within and between nations.

Overall the issues of the so-called New Economy are basically the same as those in the more traditional economy, but are even more urgent. All organisations need to get the relationship between Power and Responsibility reasonably right, if they want to be successful over any length of time; this is even more relevant for organisations in the New Economy that are even more critically dependent on sharing knowledge and the need to manage innovation effectively.

Role of Wisdom
Before I conclude I would like to make a brief comment about the role of wisdom. Wisdom is a concept that is rarely mentioned in management literature in general, or knowledge management literature in particular. Wisdom can

be the vehicle for incorporating values into the leadership and management agenda. We need to move from a physical, power driven, leadership culture, to a 'smart' leadership approach, and ultimately onto a 'wise - values driven' - leadership culture. The key to successful 'wise' leadership being the ability to put wisdom into practice effectively.

One relevant piece of wisdom that we should never forget is the comment: "People are not interested in what you know until they first know you care."
(Those particularly interested in this area might like to refer to the 'Wisdom' project on World Future Society web site: www.wfs.org.)

Conclusion

Historically learning about leadership has been more about power, rather than responsibility. But, increasingly, the focus need to be shifted to be more about how we learn about, and how we learn to live with and manage, responsibility more effectively. Hence it is vital that we spend more time reflecting on how effective learning takes place in these areas, which includes, at its core, how we learn/develop our values.

Any approach that does not have this as its starting point just runs the risk of just producing more Hitlers, which should not have any part of our approach to leadership.
So a fundamental building block of leadership - if not *the* fundamental building block - is the ability to respect each other better. That means becoming more 'others' focused and being able to demonstrate that respect in the way in which we communicate with each other. In my view every act of communication has a leadership element to it. This point is

easy to say, quite easy to improve a little technically. But it is not so easy to show that we really believe it.

We need to have our Head - Competencies; our Heart - Commitment; and our Soul - our Values working well together. If we can get that right, or even do it just a bit better, it will be enormously beneficial to us as individuals, to the organisations where we work, and society as a whole.

Overall, I strongly believe that the whole issue of leadership begins and ends with the need to combine that greater concern for 'others', with a more insightful and relevant balance between Power and Responsibility issues.

Leadership should not, in any way, be preoccupied with Power and the 'self'. Getting the relationship between the self and others, between Power and Responsibility, is critical for the sanity and success of individuals, as well as for the long-term success of organisations and society as a whole. I believe this to be the key issue in leadership. It is one that affects us all - and it is one that we can all have an effect on. It is only when we get this broader balance reasonably right that we will be able to focus on the theme of this conference to use 'Leadership for Human Development' over the long term.

We are not going to solve all our problems by some miracle, but there are small steps that we can all take in the right direction. That is why we all need to take the question of leadership more seriously in all our communications and actions. I hope this is a cause for optimism.

Leadership and Nation-Building In South Africa

Carol Allais

Dr. Carol Allais is Professor and Chairperson of the Department of Sociology at the University of South Africa.

Who would have imagined S A as an example of anything but awfulness?
(Interview with the Telegraph, London. Desmond Tutu. The Sunday Times. April 22, 2001)

Introduction

The first democratic elections were held in South Africa in April 1994. The post-election bloodshed, which was predicted and feared by all did not materialise. The Economist (Feb 24, 2001) summed up the peaceful transition from authoritarian rule to democracy as follows: *Of all the horrors of the 20th century, South Africa s was unique. It did not happen.*

Despite the euphoria generated by the smooth transition to democracy, and the rallying call of a rainbow nationí, seven years into democracy, the transformation of South Africa society is a slow and painful process. Transformation of society has been met with various measures of success.

While South Africaís transition for all practical purposes was a model transitioní it was by no means simplistic or without dangers.

The history of South Africa, which is characterised by colonialism, racism, euro centrism, apartheid, sexism and repressive laws, has created a divided society whose divisions have been reinforced and sustained by a system of separate and unequal development and segregation in virtually all spheres of social, economic political and cultural life. Patterns of inequalities are clearly linked to race as a result of the countryís history. To a unique extent race and class overlapped for decades with non-whitesí (black South Africans) on the losing end (Magubane 2000).

In order to grasp the nature of problems besetting the transformation process, one needs to understand the diverse nature and background groups of the peoples, which make up South Africa society. South Africaís population of 37.9 million people is made up of blacks (Africans) (76.3 percent), whites (12.7 percent) coloureds (8.5 percent) and Indians (2.5 percent). Africans comprise five tribesí: San (a few remaining members), Nguni (who speak mainly isiXhosa, isiZulu, siSwati and Ndebele); the Sotho-Tswana (comprise groups North, South and West Sotho/Tswana - each having their own language), Tsonga (xiTsonga) and Venda (Tshivenda).

Traditionally, white South Africans include English speakers (of British descent), Afrikaners, (of Dutch descent) and also immigrants from Netherlands, France, Germany, Portugal, Italy and other European countries who still maintain their own languages and cultures. More recently there has been an influx of immigrants from Eastern Europe and the ex-USSR. There are also a number of Chinese people (descendants of indentured labourers), who maintain a strong cultural identity, as well as more recent immigrants from Taiwan as a result of a strong relationship between apartheid South Africa and the anti-communist government in Taiwan.

The Constitution provides for 11 official languages: Afrikaans, English, isiNdebele, Sepedi, Sesotho, siSwati, Xitsonga, Setswana, Tshivenda, isiXhosa, and isiZulu. (There are also moves to make sign language the 12th official language.)

The major religious groups in South Africa are Christians (almost 80 percent) of the population, Hindus, Muslims and Jews. A large minority of South Africaís population regards themselves as traditionalists. There are over 19 denominations within the Christian faith, ranging from the African Independent Churches with indigenous ties, to the Roman Catholic and Anglican Churches. Freedom of worship is guaranteed by the Constitution (chapter 2 of the Constitution also referred to as the Bill of Rights, Section 15) and official policy is one of non-interference in religious practices.)

The main political parties range from the mainly black (African) Pan-Africanist Congress to the all white Vryheidsfront (Freedom Front). In between are the African Christian Democratic Party, the African National Congress, the Democratic Alliance (which is a recent amalgamation of the Democratic Party and the National Party). The smaller parties include the white Afrikaans Herstige Nasionale Party (HNP), the mainly Zulu Inkhatha Freedom Party, The South African Communist Party and the Socialist Party of Azania (SOPA).
These may be described as contending modelsí, all having mutually exclusive normative political ideals and visions.

Thus the diversity in terms of race, ethnicity and multiculturalism which characterises South Africa society - bridging the gap between different interest groups - presents, perhaps, its greatest leadership challenge in the short and long term.

Inextricably intertwined with the challenges presented by diverse values are the problems of poverty, unemployment, AIDS and a drastic increase in crime. It is estimated that 57 percent of the population are living in poverty; 3 million households do not have electricity, 8 million have no access to clean water. The employment scenario is bleak. Official statistics put unemployment at between 20 and 30 percent. Other sources put it at as high as 40 percent. Unemployment is currently still rising as a result of the macro-economic programme (GEAR) instituted by the post-Mandela government. It is difficult to assess when this decrease in job opportunities and resultant job losses will stabilise. The highest levels of unemployment and underemployment are amongst the black (African) population. The shadow of AIDS hangs over almost every aspect of South African life. South Africa can expect 4-6 million to die of AIDS by 2010, when the epidemic is expected to reach its peak, and leave 2 million orphans. Few Africans can even begin to afford the anti-retroviral treatments that can keep AIDS at bay.

Leadership for Nation-building

Nation-building projects, if imposed in a top-down fashion are bound to create tension and exacerbate existing social fault lines. Rather than Jacobinistic nation-building, South Africa and its leaders require an open and intercommunicative process, facilitated by visionary leadership and elements of civil society to instil a state of democratic citizenship. Rhoodie and Liebenberg (1994) refer to this as democratic nation-building.

While a very bleak picture has been painted, the small miracle, which took place in the form of peaceful elections, must not be lost sight of. **Leadership played a great role in the transformation process to a new South Africa.** However, maintaining the pace and momentum of transformation of the early days of democratic change while simultaneously rising to the challenges outlined above, requires continued leadership as a critical factor (Meintjies 2001). In South Africa leadership gaps are being experienced at all levels. Leaders are the holders of values and play a key role in supporting people in that fearful process of reshaping values. In South Africa, cultural transition is slow and grudging, largely because the top management of institutions and organisations is uncertain and insecure about aspects of the new direction. All interest groups must back common programmes such as ones to combat racism and HIV Aids. A greater openness to leadership interchange and sharing across sectors is needed to accelerate the process. Existing pockets of consensusí need to be expanded through inter-communication and networking to enhance meaningful changes.

One of the more damaging shortfalls is that experienced by the youth. Youth leadership develops best in a context of an abundance of leaders in wider society. It develops where leaders in government, business and civil society are relevant, can read the futureís pulse and are getting to grips with the problems of the day and provide not only role models for the youth but gain credibility by ensuring a rightful and meaningful process of socio-economic participation for the youth.

Globalisation, as driven by multinational business corporations, has opened up the world to an extent never before seen, but often at considerable cost to poorer countries that are treated as economic units rather than human beings (Lee 2001:3). Leadership is, therefore, as decisive for the region and the continent as it is for South Africa.

The critical task of democratic nation-building requires leaders to work together on critical issues. What is needed is the leadership to bring the assets, talents and society-building aspects together. Leaders are not only the identifiers and signifiers of growing consensus, they are, and should be, consistent cementersí of consensus. In short, leadership is not just an additive for the fuel that powers people forward, it is the fuel itself.

Meintjies (2001) describes the style of leadership required for such an endeavour as bridgingí or connectiveí leadership. This is so not least because national social and economic goals, especially in a diverse and divided society can never be achieved without pulling together a critical mass of people from all walks of life. Liebenberg (1993:40) examines the notion of transformingí leadership and observes that leaders or the masses cannot go it alone and that leaders, in interaction with their followers, play an important role in the process of transition.

The Role of Civil Society
The past twenty years has witnessed a new development in the social history of the world - the emergence of an

organised and active civil society. Civil society constitutes a dimension of society different from and sometimes even antagonistic to the state (Perlas 2001: 5). In its modern form, civil society means the active and organised formations and associations in the cultural sphere. These would include, for example, NGOs, academia and church groups, in contradistinction to, but not necessarily in opposition to the formal apparatus of governance in the political sphere. This modern conception of civil society is similar to the Gramscian conception in that civil society differentiates itself from both business and government. Business is accorded its own area of articulation in the larger sphere of the economy. (Perlas 2001: 7). One of the key activities of civil society is to build and enhance social, human and institutional capital. With this goes a critical yet active public participation in various spheres of the polity.

Much has been written on the role of political leadership. The transformative and conciliatory leadership role played by Nelson Mandela in the run up to South Africaís democratic elections, and in his capacity of President in the first four years of the countryís new democracy being a case in point and will not be repeated here. There are many less heralded leaders from civil society who may be described as bridging or connective who are active nation builders. Zachie Achmat of the Treatment Action Campaign (TAC) is one such leader. Archbishop Desmond Tutu is another. Archbishop Tutu chaired the Truth and Reconciliation Commission (TRC), which was set in motion in 1995.

In the immediate aftermath of transition to democracy, South Africa, following the example of other countries such as Chile and Argentina, decided to unearth the truthí about a past of repression and collective violence. Liebenberg & Zegeye (1998: 542) point out that there have been various paths taken by countries to at least acknowledge the past, and at most take steps against offenders to introduce corrective or restitutional steps and more significantly, take preventative measures to prevent their recurrence. The implied goal is at least to enable/inculcate socio-political tolerance, to institutionalise open and democratic practice (various forms of democracy) and to ensure stability though transparent post-conflict governance and economic justice. Examples of other Truth and Reconciliation Commissions initiated by the new democratic governments or by sectors representing civil society are those of Bolivia (1982), Chile (1992) and Argentina (1984).

Truth Commissions are characterised by a truth phaseí in which they open up the pastí, which is closely linked to the ideal of effecting justice or restitution for those wronged, or the victims of human rights abuses (the justice phaseí). In some cases a political trade-off is made to let bygones be bygonesí and to focus rather on socio-political and economic reconstruction. Acknowledgement and restitution rarely play a part. Other cases aim at acknowledgement and restitution as far as humanely possible. This is especially the case in TRCs such as Chile and South Africa (Liebenberg & Zegeye 1998: 542-3).

The TRC had been given a threefold task: to listen to all who alleged a gross violation of their human rights, at the hands of either the previous government or the liberators; to receive applications from those who had committed violations, in the expectation of full amnesty for full confessions; and to provide for appropriate reparations to the victims.

Most important of all, however, is its responsibility to provide recommendations or proposals to inculcate sound civilian overseeing of security institutions, to nuture and enhance a reprofessionalisation of armed forces within the ambit of the civil and constitutional state.

Conclusion

The South African miracle has not yet unfolded fully and there are impressive (if not threatening) challenges confronting political leadership and civil society. It is in this arena that connective (bridging) and transformative leaders can play decisive, if not historical, roles.

Lest I have struck too pessimistic a note, let me conclude with the words of Peter Davis (editor of the Durban Sunday Tribune). He reminds us that it is early days yet - You have to remember wére in the middle of a revolution here - it really is a revolution and it may go on another 20 years .

List of sources

Lee, N. 2001. Introduction in R. Shepard. Humanising globalisation: The vital role of civil society. Durban: Novalis Press.

Liebenberg, I. 1993. Transition from authoritarian rule to democracy in South Africa: The role of political leadership and some strategies to attain democracy. Unpublished MA dissertation. University of the Western Cape. Cape Town.

Liebenberg, I and Zegeye, A. 1998. Pathway to democracy? The case of the South African Truth and Reconciliation process. *Social Identities* 4(3): 541-558.

Magubane, BM. 2000. African sociology: towards a critical perspective. Asmara: New World Press.

Meintjies, M. 2001. *The secret of success lies in good leadership.* Sunday Times Business Times. May 6 2001.

Perlas, N. 2001. What in civil society in R. Shepard. Humanising globalisation: The vital role of civil society. Durban: Novalis Press.

Rhoodie, N. & Liebenberg, I.. 1994. Democratic nation building in South Africa. Pretoria: HSRC.

Shepard, R. 2001. Humanising globalisation: The vital role of civil society. Durban: Novalis Press.

Sunday Times. *Knocking at heaven s door.* April 22, 2001.

South African Yearbook. 1998. (5TH ed.). Pretoria: Government Communication and Information System (GCIS).

The Economist. *Africa s great black hope.* February 24th - March 2nd 2001.

Leadership and Conflicts in Africa

Mahy Hassan Abdel Latif

Dr. Mahy Abdel Latif is counsellor in the Egyptian Foreign Ministry

Introduction

The history of the African continent in the last 30 years can be considered one of unfulfilled dreams and betrayed ambitions. In the wake of their independence, the young African states hoped, along with other things, for unity, peace and security. Instead, war, famine and suffering turned to be the lot of a majority of the people of Africa.[1]

Currently, conflicts constitute one of the most pressing of all challenges facing the continent. Not only have these conflicts cast a dark shadow over the prospects of a united, secure and prosperous Africa, but also caused staggering losses of resources expended on carrying out wars, massive destruction of property and infrastructure, as well as environmental degradation. However, the human dimension is absolutely the most distressing; men, women and children have been uprooted and forced to become refugees as a result of conflicts. [2] Africa has the unenviable record of hosting the largest number of uprooted communities in the world accounting to 7 million refugees and almost 20 million displaced persons.[3]

The vast majority of the more than thirty conflicts that have taken place in Africa since 1970 were intra-state in origin.[4] This fact has led many to argue that the nature of conflicts in Africa has changed from inter-state conflicts to intra-state conflicts, which represent the current challenge Africa has to face up to. However, it is the contention of the author of this paper, that the nature of conflicts in Africa has not so much changed, it only became more pronounced. The current eminence of intra-state conflicts in Africa does not represent a change in the nature of conflicts in the continent. In fact, the potential for this type of conflicts has only been suppressed by nationalist and liberation movements and governments seeking independence, and also to some extent by super-power rivalry during the Cold War. The end of the Cold War and the deteriorating political, socio-economic situation in Africa in the eras of the 80ís and 90ís, have unleashed the hitherto simmering ethnic, religious and political intra-state tensions and allowed them to run their full course. It could be, nevertheless, argued that the novelty is in the form, which some of these intra-state conflicts have taken and that is what has been called anarchic conflicts. It is the contention of the author also that intra-state or anarchic conflicts are not the only challenge that Africa has to face up to in the next millennium. There is a whole list of potential sources of conflict that could trigger not only intra-state conflicts but also inter-state conflicts, two types that in fact could not be considered in isolation.

This discussion is an attempt to look at conflicts in Africa, their root causes, changing nature, implications, and the potential challenges facing the continent in the next millennium.

I. Conflicts And Their Roots In Africa

Towards a Definition of Conflicts
Conflict as a concept has been perceived as a pervasive social process that takes place at all levels be it personal, group, organizational or international. This multidimensional character of conflict has been the stumbling block in the way of researchers attempting to define it. Struggle, strife and/or collusion are the main ingredients of most definitions of conflict. Most definitions have also attempted to differentiate between conflict and competition. Some have defined conflict as a struggle over values or claims to status, power or scarce resources in which the aim of the group or individuals involved is to gain these objectives simultaneously and to neutralize, injure or eliminate rivals. [5] A. Oberschall noted that social conflict is one of the ubiquitous events that encompasses a broad range of phenomena including class, racial, religious, and community conflict, in addition to riots, rebellions, revolutions, strikes, marches, demonstrations and protest rallies. [6] Peter Wallensteen defined conflict as a situation in which a minimum of two parties strive at the same moment in time to acquire the same set of scarce resources. [7] The crucial condition of conflict is perceived to be scarcity which has three requirements to materialize; a group of organized actors, (with)

incompatible objectives, and a conscious behaviour to attain set goals.[8]

Roots of Conflicts in Africa
Be it as it was wars of liberation, decolonisation or as it currently is, intra, inter or regional conflicts, the sources or roots of conflicts in Africa are said to reflect, or to have reflected, the diversity and complexity of the make-up of the continent where different African countries have different historical, geographical conditions and different stages of economic development, as well as different patterns of public policies, internal and international interactions.[9]

In spite of these differences, the sources or roots of conflict in the continent are closely inter linked by some common experiences and factors, out of which the main ones are:

Historical Factors or Legacies
The arbitrary partition of the African continent by the Colonial Powers, at the congress of Berlin 1885, has joined unrelated areas and peoples and thereby posing a great challenge to the newly independent states. Although the era of serious conflict over state boundaries in Africa has largely passed, to a great extent because of the OAUís decision in 1963 to accept inherited boundaries from colonial authorities, African states still face the challenge of forging a genuine national identity among diverse and often competing communities.[10] In other words, the imposition of borders as well as colonial institutions on traditional African societies have made conflicts inevitable. Colonial rule has divided African societies along several fault lines that were to impact negatively on post-colonial Africa.[11]

Internal Factors
A key source of conflict across the continent is considered to be the nature of political power along with the real and perceived consequences of capturing or maintaining it. Assuming power means control of wealth, prestige and prerogatives of office. Insufficient accountability of leaders, lack of adequate checks and balances, non-adherence to the rule of law, and the absence of peaceful means of changing leadership combined with centralized and personalized forms of governance where the state is the major provider of employment and political parties are either regionally or ethnically based, create a dangerous situation where rival and ethnic communities perceive their security and survival in controlling state power and, therefore, conflicts become inevitable. [12] One could argue within this context that most conflicts in Africa boil down to unaccountable leadership and poor governance.

External Factors
Not only has Africa become the casualty of colonial arrangements but also of post-colonial ones. Africa was caught in the vortex of the ideological conflagration of the Cold War era. Accordingly, many African states were divided along ideological and pro-west, pro-east lines. Many conflicts in Africa had their roots anchored in these imported ideologies and as a consequence some nationalist saw the one-party system as a way out in conformity with traditional African values. This system has proved intolerant of dissenting views and excluded popular participation, which led to alienation. In some cases, this alienation took the form of depriving some ethnic groups that were considered as anti-establishment. [13]

Although external intervention in Africa has diminished with the end of the Cold War, it had not stopped to play an important, and sometimes, decisive role in instigating or suppressing conflicts in the continent. External intervention is not limited, however, to forces outside Africa. The role of other African governments in provoking or sustaining a conflict in a neighboring country has to be acknowledged. [14]

Economic Motives

Economic motives often stand behind provoking a conflict or prolonging it. In spite of all the havoc caused by armed conflicts, there are those who profit from conflicts in Africa or have no interest in stopping one. On top of the list are international arms merchants and sometimes the protagonist themselves. The examples of Liberia, Angola, and Sierra Leone reflect the fact that control and exploitation of natural resources and reserves was one objective of the warring factions. Besides, it provided them with the means to sustain the conflict. [15]

Other Factors

A number of other factors of conflict in Africa are specific to particular situations and sub-regions. For example in central Africa, competition was for scarce land and water resources in densely populated areas. In Rwanda, successive waves of displaced persons have made several families claim rights to the same piece of land. Where oil is extracted, conflict has arisen over the degradation of the environment or inadequate benefits from such resources. In North Africa, opposing visions of governance led to serious tensions and conflicts. [16]

The Changing Nature Of Conflicts In Africa

Repercussions of the End of the Cold War
The end of the Cold War, officially proclaimed the 21st of November 1990 in Paris through the adoption of the Paris Charter for a New Europe by the Conference on Security and Cooperation in Europe (CSCE), had a negative impact on African security and peace. It has led to what could be called a geo-strategic devaluation of Africa. [17]

The International Context
The end of the Cold War has created a new eagerness by the international community to exercise its newly acquired capacity for collective decision-making. The early 1990ís witnessed the launching of ambitious peacekeeping and peacemaking initiatives in Africa and elsewhere. Despite its many successes, the abysmal failure of the UN to restore peace in Somalia or to prevent genocide in Rwanda has had profound consequences in Africa. The perception, throughout the continent, of near indifference on the part of the international community has created a poisonous legacy in Africa. [18]

The Continental Context
On a continental level, the end of the Cold War, led to a simultaneous dissolution of East/West rivalry in Africa leading to long awaited transitions such as the independence of Namibia and the end of Apartheid in South Africa. At the same time, leading to changes in the nature and manifestations of intra-ethnic conflicts and civil strife. Africa had to expect dramatic changes not only in the international but also in the national environment of its

politics. The hitherto suppressed ethnic and political tensions were unleashed. Some African states ushered in a process of disintegration into conflicting ethnic, cultural, or religious factions. Conflicts that have been so far overshadowed by strong nationalist governments and superpower rivalries have been exposed and brought to the fore by the end of the Cold War. [19]

It is a truism that superpower rivalry, during the Cold War, has fuelled some of Africaís deadliest conflicts (e.g. Angola), however, there was a premium placed on maintaining order and stability among friendly states and allies. Consequently, once the Cold War was over, many African regimes lost their grip on political power and were unable to sustain economic development leading to internal unrest and violent conflicts. [20] Conflicts that have passed regional, ethnic divisions to clan and even sub-clan lines.[21] The examples of Angola, Burundi, Congo, Liberia, Mozambique, Rwanda, Sierra Leone Somalia & Sudan, are examples of countries torn apart by violence and intense conflicts demonstrating the failure of African states to manage change in an effective and non-violent manner in the post Cold War era. [22]

The Changing Nature of Conflicts in Africa
In addition to the negative repercussions of the end of the Cold War that we have mentioned earlier, the eras of the 80ís and 90ís have ushered a path stream of contradictions and negative complications from an unfair international economic order, and the disappointment of Africaís performance in the areas of good governance and political emancipation along with a decreasing level of economic development and a record of human rights abuses.[23] By the mid 90ís, waves of democratisation and partial economic

liberalization plans have at best been a mixed blessing. In almost every African state there was a faction in society that felt aggrieved, under represented, excluded or alienated from the system.[24]

This combination of unfavourable factors that existed in the continent, can lead us to argue that indeed a recognizable change has taken place in the nature of conflicts in Africa, from inter to intra (internal) conflicts. The Declaration on the Political and Socio-Economic Situation in Africa and the fundamental changes taking place in the World of 1990 adopted by the OAU Assembly of Heads of State and Government, was perceived as a decisive turning point because for the first time in Africaís history, the OAU recognized this changing nature of conflicts which demanded a more dynamic approach given the African preoccupations with the sacrosanct principles of sovereignty and non-interference in the internal affairs of states enshrined in the OAU Charter (Art. III).[25]

However, it is the contention of the author of this paper that the nature of conflicts in Africa has not so much changed but rather that the nature and manifestation of intra-state conflicts have become more pronounced. The driving forces for these conflicts have always existed. Suffice it to reiterate the fact that Africans from different religions, ethnic identities and communities were arbitrarily joint together by the colonial powers in 1885. This nature or type of conflict has only been suppressed, as mentioned before, by nationalist, liberation movements or governments seeking independence, also to some extent by superpower rivalry during the Cold War.

However, as argued earlier, the end of the Cold War and the loss of international interest in Africa, coupled with the deteriorating political, socio-economic and humanitarian situation in the continent during the 80ís and 90ís have unleashed the simmering ethnic, religious and political intra-state conflicts and allowed them to run their full course. It can be argued, though, that what represents a novelty is the new type of intra-state conflicts i.e. Anarchic Conflicts . In the part to follow we are going to discuss in more details the nature of anarchic conflicts, their causes and their implications.

Anarchic Conflicts, their Nature and Causes
The nature of this conflict is reflected in the definition of the word anarchy (Greek origin anarkhia), which means disorder resulting from an absence of authority or confusion due to the absence of rules or precise order. This type of conflict is defined as global violence generated either by the total bankruptcy (collapse) or the decadence of rules and structures of the state. It is an expression of a double crisis of the state and the society, which ravaged the African continent at the end of the 20th century. [26]

These kinds of conflicts are characterized by their complexity and diversity. The crumbling of political entities, putting into question whole societies, new quests for independence and identity, popular aspirations for democracy, demands for good governance, existence and emergence of ultra nationalist movements, forced displacement of populations, massacres and ethnic cleansing. In this new type of conflicts, structures of the state break up to the extent that no authority exists to exercise power, no minimal public service, no respected norms, total decadence of all civil, social or even military structures. The disintegration of the chain of command reaches an extent that the multiplication of factions leads to large scale violations of human rights.[27] In sum, in what has been also called collapsed or failed states, the disintegration of social and political structures renders the state ungoverned or ungovernable.[28]

As for the goal of this type of conflict, it is the struggle for state power be it to maintain or to acquire it. The course of this conflict is bipolar. On one side, since this conflict is related to the maintenance of power, the principal actor is the state or the government in power, which uses or abuses the monopoly over its armed, police and security forces against its own citizens or other ethnic groups in the country. On the other side, when the struggle is for the conquest of power, then the principal actors are either the citizens (individual actor) or what is called para-colonial or historical ethnic communities (collective actor). The first kind of violence is called a conflict of citizenship, while the second is called a conflict of nationality.[29]

The main causes given for such type of conflict are as follows:

1. The Inescapability of Change: stability cannot be valued as an end in itself at the detriment of progress. All societies have to adapt to continuous change with regards to redistribution of powers and resources, something that is in the nature of the state.
2. Despotism and Confiscation of State Power: by an individual or a group at the detriment of citizens and ethnic minorities. Generally speaking, injustice and inequality in the distribution of the revenues of material or moral resources make violence erupt.
3. Inadaptability of the Western Model of the Nation-State: to the social logic and to the pluralistic structures of the African societies is considered to be one of the

fundamental causes for this type of conflict. It was argued that the model of a Federal state which includes different ethnicities, languages, religions, cultures, and laws and which can be called a multinational, multiethnic or post-national state is the best model for African states.[30]

Some other causes can be discerned such as:
1. A small rich elite and poverty stricken masses.
2. Shortage of resources including land and basic sustenance.
3. Sharp decline in family or traditional authorities.
4. Erosion of social rules and emergence of alternative social structures as gangs, warlords and even revolutionary parties.
5. Disappearance of common social restraints on violence.
6. High levels of unemployment
7. Manifestations of social tension between rural and urban, traditional and modern, uneducated and educated, ethnic insiders and ethnic outsiders.[31]

Implications
A situation where there is total collapse of state institutions and disruption of government functions renders attempts of intervention or assistance, either by African states or others, severely difficult. Attempts to ensure a settlement, resolve a dispute, or to deploy forces for preventive purposes, or to provide assistance (humanitarian or other) are bound to be limited and require substantial resources. In this context, peacemaking and peacekeeping become more complex and more costly. As in the case of Somalia and Rwanda, outside intervention had to extend beyond military and humanitarian tasks to include the tasks of re-establishing an effective government and promoting national reconciliation.[32]

Moreover, in these conditions where there are warring factions and no recognized government the question arises: will all these factions be considered parties to the conflict and be cooperated with? Or which faction to talk to? This is considered as a new challenge, especially to the OAU, which is an intergovernmental organization, can it then negotiate with anti-government factions? This gives rise to a legal problem of international relations. For many years, the OAU refused to deal with political and military well-organized movements like RENAMO or UNITA and regarded them as armed bandits. The task becomes even harder for the OAU since it is difficult to get the consent of the parties when there is a multitude of them. The case of an absence of state was never anticipated or foreseen by the Cairo Declaration of 1993, which established the OAUís Mechanism for Conflict Prevention, Management and Resolution. [33]

Weíve talked about difficulties facing the OAU in situations of anarchic conflicts. The report of the International Committee of the Red Cross (ICRC), which mentions seven challenges facing it in Africa today, is indicative of the implications of anarchic conflicts in the case of humanitarian assistance.

These seven challenges are:
1. The Relevance of International Humanitarian Law (IHL): The instruments and ideology of the IHL (codified in the Geneva Protocols of 1949, their Additional Protocols of the 1977 and other instruments such as the Ottawa Treaty banning the use of landmines) tend to be inappropriate to the type of anarchic conflicts. How to deal with child-soldiers waged conflicts? How to evacuate a Tutsi through a Hutu area or vice-versa? The main interlocutors of the ICRC become local leaders who often fight for purely commercial

or selfish interests away from any humanitarian preoccupation.

2. The Ethnic Dimension in Conflicts: The Geneva Conventions or other IHL instruments, become inapplicable in ethnic conflicts. What can be said to leaders who order killing of other on the basis of their religion, tribe or ethnic group?

3. The Weakening or Disintegration of the State: In this case the interlocutors of the ICRC cannot anymore impose their power on warriors in the field and therefore this can impede the delivery of relief and protection activities from the capital. ICRC movements have to be negotiated with a multitude of checkpoints, armed groups, regional commanders (case of Somalia, Zaire and Liberia).

4. The weakening of the state also leads to a reduction in public social services provided by governmental institutions. In substituting these services, the ICRC is obliged to provide care and assistance to victims over whom it has no direct mandate to protect.

5. The Humanitarian Competitions: Humanitarian activities are becoming big business. There is a problem of coordinating the different NGOs and their approaches in a context of anarchic conflicts. The Politicization of Aid: In a country where thereís no government or any internationally recognized monitoring capacity, the various NGOs that exist might serve a hidden agenda of their particular donors.

6. The loss of Ideology and the Role of Economics: With the Cold War over, the traditional sponsors of the different fighting groups are replaced by new ones that are not motivated by politics or ideology but by big business. These tend to be multi-national conglomerates trading in African diamonds, oil, minerals etc. The Geneva Conventions are binding states not multinational conglomerates, so whom

could the ICRC talk to? These are not interested in IHL but in business.

7. **The Lack of International Interest to Find a Political Solution:** The Somali Case is an example of the Zero Casualty Requirement by the developed countries which meant that their armies would not intervene in any dispute if their forces or troops are at risk. More generally they are not interested or willing to bring about a political settlement of a dispute in a conflict where their national interests are not involved.[34]

Challenges Facing Africa In The Next Millennium

The Interaction Between Inter and Intra-State Conflicts

Given the fact that very few African states are genuine nation states, with a significant multitude of internal, ethnic and religious dimensions, the prospects of intra-state conflicts in Africa are considerably high.[35] However, the eminence or high prospects of intra-state conflicts in Africa does not mean that this is the only nature or type of conflicts that Africa has to deal with in the future or that this is the only challenge that Africa has to face up to in the next millennium.

The recent Ethio-Eritrean war offers a good example. The conflict in the DRC provides another example of the fact that it is almost impossible to reflect upon intra-state conflicts without taking into consideration the larger neighbouring and even regional situation. Intra and inter-state conflicts cannot be considered in isolation. Few intra-state conflicts in Africa could be considered as completely internal affairs. Ethnic affinities, refugee problems and political sympathies are major reasons for involvement in neighbouring countries´ domestic problems. The more recent examples are Liberia/Sierra Leone, Chad/Togo, and Sudan/Uganda. A nation´s own security has to take into consideration that of its neighbours.[36]

Consequently, we can maintain that Africa has to expect both inter and intra state conflicts, for there is a number of potential sources that could trigger either one or both types of conflicts.

Potential Sources of Conflict in Africa
It is argued that if Africa is to face up to the challenges awaiting it in the 21st century, there is an urgent need to look at a whole list[*] (perceived as a non-exhaustive one) of potential sources of conflicts that threaten the security of the continent and bear negative implications on its prospects for sustainable peace and development. In what follows we are going to go through this list.

Border Conflicts
Border conflicts in Africa could result from;
    1. Fluid, porous or mal-demarcated borders.
    2. Political ambitions.
    3. Cross-border ethnic mixes and structures.
    4. The desire of controlling scarce resources

Some examples of actual or potential border conflicts are between Algeria-Morocco, Somalia-Ethiopia, Ethiopia-Eritrea, Sudan-Eritrea, Uganda-DRC, Sudan-Uganda,

---

[*] This list was provided by Vasu Gounden concerning the Southern African Region, however, it is taken here to apply for the whole continent since it applies not only to the S. African Region but to all regions in the continent as the author here perceives it to be so.

Zambia-DRC, and Botswana-Namibia. Although for the rest of Southern Africa there are no current border disputes, the spill over can threaten the security of the region. Accordingly, border problems have to be studied carefully so that strategies of actions can be formulated in case of eruption of border conflicts[37].

Ethnicity
There are different types of multi-ethnic societies, fragmented where there are more than 4 major ethnic groups e.g. Nigeria and the DRC (former Zaire). Dominant Minority Societies where this minority wields power to the exclusion of a considerable majority for e.g. Rwanda and Burundi. The formation of an ethnic identity can be affected by the struggle for resources, rights and privileges whether with other ethnic groups or with the state which dominates it. Ethnicity is often manipulated (through the use of symbols, religion, languageÖetc) for political purposes. Non-oppression, respect for institutions, stable power structures, peaceful change of government, and the establishment of strong mediation, peacekeeping and peace enforcement authorities, early-age education of tolerance are all believed to reduce the threat of conflicts due to ethnic reasons[38].

Refugees / Migrants
Out of the 24 million internally displaced persons in 1992, it is estimated, by the Refugee Policy Group, that 65% were to be found in Africa. The movement of large numbers of people due to wars, internal, ethnic conflicts and population growth poses great security threats in Africa. Host governments face substantial financial, social, and public service burden, which creates tension and conflict over scarce resources and employment. In addition to the increase in crimes, diseasesÖetc. For example, civil war and

genocide in Somalia, Sudan in the Horn, Rwanda in the east, Liberia in the west, Angola in the south, which have led to the increase of the number of refugees and migrants into the Southern African region. [39]

Religious Conflicts
Within this context, greater attention is needed since the threat of religious conflicts appears to be of great eminence. Conflicts of this nature have intensified recently through extremists groups. Examples are: Algeria, Sudan, Ethiopia, Nigeria and Egypt. [40]

Small Arms Proliferation
The spread of intra-state conflicts has led to the increase in the demand for small arms where they are used for close range combat, irregular fighting and need little training and maintenance. In return, the proliferation of small arms (due to the lack of inspection facilities and border patrols) heightens the potential for intra-state conflicts at the political, socio-economic, and ethnic levels. Moreover, it has short and long term negative consequences on development due to rising levels of violence, crime and instability. [41]

Urban Growth Management
While urban growth is dropping in developed countries, it is rising in developing ones. In the latter, urban growth rate has increased from 63% in 1990 to 71% in 2000, and shall increase to 81% in 2025 resulting in increased urban poverty, health problems, concentration of economic activities in large cities, growing demands and pressures on urban services and infrastructure, as well as environmental degradation. Given these facts, focus is required for

establishing a policy of alleviating poverty, creating jobs, and improving the urban environment.

The latter includes, providing urban infrastructure and services, as well as strengthening the urban local government and administration. Another requirement is the establishment of small and medium size cities with good economic potential which will help in creating new locations for economic development, in expanding job opportunities, and in achieving a sort of a balanced urban development.[42]

Difficulties of Integration and Transformation
Since 1952, 78 violent changes of government have taken place in Africa with about 88 leaders deposed. In cases of total collapse of the structure, political and legal order of the state (anarchic conflicts), the problems of reconstruction and integration (involving restoring order, rebuilding state legitimacy, and restructuring the economy) have to be faced. Some of these problems are:

1. Creating a suitable environment for political tolerance.
2. Establishing strong political structures and leadership.
3. Handling extremist groups.
4. Engaging in confidence-building projects.
5. Meeting high expectations by the people.
6. Developing good infrastructure and communication systems.
7. Addressing atrocities of the past.
8. Developing a culture of peace and tolerance.
9. Redistributing wealth.
10. Addressing ethnic and racial tensions. [43]

Economic Conflicts
Conflicts, accompanied by the application of inappropriate economic policies and management, have meant that African development suffers. Physical productive capital is destroyed, production disrupted, infrastructure is destroyed or deteriorates, new investment is discouraged, market processes and exchange relations are inhibited, and living standards decline. The loss of human lives as well as the presence of large numbers of homeless people greatly affect the stock of human capital and large of amounts of state capital are used for emergency needs . [44]

Developing countriesí debts rose from US$658 billion in 1980 to US$ 1,945 billion in 1994. Africa has some of the poorest countries in the world. The economic situation in Africa shall further deteriorate given the high prospect of potential conflicts. [45]

Environmental Conflicts
The main cause behind deforestation and land degradation is poverty, which leads people to over-use their environment to be able to survive. Over 250 million people are living below the poverty line in sub-Saharan Africa alone. Pressures on the environment, pollution of land, sea and air, and the destruction of natural vegetation are aggravated by population growth. Over half of Africaís arable land is threatened by desertification. Depletion of the Ozone layer and the phenomenon of global warming are additional factors threatening the environment in Africa.

The latter will impact on the weather in Africa making it hotter and drier while at the same time affecting wild life in the region. Crop failures have made many villages dependant on food aid. Africa has to face the problem of self-sufficiency since food aid is only a short-term solution. While weather factors result in famines, wrong political decisions, corruption, mismanagement, ignorance, neglect, and conflicts are other important reasons for famines. Increasing global temperatures shall lead to a spread of fevers (yellow and dengue), malaria and other diseases. Finally, nuclear waste is still another real threat to the environment. Not only can marine life be destroyed but also fresh waters used for human and agriculture needs, can be contaminated by toxic chemicals. [46]

Conclusion

This discussion has presented an overview of conflicts in Africa, their roots, nature or type, and their implications on African security and socio-economic development. The paper has also identified some of the potential sources of conflicts that represent current or future challenges that Africa has to face up to in the next millennium. The author here has tried to argue that the nature of conflicts in Africa has not so much changed.

The fact is that intra-state conflicts, including their new manifestation or form i.e. anarchic conflicts, has gained pre-eminence over inter-state conflicts in the recent eras of the 80ís and 90ís due to international and internal factors, the inter-play of which, has unleashed the hitherto suppressed potential for intra-state tensions and allowed them to run their full course. The author has also argued that intra-state conflicts do not represent the only challenge that Africa is facing, but that it is impossible to reflect on intra-state conflicts without considering the dimensions that could trigger inter-state conflicts as well.

The reflection on the afore-mentioned issues leads us to conclude that conflicts, of whichever nature or kind, have adverse and negative ramifications on peace, security and stability in the African continent as well as on its prospects of socio-economic and human development. We can very easily pinpoint the interlocking nature of peace, security, stability and development in Africa. Moreover, we can easily discern a vicious circle of roots or causes of conflicts, their negative repercussions on socio-economic development, the impact of poor economic performance on the society and on the state's capacity to respond to internal tensions, demands and pressures, and the eruption of conflicts in Africa. These facts show the predicament in which Africa finds itself.

If Africa does not want to find itself, in what is called a new world order that was established on the heels of the bipolar order of the Cold War, completely marginalized and utterly insignificant geo-strategically, politically and economically, difficult decisions have to be taken and serious efforts have to be enacted.

It is high time for Africans to realize that only united and conscious African efforts can solve African problems. Africansí determination and strong will have to be summoned to handle the African predicament. Below, we shall review some of the crucial recommended elements that could promote durable peace and sustainable development in Africa, thereby, helping the continent in dealing with current and future challenges facing it.

1. First of all, the real causes behind conflicts in Africa whether intra, inter-state or other, have to be seriously and properly addressed. We can never hope to pre-empt, prevent or solve conflicts without eliminating their root causes.

2. The proper approach to solving a problem is usually the second step in handling it. As we have argued before, that all aspects of African security, peace, stability and development are closely interlinked, the proper approach to African problems becomes then a holistic, comprehensive one that encompasses all facets of these problems.
3. There is a dire need in Africa for a visionary, far-sighted political leadership. A leadership with a clear vision and understanding of African problems, their different causes and interactive dimensions, as well as the appropriate strategies and policies for addressing them.
4. This leadership has to endorse concepts of good governance, the rule of law, and democracy in its attempts to solve African problems, address their causes and face future challenges. This would entail:
(a) Decentralization of power and depersonalised forms of government.
(b) Ensuring high standards of transparency, accountability and probity.
(c) Creating pluralistic democratic states based on free elections, multi -party systems that could accommodate and ensure that all religions, ethnic, linguistic, minority or opposition groups are adequately represented at all levels of decision-making. Consequently, giving different groups in the society a stake in a system where their interests are represented.
(d) Promoting respect for human rights and guaranteeing fundamental freedoms including freedom of the press, freedom of speech and belief.
(e) Ensuring proper and impartial enforcement and institutionalization of the rule of law.
(f) Promoting a culture of peace and tolerance of diverse ethnic, religious, as well as of dissenting opinions and opposition parties.

(g) Encouraging womenís full participation in political life at decision-making levels.
(h) Building constructive partnership with civil society organizations for peace and development in Africa.

5. Within the context of sustainable socio-economic and human development in Africa; education, womenís empowerment, investment, competitiveness, cooperation and integration become key passwords;
(a) Education is the key to all kinds of development is it political, socio-economic or human. Eradicating illiteracy, providing African people, men and women, with technical training and professional skills, represent the basic foundation for African development. Ignorance is the major source of all troubles in any society and the main reason for its staying backward in all fields.
(b) African womenís empowerment^Θ and the enhancement of their capabilities are essential for current socio-economic and even political development or progress. Women can play a decisive role in the preservation of African environment, and natural resources such as water.
(c) Investment* is another key word for economic development. African countries have to adopt adequate economic policies and provide proper infrastructure in order to create the suitable environment for national and foreign investment.
(d) Africa has also to adopt the appropriate strategies and policies so that it can compete on the global level and be included in the new international economic order

---

^Θ The UN Secretary General report, The Causes of Conflict and the Promotion of Durable Peace and Sustainable Development is especially enlightening on recommendations to responding to African problems.

symbolized by the Uruguay round and the World Trade Organization.
(e) Cooperation and integration, regional and sub-regional, is the hope for African development. Africans have to enhance and strengthen their cooperation in all economic, scientific and technical fields, sub-regional organizations seem to represent a first positive step towards the long-term objective of the African common market on the model of the European common market.

6. At the continental level, comes the indispensable requirement for an early warning system and a mechanism whereby to anticipate conflicts before they erupt, manage them once they erupt and after their eruption, ensure collective action to diffuse and solve the conflict, and to subsequently engage in post- conflict reconstruction:
(a) The OAU has, as referred to earlier, founded the Mechanism for Conflict Prevention, Management and Resolution established by the Cairo declaration of 1993. The Mechanism provided an institutional framework for conflict prevention, management and resolution in Africa. It was designed to encompass measures such as preventive diplomacy, mediation, conciliation, peacemaking, peacekeeping, and confidence building in cooperation with the UN, African sub-regional organizations and NGOs.
(b) The Mechanism is, however, facing some constraints* (conceptual, political, Institutional and resource related).

---

* See Magdy A. Helfny, The OAU Mechanism for Conflict Prevention, Management Resolution, Presented to Meeting of African & ME Council, Aswan-Egypt, 16 18 Feb. 1997.

Accordingly it has to be strengthened and its effectiveness enhanced through addressing these constraints. That means, handling the sensitive questions of sovereignty and non-interference in contrast to the concept of the right to interfere or le droit diing rence (which was developed in the field of international law after the end of the Cold War) in cases where it is absolutely necessary to end cases of human suffering for example. For that purpose, the rules of intervention have to be clarified and agreed upon by all states.

(c) Moreover, the Mechanismís effective functioning requires its being equipped with a highly qualified and professional staff. There is as well a need for a well-studied resource mobilization and fund raising plan to support the work of the mechanism.

7. Within this respect, cooperation, collaboration and coordination in contrast to confrontation, are the secrets to durable peace and security in Africa. African indigenous capabilities have to be enhanced in the field of conflict prevention, peacekeeping and peace making. Training centres such as the Cairo Centre for Training on Conflict Prevention and Peacekeeping in Africa, which coordinates closely with the OAU, have to be encouraged. Another possibility would be to establish logistic bases in Africa to prevent delays in sending peacekeeping troops to the fields of operations.

8. Sub-regional organizations, such as for e.g. The Economic Community of West African States (ECOWAS) that established a Cease-Fire Monitoring Group (ECOMOG) to keep the peace, restore order and ensure respect for cease-fire agreements, have proved

their effectiveness in dealing with some conflicts in Africa (Liberia) and therefore their role has to be encouraged while at the same time ensuring modalities for coordination with other sub-regional organizations, the OAU, and the UN.

The task is gigantic and the challenges are awesome but only an African visionary leadership, determination, commitment and strong will combined with concerted and conscious African efforts can meet the challenges that Africa has to face up to in the 21st century both at the regional as well at the international level.

Endnotes

1.   Col. Gustave Zoula, Les Conflits Anarchiques : Un nouveau Defi pour líOUA. 5 me S minaire, OUA / ICRC a líintention des Ambassadeurs Accr dit s aupr s d líOUA, Addis Abeba, 30   31 mars 1998, p.1.

2.   Madgy Abdel Moneim Hefny, The OAU Mechanism for Conflict Prevention, Management and Resolution : Lessons of Experience and An Agenda for Action, Meeting of African and Middle East Council, Aswan   Egypt, 16   20 Feb., 1997, p. 3.

3.   Chris J. Bakwesegha, The Role of the Organization of African Unity in Conflict Prevention, Management and Resolution in the Context of the Political Environment of Africa , African Journal on Conflict Prevention, Management and Resolution, Vol. One, No. One, Jan   Apr. 1997, p.4.

4.   The Causes of Conflict and the Promotion of Durable Peace and Sustainable Development in Africa, Report of the Secretary-General to the UN Security Council, N.Y : UN Department of Public Information, 16 Apr., 1998, p.1.

5.   Magdy Abdel Moneim Hefny, International Water Issues and Conflict Resolution: Some Reflections. Paper presented to the Eight IWRA World Congress on Water Resources, Cairo   Egypt, 21   25, Nov., 1994, p. 361.

6. Anthony Obserchall, Theories of Social Conflict , Annual Review of Sociology, Vol. 4, 1978, pp. 291 315, in Magdy A. Hefny, International Water Issues and Conflict Resolution, op, cit., p. 361.

7. Peter Wallesteen, ed. Peace Research and Challenges, Boulder and London: West view, 1988, p. 120, in Madgy A. Hefny, International Water Issues and Conflict Resolution, op. cit., p. 362.

8. Madgy A. Hefny, International Water Issues and Conflict Resolution, op. cit., p. 362.

9. The Causes of Conflict and the Promotion of Durable Peace and Sustainable Development in Africa, op. cit., p. 2.

10. Ibidem, p. 2.

11. J. Sorie Conteh, Colonial Roots of Conflicts in Africa. A Historical Perspective, Prevention and Resolution , African Journal on Conflict, Prevention, Management and Resolution, Vol. Two, No. One, Jan Apr., 1998, p. 18.

12. The Causes of Conflict, op. cit., p. 3.

13. J. Sorie Conteh, op. cit., pp. 19 20.

14. The Causes of Conflict, op. cit., p. 3.

15. Ibidem, pp. 3 4.

16. Ibidem, p. 4.

17. Col. Gustave Zoula, op. cit., p. 5.

18. The Causes of Conflicts, op. cit., pp. 2 3.

19. S. Bassey Ibok, The Dynamics of Conflicts in Africa: Evaluating OAUís Past and Present Approaches to Conflict Prevention, Management and Resolution and Future Prospects, African Journal on Conflict Prevention, Management and Resolution, Vol One, No. One, Jan Apr. 1997, pp. 67 8.

20. The Causes of Conflicts, op. cit., p. 2.

21. Chris J. Bakwesegha, The Role of the Organization of African Unity in Conflict Prevention, Management and Resolution in the Context of the Political Evolution of Africa, African Journal on Conflict Prevention, Management and Resolution, Vol. One, No. One, Jan. Apr., 1997, p. 4.

22. Report of the Joint OAU / IPA Task Force on Peacemaking and Peacekeeping in Africa, N.Y. Mar., 1998, p. 1.

23. S. Bassey Ibok, op. cit., p. 67.

24. Jakkie Cilliers, Some Practical Proposals Regarding Early-Warning of Inter-State Conflicts in Africa, in OAU Early Warning System on Conflict Situations in Africa, OAU: Addis Ababa, 1996, p. 73.

25. S. Bassey Ibok, op. cit., pp. 66 8.

26. Mwayila Tshiyembe, D finitions, Formes et Perspectives Historiques des Conflits Anarchiques, Colloque OUA / CICR, Addis Abeba, 30 31 mars, 1998, p. 3.

27. Col. Gustave Zoula, op. cit., pp. 3 4.

28. Jakkie Cilliers, op. cit., p. 74.

29. Mwayila Tshiyembe, op. cit., p. 4.

30. Ibidem, pp. 6 7.

31. Jakkie Cilliers, op. cit., p. 73.

32. Ibidem, p. 72.

33. Col. Gustave Zoula, op. cit., p. 4.

34. Vincent Wicod, The Anarchic Conflicts: 7 Challenges for the ICRC Humanitarian Activities Development, Speech for the Joint OAU / ICRC Seminar, Addis Ababa, 30 31 March 1998, pp. 1 5.

35. Jakkie Cilliers, op. cit., p. 71.

36. Ibidem, pp. 77 8.

37. Vasu Gounden, Potential Conflict Areas Confronting the Southern African Region, African Journal on Conflict Prevention, Management and Resolution, Vol. One, No. Two, Aug. 97, pp. 24 6.

38. Ibidem, pp. 26 8.

39. Ibidem, pp. 28 31.

40. Ibidem, pp. 31 3.

41. Ibidem, pp. 33 4.
42. Ibidem, pp. 35 7.
43. Ibidem, pp. 37 9.
44. Ibidem, p. 41.
45. Ibidem, pp. 41 2.
46. Ibidem, pp. 43 5

Leadership in Russia: The Phenomenon of President Putin

Anjelika Baravikova

Ms. Anjelika Baravikova is a Political Analyst with the Atomic Energy Agency in Vienna, Austria.

I want to start by thanking Dr. Safty for making this important gathering, and especially the reunion of the United Nations Leadership Conference Committee, possible.

Russians view Putin as Andropov of today

A poll conducted by ROMIR-Gallup International and reported by Interfax on 15 May 2001 found that 37.5 percent of Russians consider President Vladimir Putin to be unique and not at all like any of his predecessors. But 18 percent said that he is similar to former CPSU General-Secretary and KGB leader Yuri Andropov. Smaller percentages said that Putin resembles Boris Yeltsin, Peter the Great, Mikhail Gorbachev, Vladimir Lenin, Bill Clinton, and even Mahatma Gandhi.

Historic annotation
Ten years ago the institution of presidency was introduced in Russia. Only in this way Russian power could resist union power. On 15th March 1990 General Secretary of the USSR

Communist Party Mikhail Gorbachev was elected President of the Soviet Union with virtually unlimited authority. The elite tried to escape control of the centre. The position of the USSR president proved to be unstable, as the forces of disintegration became stronger than the central governmentís motivations. In the first Russian elections for a republican president Mr. Yeltsin received 57% of votes (Ryzhkov - 17% and in third place Zhyrinovsky). Yeltsin was to win over Gorbachev in the struggle for power and eliminate the Communist Party and Soviets.

The attempted coup díetat of 1991 helped Yeltsin become president-liberator and gained him enormous popularity. His presided over the breakdown of the Soviet Union (but the USSR was ready to disintegrate by itself, although many saw it as a plot of the republican elite against the Union President and the Union centre). The second error of Yeltsin was the shock therapy initiated by Egor Gaidarís team. Yeltsin, who had no party of his own, no power basis, faced the opposition parliament and lost war in Chechnya. He won his second term only with the support of oligarchs. That was a Pyrric victory, because those who helped him win immediately asked for dividends (positions in Yeltsinís government 1996 were distributed according to package principle (oligarchs had their representatives at leading posts and controlled middle management)). Yeltsin found himself at a loss. He took the risk of trusting Putin, relying on his experience in secret service, his coolness and presence of mind, on his democratic principle, human decency and youth (everything that Yeltsin himself lacked). But he left the system of practically unlimited power of president, which still depended on the presidentís personal qualities. Because of this, the Russian presidency could become authoritarian and there could be limitations of civil freedoms under the pretext of bringing back the order . However, there are signs that

Putin is trying to develop civil society, legal system and liberal economic initiatives. This gives cause for optimism.

Speaking at a Kremlin session on Russian Sovereignty Day (12th of June 2001) during which he presented former President Boris Yeltsin with the first Order of Merit of the Fatherland and gave awards to writers and artists, Russian President Vladimir Putin noted that "everything we endured over the past decade, all our experiences, successes and failures, shows one thing -- any reform only makes sense when it serves the people." Putin added, "If reforms do not benefit citizens, then they will fail." Putin also said he remains committed to "democracy and civic freedoms -- they are the essence of society and have to be fought for every day."

In an interview broadcast on ORT television on 12 June 2001, former President Yeltsin said he is proud of the fact that over the last 11 years since the declaration of Russian sovereignty, the foundations have been laid for further reforms. The task 11 years ago, he said, was "to free Russia, to free people, to make them free." And to that end, it was necessary to make the press and markets free as well. Yeltsin said he is confident that the foundation laid during this period will withstand any future problems and will "hold up the house which will be built by future generations." Yeltsin praised Putin.

Yabloko leader Grigorii Yavlinsky told Interfax-Northwest on 12 June 2001 that the adoption of Russian sovereignty was "the day of Russia's liberation from communist ideology and the first step to its integration into the world democratic community." Yavlinsky also said the appointment of members of the Federation Council is a retreat from democratic values, that a revival of the death penalty is completely unacceptable, and that any appearance of bureaucratic authoritarianism could "completely liquidate all the positive achievements which have taken place since the proclamation of the independence of our Motherland."

Federation Council Chairman Yegor Stroev told the St. Petersburg Economic Forum in June 2001 that Putin's policies have brought an end to Russia's "time of troubles." Stroev described the last decade in Russia as "a time of mindless destruction and revolutionary ideas." But Stroev added that despite the progress made so far, the future of Russia and of the Commonwealth of Independent States (CIS) will depend "on which takes place more quickly" the introduction of new technology or the exhaustion of natural resources.

Personal

Vladimir Putin, born in 1952, in St. Petersburg, received higher education from the law faculty Leningrad State University. He speaks excellent German.

In 1975 after graduation he was sent to the state security organisation, until 1990 he worked for the KGB, and worked in DDR. Later Putin worked as adviser to Sobchak, St. Petersburgís controversial mayor. From 1990 to 1995 he worked for the St. Petersburgís government, then was transferred to Moscow. Since 2000 he became temporary President, since March-May 2000 - elected president of the Russian Federation (with 52.52% majority).

While working in St. Pete City Hall he had a nickname Grey Eminence because though never exposed, he was informed about everything going on within the city hall walls. He remained a mysterious and influential figure.

Putinís relations with Sobchak, former St. Petersburgís mayor, prove his integrity. The signs of personal loyalty staying true to his patron who fell from public grace, paying him tributes publicly after his death are a sign of personal decency in Putinís character. This strong sense of loyalty could be attributed to the KGB esprit de corps.

Style

His speeches are characterised by brevity, sharpness and are succinct.

Many think he might become a cult figure. He has three components for this: mythology (came from mysterious and horrible KGB, appeared as deus ex machina, suddenly). Fear - KGB equals fear (especially for older generations), and hope for salvation - save Russians from being a disgraced nation, raise them to the level of self-respect. However, his dour, bureaucratic-style personality and general lack of charisma might be obstacles on the way to become a cult figure.

Many explain Putinís actions by his natural wisdom and caution inherited from the KGB intelligence college.

However, he is not an ordinary politician, because he skipped several steps on the way to the presidency: his first elections were presidential, he became the country leader without his team, programme and idea what, how, with whom and by what means he would implement. First year he was busy establishing a famous vertical line of power.

In my opinion he is a statesman, for whom Russian interests are most important. He has a sharp sense of state interests, which is a rare quality in todayís Russia. Strengthening of the state machinery destroyed during the last years is the main topic on his agenda. In it he sees the ground of further changes in Russia. But the question remains: how will the strengthening of the state affect social reforms. It is a complex issue, there is a danger that strengthening of the state machinery will be at the cost of the weakening of civil society. Much will depend on the circumstances and foreign factors. Putin wishes to modernise Russia, it is the same familiar modernisation from above, in a different way, as those of Peter the Great, Lenin or Stalin. He is not an anti-west politician, he strives for Russian integration in the world politics and global processes - on the condition that globalisation should take into account Russian national interests and be carried out according to a scenario written in Moscow and not in Washington. This remains to be seen.

Putin tries to strengthen the state and modernise Russian economy. He tries to do it without looking at the West, not blindly following imported prescripts. This is irritating for many there. Therefore they consider that he has a more autonomous policy than Yeltsin. The West is very cautious about Putin, as they think such independent policy could lead to less democracy in Russia and more authoritative/authoritarian style of leadership in Russia. Putin should be supported, because he represents the best hope of democratic development in Russia.

People around him

It is known that President Yeltsin during the last years of his reign appointed staff according to their loyalty and not professionalism. Putin at the very beginning tried a different way. He appointed Kasyanov who was known as a technocrat-reformist, pragmatic, supporter of the market reforms. Kasyanov has respect in the West. Besides, and this was a novelty for a politician, he speaks English fluently. His career developed spectacularly. He was vice minister of finance and became a prime-minister. He is quite ambitious. In contrast to other prime ministers, he did not use his power to influence political processes in the country. This way he confirmed his reputation as a technical prime minister.

The other people close to the president are two liberals from St. Petersburg - Gref and Kudrin.

During Putinís election campaign, 37 year-old Gref headed the Centre of Strategic Innovations - kind of intellectual headquarters of Putinís team. He plays a role of economic strategist in the government.

Kudrin is a friend from Putinís times in the St. Petersburgís city hall. Mr. Illarionov, presidential adviser on economic questions is a radical liberal. Putin admitted that he needed an extreme economist in the government to have the whole spectrum of opinions.

Overall, people from St. Petersburg form a major part in the government - vice prime ministers Klebanov and Matvienko, chairman of energy company RAO EAS Chubais, head of Counting Chamber Stepashin. Other Peters (piterts) are minister of communications Reiman and minister of health care Shevchenko, new inner security minister Gryzlov, recent appointment of Alexei Miller as head of Gazprom, and a number of others.

Phenomenon

According to Helene Carrere díEncoss (French historian, sovietologist and now specialist on Russia) Russia should be grateful to Yeltsin for the following 2 decisions: introduction of democracy and proof that going back to communism/socialism is impossible, and initiation of market reforms. On its way, Russia found many hindrances: incompetence, corruption, organised crime, and capital flight. Russia became poorer, its economy is in hardships, but there are conditions for Russia to become a normal state. President Putin could make the difference; his popularity in the country is quite stable. He has not offered any solutions yet, but started the process of analysis and discussion. In the country a new post Soviet elite is being formed (those who are over 30 now), many of who got their education abroad and would like to use it for the betterment of their country. However, some dangerous (or comical) tendencies should be noted, such as young peopleís organisation Going next to (Iduschie ryadom). Many think they are organised and sponsored by Kremlin, but they could only create repulsion by their similarity with infamous Komsomol (Soviet organisation of young people).

Success and failure since Putinís election practically does not affect his popularity. Although some lost confidence in the Russian president, there is a very high level of hope for better future related to his activities. More than   of the population believe he could bring the country into order. Important in this analysis is the initial ambiguity of Putinís programme, which provided the ground for hopes among various groups of population. And lack of alternatives - both political and personal - which is a sure sign of coming stagnation. His promise to remove the gap between the past (Soviet) and present found support and was reflected in renaissance of Soviet state symbols (military banner, state hymn music and style). The Achilles heels here are: Chechnya, catastrophes (Kursk, Yakutia) and media (NTV).

Politologists believe that Putin is a person with the sense of mission. He has not prepared himself for a position of the president. He is very serious to the burden of power and responsibility and carries it decently. He has inherited a broken economy, unmanageable state and society in the state of anarchy and has all intentions to repair them. He would like to turn Russia into an economically flourishing country and pragmatically tries to solve its problems.

Popularity of Putin is explained by his image - president of hope. But according to some opinions he has lesser tasks than his predecessors, for example, neutralisation of oligarchs, increased independence of courts of justice and housing reform are smaller tasks than communist party liquidation, USSR disintegration, creation of multi party system in the former totalitarian state and introduction of private property.

Two years ago when asked who ruled Russia, most Russians would have said: Berezovsky and oligarchs, now - they would say the President.

He is an information president, making effective use of TV, radio, news media and Internet. He tries to put information pressure on Russia and the whole world. This information presence helps him maintain high rating and positive image in the eye of the Russian and foreign audiences. Some information problems (e.g. situation with NTV raising to the problem of freedom of media in Russia) hinder coverage of important events and tendencies, positive political initiatives. The question of information security arises, as well.

Putin and mass media

For Putin mass media is a collective propaganda machine and organiser. This is no means of interaction between the executive branch of government and the people, but one of the elements of power vertical . It seems that Putin accepts free mass media as part of democracy but also as a force, which could become a hindrance on the way of realisation of his plans. It looks like the Kremlin tries to control parties, parliament and press. He still has to realise that free press guarantee access to any and truthful information, and gives life to such democratic institutions as independent elections, local self-governance, parties, and real opposition.

The crisis of NTV proves it. The United States expressed their concern about the lack of an open and transparent process in Gazprom's takeover of NTV, Reuters reported. Washington was also concerned about "the overall issue of freedom of speech and freedom of the media in Russia. According to Washingtonís spokesperson " it would be a great loss to the people of Russia if the changes at NTV reduce their access to a wide range of news and views over the airwaves." The other issue is how sincere these concerns are.

Meanwhile, in the wake of Gazprom's takeover of NTV, U.S. media magnate Ted Turner was revising his plans to buy a share of the NTV Company.

In an analysis published in "Novye Izvestiya" on 17 April 2001, commentator Otto Latsis argued that President Putin "is doomed -- he has won." Latsis said that the NTV case has shown "the full extent of the contradiction between democracy and authoritarianism in Putin's methods" and also "the professional methods of the secret services," which are "becoming characteristic of the business known as the Russian state." But precisely because Putin is operating on such a narrow circle, Latsis warned, he may find himself in trouble. At the same time, Latsis said, groups like SPS have "compromised themselves by not defending NTV" more actively.

Writing in "Novye izvestiya" on 9 June 2001, the same political commentator Otto Latsis suggested that President Putin has adopted a conservative political approach, one that reflects an effort to find agreement with the country's bureaucratic elite rather than the population at large. Such an approach, Latsis argued, leads to "stagnation" of the kind the country experienced under Soviet leader Leonid Brezhnev rather than the reforms that Putin said he wanted to implement.

The scandal with NTV brought an important element to the fore: Putin became enemy of world press and was placed in the first dozen of such enemies in the black list prepared by the Committee to Protect Journalists. Mentioned were Chechnya, secret services, Media Most, and general conditions for journalists. However, the other opinion is that it is all connected with media kingdom of Gusinsky (Russian media magnate and oligarch) and that Putin is no enemy of free press but rather Gusinskyís enemy. The fact is that the new NTV has not really become a puppet station, a mouthpiece for the government thus far.

In a message to the Media Forum 2000 in St. Petersburg in June 2001, President Vladimir Putin reaffirmed his commitment to a free media, noting that it is a precondition for the development of a democratic society and "the most important" protection against any retreat to the authoritarianism of the past, Russian and Western agencies reported. Viktor Cherkesov, the presidential envoy to the Northwest federal district, said he considers the effective interaction of the authorities and the media to be one of the most important tasks before Russia today. Aleksandr Lyubimov, the president of the Media Union, told the meeting that he does not see his group as duplicating the Union of Journalists. And Media Minister Mikhail Lesin noted in his comments to the group that the situation around NTV has still not stabilized, largely because of the inadequacy of legislation governing the media.

Achievements, first year

The news from Russia is good, or so it seems. Vladimir Putin has stopped his countryís financial downfall, filled the state budget with petrodollars and is presiding over steady economic growth. He has installed a government of liberal-minded professionals, revamped the tax system and plans to fully legalise private ownership. Even the taxes started to flow in. The market framework is in place what Russia needs next are foreign investments. But the West does not applaud these positive changes: it remains sceptical.

A glance behind the stage indicates that real power in Russia is now concentrated in a handful of Putin loyalists from Leningrad and the KGB. They have embarked on the self-set task of building a market economy without a civil society. Russia is developing according to a quasi authoritarian guided democracy model typical of Latin American countries, rather than according to Western market values. Never before in Russiaís modern history has a state leader tsar, general-secretary or president achieved such public support within one year. Putin faces no opposition. Chechnya has been recaptured by force, other republics and regions have been returned to central control more gently than Chechnya but nevertheless resolutely. The two chambers of parliament, the Duma and the Council of the Federation, have been emasculated. Journalists who had for the past decade defended press freedom, have deliberately subjected themselves to Putinís strong hand. The majority of Russians, who lost faith in state and prosperity during Boris Yeltsinís confusing reform era, enthusiastically applaud. The West can do little to change the mood inside Russia. It is, however, worried about how Putin will handle his powers. Is he going to translate economic stability into the creation of a civilised market and prepare Russia for globalization in partnership with the West. Or will he establish authoritarian rule and chose confrontation?

According to Alexander Rahr, Western leaders are worried about their loss of influence over Russian policy. Appeals to stick to European democratic norms were com pletely ignored during the Chechen war. The former Western approach was softening Russiaís stance during the debates over NATO-enlargement or the Kosovo conflict. At the moment, such threats mean little to Russia. One last tool remains, however. The West might try to prevent Russia from choosing a confrontational path: the huge debt of $160 billion, which Moscow is meant to repay over the next years. The private creditor institutions, assembled in the London Club, have already made an agreement to restructure part of the Russian debt. But the creditor nations, particularly Germany, organized in the Paris Club, were reluctant to follow suit. Russiaís recent suggestion that it will postpone due payments to the Paris Club has provoked an outcry in the U.S. and Europe.

The West is not interested in seeing Putin investing his petrodollars into the modernisation of his army and fleet, or possibly in a Russian anti-missile system. Putin understands the West. He studied Western policies throughout his career. He wants to make Russia strong while not annoying the West. His recovery program involves regaining lost markets for arms and energy. Ambitious pipeline projects have secured Russiaís monopoly over energy flows from the Caspian region and Siberia to Europe and

Asia. But this does not necessarily mean alienating the West. The recently announced German-Russian co-operation on modernising Russian MIGs for customers in Asia and Central Europe is another cornerstone in Putinís skilful strategy to involve his Western partners into a new pragmatic relationship [15].

Some people criticise Putin for doing too little during his first presidential year. The answer is that he was busy gaining popularity and support of the liberal and right-win forces, left movements, IMF, foreign governments, Duma, Federation Council, government, etc. Many of the reforms would have been impossible to realise one year ago. There was no agreement with parliamentary forces, regional leaders, and oligarchs many of whom controlled by the media. The first year was dedicated to prepare a favourable political field to start economic changes. Theoretically, these two processes could have gone hand in hand but the President concentrated one at a time. This explains his attention to governors, oligarchs and deputies and their discipline; spreading of pro-presidential coalitions within Duma, change in Federation Soviet, and the situation with Gusinsky. This power concentration and centralisation were considered by many as totalitarism and authoritarianism. However, it is a way from unlimited anarchy to controlled anarchy.

Putin power control grew. It started with appointment of seven region envoys to newly created federal districts. While the Magnificent Seven have only a few accomplishments to their credit, it is already clear what at least some of them hope to create: a new state order in which the seven federal districts constitute a bureaucratic layer separating Russia's 89 federation subjects from Moscow. If their wish becomes reality, the seven federal districts will have their own media, their own long-term economic plans, and their own State Councils.

---

[15] Alexander Rahr is Program Director at the German Council on Foreign Relations, Berlin and the author of a recent Putin biography: Vladimir Putin, Der Deutsche im Kreml , (Universit as, 2000), soon to be published in English by Wuerz Publ. Ltd., Winnipeg.

The envoys' ability to achieve these goals remains questionable, however. To date, the presidential representatives appear to have done little other than set up offices, hire personnel, gather facts about their regions, and organize meetings and conferences. But their public comments reveal how they see their jobs evolving. Currently, they have four key tasks: ensuring that regional laws conform with federal legislation, overseeing cadre issues, developing economic strategies for their macro-regions, and organizing new bureaucratic and other structures at the new district level, including media organizations. Each envoy has already presented to the regions within his district a list of local laws that do not conform to federal legislation. However, on cadre issues, they have moved more slowly, possibly because they anticipate a stronger negative reaction. In the Urals district, envoy Petr Latyshev dismissed the head of a customs office in Yekaterinburg and is reportedly preparing to dismiss a local prosecutor and police chief as well. Sverdlovsk Governor Eduard Rossel called Latyshev's moves inadmissible "muscle- flexing." Latyshev responded that he was given the right to make such appointments and intends to keep doing so. In the longer term, the envoys hope to concern themselves with their macro-regions' economic development. Latyshev reported that at a meeting in April 2001, President Vladimir Putin advised the envoys to establish Centres for Strategic Development in their districts' capitals, along the lines of the Moscow-based think-tank of the same name. As head of that centre, Minister for Economic Trade and Development German Gref coordinated the drafting of a 10-year economic plan for Russia. Presumably, the districts' seven centres will each draft such a long-term development plan.

But judging from the envoys' statements, they consider a key ingredient to economic success to be getting the regions to regard themselves as smaller units of a larger whole, namely, the federal district. In a recent interview with "Nezavisimaya gazeta," presidential representative to the Northwest district Viktor Cherkesov complained that one problem with the local media, particularly newspapers, is that 80 percent of coverage is about local news and 20 percent about national developments but there is no information at all about neighbouring regions. He noted that "for the development of large business, it is necessary to push forward business information beyond an oblast's or republic's borders." Cherkesov was one of the first envoys to suggest the creation of district-level media with district-wide broadcasting and distribution capabilities, but others soon followed. Latyshev, for example, recently hosted a conference on how to create a "single information space" in Russia's federal districts. District-wide media, however, is only part of a much larger plan. Soon after his appointment, Putin's envoy to Siberia, Leonid Drachevskii, announced he is forming a council of all leaders of the regions in his district. And in May, Georgii Poltavchenko, envoy to the Central district, announced the formation of a similar council in his district. According to Poltavchenko, analogous bodies are being planned in the remaining federal districts.

These new mini-State Councils will coexist with district level entities of Sberbank, Rostelecom, and the All Russia State Television and Radio Company. Almost as soon as the new office of presidential envoy was created, analysts queried what powers -- if any -- those envoys would be given to enforce their decisions. Khakassia Republic President Aleksei Lebed recently suggested that the new envoys are mostly "paper lions" and that regional leaders cooperate with them only when it suits them. However, Rossel's negative reaction to Latyshev's dismissing some of his local appointees suggests the paper lions do have teeth. In fact, the ability to hire and fire local officials may be one of the envoy's most effective weapons, undercutting regional leaders' ability to distribute jobs and contracts to their local associates and thus diminishing the leaders' influence over local elite. And the ultimate weapon -- control over money -- may soon become part of the envoys' arsenal.

Far East Envoy Konstantin Pulikovskii recently declared that envoys would have the ability to "guarantee" the transfer of federal monies to the regions. He also suggested that the envoys will ensure those monies are used properly. Meanwhile, presidential envoy to the Volga region Sergei Kirienko suggested in an interview with "Nezavisimaya gazeta" this week that rather than being given more powers, the office of the presidential envoys might simply fade away. At the same time, he maintained that the system of seven districts is needed to make the Russian Federation more governable. Therefore, the number of district-level organizations and personnel may continue to proliferate. If that happens, it may become increasingly clear that the Kremlin's aim is to create a new hierarchy in which regional leaders are bumped down in the chain of command. Soon regional leaders will be deprived of their forum at the Federation Council. But they may have at least one comforting thought: one level below them will remain, namely that of city leaders. These officials, with few weapons at their disposal, have battled against the governors for their fair share of tax proceeds -- usually in vain.

Since the appointment of Russia's governors, more than half of Russia's 89 regions held gubernatorial elections. With nearly two-thirds of the incumbents re-elected, the face of Russia's regional elite remains much like it was at the beginning of last year. However, there are a few incipient trends worth noting. The average age for a governor is just under 53, down slightly from the average age of 53.5 at the beginning of 2000. All the governors are male, except Koryak Autonomous Okrug Governor Valentina Bronevich, the only female.

The other achievement is the support of the parliament. Four parliamentary groups -- Unity, Fatherland, Russian Regions, and People's Deputy -- who combined hold 234 of the 450 seats in the Duma, agreed to coordinate voting on some economic and political issues and thus give President Vladimir Putin a working majority on those questions in April 2001. In a joint statement, the parties declared their "intention to create a coordination committee of centrist groups with a view to forming an inter-faction committee to achieve a solid parliamentary majority. However, several deputies and commentators suggested that the four-party group was far from united and might fall apart at any time. Among those making that point was Communist Party leader Gennadii

Zyuganov, who said that the party lacks a clear ideological base and that "when they meet their first failures, this company will soon split." Meanwhile, Duma deputy Viktor Pokhmelkin (Union of Rightist Forces, or SPS) said that the formation of the group would make it easier for his party and Yabloko to cooperate. In addition, he warned the creators of the coalition that they must not have any "illusions that the creation of such a monster means its victory."

The next issue is that pension and the future pension reform. President Putin signed a decree on 17 April 2001 raising average pensions to approximately 2,300 rubles ($80) per month. Putin said his decree would help some 18 million pensioners. Meanwhile, Putin has said that work on pension reform is going well.

Critics

In an interview published in the Madrid newspaper "El Pais," Yabloko leader Grigorii Yavlinsky said that there are clear signs that "a certain type of corporate state is being created" in Russia under President Vladimir Putin. Yavlinsky also said that "it is possible to say that the majority of Russian mass media outlets are constituent parts of the state machine." He said that Russia must create an independent judicial system, find "a political alternative" to the war in Chechnya, and introduce "a more transparent and rational" tax system. According to an analysis in "Vremya MN", Putin is aiming to create "a corporate state," one in which government and business will be separated, there will be a liberal economy with the opportunity for foreign investments, and strict administrative control. The article's author, Andrei Neshchadin, said that this state would create a classical balance between state, society, and business.

Embattled oligarch Boris Berezovsky said on NTV on 31 May 2001 that he thinks "[Russian President Vladimir] Putin will not even make it through the very next stage of his term." Berezovsky acknowledged he made a major mistake during the last presidential elections by supporting Putin, who he believed at the time would continue former President Boris Yeltsin's reforms. "Putin's view," Berezovsky said, "is that Russia cannot be ruled other than by authoritarian methods, whereas I am deeply convinced -- and the past 10 years have shown as much -- that Russia can develop for real as a liberal country."

Writing in "Vek" on 1 June 2001, commentator Aleksei Bogaturov argued that President Putin has created "a tripod of power" based on the cabinet, people from St. Petersburg, and officials in the presidential administration. But tripods, Bogaturov said, are "only relatively stable" and this one might be knocked over by any of four major problems: the war in Chechnya, state policy toward the media, relations with the United States, or international energy prices.

Human rights

From afar, Russia seems icy and monolithic these days. Yet, on closer view, many "grassroots" activities are pushing through the ice. These initiatives -- ranging from human rights and charity work to media and micro-finance projects -- are starting to take root in various parts of Russia. While the Kremlin seems increasingly obsessed with restoring state power and glory, civic initiatives have begun to touch the lives of some one million ordinary Russians. Feeling the Kremlin's icy hand, fragmented groups are starting to recognize and defend common values and interests. Even the power elite -- the business community and local governments -- sometimes now initiates cooperation with its erstwhile civic opponents. In short, Putin's vertical power politics may result in unusual social consolidations or political alliances in the future. News reports on the January "extraordinary" congress in Moscow of some 1,000 human rights activists from throughout

Russia focused on Sergei Kovalev's stirring speech on the dangers of having a "resident" as president of Russia.

Much less attention was paid to Lyudmila Alekseeva's description of human rights initiatives -- all of the country's regions (except Chechnya) last year contributed toward a national report, sometimes in parallel with regional governments' human rights commissions. In other areas, such as Rostov or Yaroslavl, local groups cooperate with regional governments on efforts to improve conditions in prisons or orphanages. Alekseeva, head of the 25-year-old Moscow Helsinki Group, noted that even the Russian Federation bureaucracy has expressed interest in human rights lawyers working with its officials to sort through thousands of citizen appeals and helping to decide which merit closer attention.

The Russian business community -- not just the digarch Boris Berezovsky -- has organized funds to assist human rights groups, Alekseeva reported. Legitimate Russian businessmen now have begun to understand that it too may need to turn to the human rights community expertise on legal defense of individual rights. The Russian Women's Microfinance Network (RWMN), organized by three prominent Russian business people in 1998, shows the business sector's greater involvement in social issues. The private RWMN has affiliates in Kaluga, Tver, Kostroma, Vidnoe, and Kazan and provides three-month loans to sustainable micro enterprises. While RWMN loans are not restricted to women, so far most loans have been to women- owned businesses in the service sector, with a repayment rate of well above 90 percent. "Memorial," a good example of a national civic organization, was founded in 1988. Today, the organization has over 100 affiliates throughout Russia and other countries of the former USSR.

While best known for its work with victims of Stalinist repression, "Memoria l" also conducts timely human rights monitoring of "hot spots," such as the breakaway Russian enclave in Moldova and continuing brutalities by Russian troops against civilians in Chechnya. In addition to research in its extensive historical archives on Soviet dissent, "Memorial" provides practical assistance to former political prisoners. Today, the local government in Komi -- an Arctic area where many Stalinist camps were located -- works with "Memorial" in maintaining a network of social services for thousands of camp survivors and their families.

Much has been written about the Kremlin's steady onslaught against the Moscow-based broadcast media, particularly its campaign against NTV and the Media-MOST group. Yet the Russian regional media have long been subjected to threats, reprisals, killings, attempted and actual censorship, and various administrative pressures at the hands of powerful local authorities or criminal business groups. Less well known is media monitoring by the Russian Union of Journalists, Index on Censorship, the Glasnost Defense Fund, and the Centre for Journalism in Extreme Situations and Internews Russia. Their reports include timely and accurate information on violence against journalists, various problems faced by the media in all the countries of the former Soviet Union, and training seminars and materials. Recently, several of these media watchdogs produced an 800-page review for the year 2000 of the state of media freedom in 87 of Russia's 89 regions -- except Chechnya and Ingushetia. The report found that "each region violates media freedom differently but each does so." Moscow and St. Petersburg were rated the most free, with non-Russian ethnic republics getting the worst ratings. Another useful new project is a Russian-language textbook on investigative journalism produced by a St. Petersburg-based NGO, the Centre for Investigative Journalism. Internews in Russia, trains journalists and supplies news to 162 independent broadcast entities throughout Russia with a potential total audience of at least 40 million, and plans to organize an Internet portal for Russian journalists this spring.

The Kremlin -- and some Westerners – are quick to dismiss Russian non-governmental groups as having only marginal support from the Russian public. Admittedly, these organizations do not have mass backing, but they do express the interests of many educated groups and serve the needs of thousands of disadvantaged people in Russia. Russian civic organizations are accused of depending on Western foundations while the independent media are supposedly in the pay of Russian oligarchs. Russian business tycoons often are the deep pockets behind the media -- just as they are for thousands of corrupt Russian government officials. And many Russian civic groups depend on funding from Western foundations -- just as the Russian government is deeply in hock to the Paris Club. But on balance, it appears likely that Russia's civic organizations are likely to pay a much larger future social dividend than the current Kremlin ever will.[16]

Civil societies

Putin on 12 June 2001 met with representatives of non-governmental organizations and told them that he seeks "a constructive, positive, and continuing dialogue" between the Kremlin and civil society, Russian agencies reported. He said that these organizations, which were established without the state playing a role, often have "a more effective influence on society than do political parties." At the same time, he said he regrets that many NGOs now receive support from foreign rather than Russian sources. He noted that he has worked to strengthen the state and will now promote a stronger society, because "a weak state is a threat to democracy in no less a degree than a despotic power."

Putin told the NGO leaders that there are now approximately 300,000 NGOs registered with the Justice Ministry, and that "even if half of these organizations fulfil their stated obligations, then this will be a major force." At the same time, he said that "society as a whole must divide with the authorities responsibility for the social-economic situation in the country, but this can happen only

---

[16] according to Catherine Cosman (Un)Civil Societies, Volume 2, Number 6 (7 February 2001)

when society is given access to the development of these decisions." He also said that "power in Russia has been sufficiently strengthened that it can support democratic rights and freedoms of citizens."

The NGO leaders in attendance welcomed Putin's attention to their work and told him that during the past year 12-13 percent of Russia's population received assistance from non-commercial and non-governmental organizations, Interfax reported. The leaders requested that the Russian government promote the kind of conditions, including legal support for charitable donations that would allow the NGOs to perform more effectively.

Aleksei Leonov, the president of the international organization "Slavs," said after taking part in the meeting between Putin and NGOs on 12 June that Putin has accepted his invitation to speak at a congress of non-political, non-governmental organizations planned for November 2001, Interfax reported. Leonov said that at that congress, the various groups plan to form a chamber or committee of civil unions of Russia.

Foreign policy

Foreign policy under Putin raises numerous questions. He is neither pro nor anti-westerner. He is a pro-Russian politician. His aim is to reach feasible integration into world economy, increase competitiveness in world markets, attract investments under the appropriate condition to safeguard Russian political and economic interests. Therefore his policies are logical. However, there is no driving force for reforms, for the development of which too little has been done yet. He has achieved good personal relations with many foreign leaders and is considered a serious politician. He opposes the idea offered by President Bush to withdraw from the Soviet-U.S. ABM Treaty of 1972 system and NATO expansion eastwards.

Igor Sergeev, the Security Council adviser to Putin, said that Russia would not agree to any overhaul of the 1972 ABM Treaty or agree to Bush's plans on national missile defense. But Bush could perhaps take heart from LDPR leader Zhirinovsky's statement that he agrees with the U.S. president that the ABM accord is out of date given technological advances.

The Western media contributed to this process by negatively covering events in Russia, for example as far as relations with the new US administration go.

Very perspective directions in the future foreign policies are: creation of effective international system of nuclear arms and nuclear military technologies non-proliferation, and effective system to combat international terrorism and crime.

Russia took active steps to become a friend with the European Union. To achieve this, Russia has to pay its external debts, respect the freedom of press and use its potential for achieving stability and security in Europe. Putin is a supporter of close partnership relations with EU. This is not a new Russian dream; it is suffice to recall President Gorbachevís common European House and similar Yeltsinís dream s.

Russian President Vladimir Putin met with his American counterpart George W. Bush in Ljubljana on 16 June 2001 for a get-acquainted session. The two men traded compliments about each other -- Bush said he could "trust" Putin now that he had looked him in the eye and Putin said that the conversations had "surpass[ed] expectations" -- and invitations to each other's country. The two directed their top aides to work on common security architecture -- "a new approach for a new era" -- but they agreed that they would not set up any special bilateral commissions of the kind that existed earlier. They also agreed to promote economic ties between Russia and the United States. The only discordant notes sounded in public were Putin's suggestion that "any unilateral actions" on the U.S. missile defense initiative or the ABM treaty could "only make more complicated various problems and issues" and the Russian leader's complaint that he does not understand why NATO enlargement is still on the table if Russia is a partner. Following the summit, Putin visited Belgrade and Prishtina before returning to Moscow. In both places, he called for a Balkan conference and a new commitment to fight religious and ethnic extremism in the region.

In an article published in "The Washington Quarterly" and in "Nezavisimaya gazeta" on 15 June 2001, Foreign Minister Igor Ivanov said that Russia would pursue its national interests rather than any particular ideological course. He explicitly rejected any return to an "imperial" foreign policy of the kind pursued "both in pre-revolutionary Russia and in the Soviet period." And he said that Russia rejects any "'neo-imperial'" ambitions. Ivanov added that Russia rejects the ideology of "global messianism" of the kind the Soviet Union pursued.

The other problem for Russian foreign policy is the self-determination of Commonwealth of Independent States. Most probably, Belovezh agreements would need to be modified and a new scheme of post-Soviet territory development would need to be created (recent political issues with Ukraine, Georgia, Azerbaijan and Asian republics).

In general, President Putin has a vision of multi-polar world. He strengthens relations with China, India and Iran on the one hand, on the other - conducts charm offensive in Europe. Apart from this, future relations with the new US administration are to be built.

Difficulties

One of the features of the Putinís politics is the lack of professional staff, and related to it the tendency of clan-geographical proximity of new appointments. According to an article in "Versiya," No. 21, President Putin has now named 19 people from his native St. Petersburg to senior positions in the government. Many of them worked with him when he served there, but at least some are linked to him only by friendship ties from his time as a university student, the weekly said.

The other destabilising factor is Chechnya. The military operation is over but the republic has not started its peaceful development yet. It is admitted that political solution to Chechnya wonít be found in the nearest 5-7 years within the framework of present attitude.

The other problem is organized crime. According to St. Petersburg's "Ekonomika i vremya , organized crime structures in Russia have concentrated such power in their hands that they now threaten the country's political institutions. Criminal enterprises have increased their control of the economy from 27 percent of turnover in 1993 to more than 50 percent now, the paper said. Moreover, Russian criminal groups are now operating in 58 foreign countries, with significant footholds in the U.S., Israel, Turkey, Hungary, and Poland, among others. Meanwhile, in an article published in "Vedomosti", Mikhail Delyagin, the director of the Institute of the Problems of Globalization, said that Russia's natural monopolies have so much power that they are dictating to the Kremlin.

Overall, there is a great need for legal and land reform, as well as concentration on fighting corruption.

Plans for the next year

Prime Minister Mikhail Kasyanov on 30 May 2001 presented his midterm economic strategy to take Russia through 2004, RIA-Novosti reported. That strategy calls for the simultaneous reform of the military and defense sectors; banking and taxation; energy and transport; communal services; and the pension system. Kasyanov said that the reforms must proceed regardless of fluctuations in the price of oil. In addition, the Russian government plans to promote the north-south and east-west transport corridors Putin has long advocated. The Trade and Economic Development Ministry said that it expects Russia's GDP to grow by 15-18 percent during this period but that it believes the country's positive trade balance will fall from $61 billion in 2000 to $37-42 billion in 2004.[17]

Emphasis is put on the economy. Here it is important to determine the balance between radical market drive and social policies. The other problem could be the impossibility to realise liberal economic reforms with the help of the present machine of bureaucracy.

Most probably, in the nearest future, the question related to State Duma (Lower House of Parliament) will have to be addressed. It will need to be either radically reorganised (as creation of super-party Otechestvo - Motherland (nickname Den) showed) or dismissed. This will be accompanied by a swift election campaign and formation of a new Duma where Putin could get a guaranteed constitutional majority. Then it will be possible to make serious changes. The executive power will have no opposition. Council of Federation and State Council wonít be the countervailing forces.

Putin is in a difficult situation. He needs to give life to military, legal, tax, pension system reforms, and others.

Putinís failure at different fronts will not mean failure of a president only. It will be a heavy moral blow for the population,

---

[17] Note: The Economic Development and Trade Ministry has concluded that the basic macroeconomic measures of the Russian economy in 2000 were "the best for the entire period of reforms," Interfax reported on 7 June. "For the first time in the last 30 years, the physical quantity of GDP rose 8.3 percent in comparison with the previous year, and the amount of industrial production increased by 9 percent," the ministry said in documents prepared for the cabinet. Among the other achievements of 2000, the ministry added, were financial stability, a decrease in energy use per ruble of GDP, and inflation close to predictions.

because there wonít be the third President of Hope. Inevitable, a president of disappointment will take his place with all the consequences.

In a documentary film about his life shown on ORT on 12 June 2001, Putin said he is not yet thinking about a second presidential term. Instead, he is continuing to try to demonstrate to others and himself that it was a good thing he was elected to the first one. Summing up the results so far, Putin said that what he has achieved is significant, but not as much as he had wanted. But he stressed that the first year was "only the beginning." Putin also said that the sinking of the "Kursk" nuclear submarine was "the most difficult" event of his time in office.

Your opinion or a question to President Putin could be send via http://www.president.kremlin.ru

Leadership in China: Social Stability and Freedom of Expression

Jiang Xuewen

Mr. Jiang Xuewen is an award-winning national radio broadcaster in China.

Introduction

The ancient Confucian aphorism Xiushen, Qijia, Zhiguo, Pingtianxia, meaning Cultivate one's moral character, manage his family affairs, run the country well and make equality and justice reign over the world, had always been the ancient Chinese people's lifetime ideal. The Confucian political philosophy takes Cultivate one's moral character, manage his family affairs as the starting point, and run the country well and make equality and justice reign over the world the ultimate aim. Whilst Cultivate one's moral character, manage his family affairs is the lifetime goal for the ordinary people to pursue, run the country well and make equality and justice reign over the world, the unshakable responsibility for Chinese leaders. To some extent, it is the great talent and forward-looking vision to run the country well and make equality and justice reign over the world that well testify the able leadership for a certain country.

The leaders under discussion here specifically refer to the national elite politicians and thinkers in the long span of Chinese history. They are, as Sidney Hook stated in The Hero in History, not only the distinct symbols of the country, but also the core of responsibility, decision-making and action. The leaders in Chinese history have played very important roles for the development and progress of China. Their concept and ideas about administering the country greatly influence the direction and process of development of China today.

Stability and Tao of Rule

Human beings are cultural beings in that they are the product of culture. Any person, regardless of earth-shaking historic heroes, or common people cannot be separated from the cultural environment where they live. To a great extent, Culture influences peopleís value, behaviour, and certainly the Tao of Rule of Chinese leaders of all times.

The civilization of China has come through 5000 years so far. As early as 4000 years ago emerged the first dynasty in Chinaís history, the Xia Dynasty (21st – 16th century BC). In 221BC, Emperor Qinshihuang established the first unified nation in Chinese history, the Qin Dynasty. Thence, although the rises and declines of dynasties alternated one after another, Chinese civilisation has come down in one continuous line till today. All through the thousands of years, generations after generations of elite have been seeking the path of national development, have accumulated into rich treasury-house of ideas. The culture of China gave birth to the Tao of Rule which have been carried on by all succeeding generations, and finally became the important component of Chinese culture.

Letís examine the Tao of Rule against the background of Chinese culture. A Country means giant mechanism under the heaven, also high responsibility, so said our ancient ancestor. One who assumes the high responsibility to administer a country is LingXiu (head of state). In Chinese language, the term LingXiu consists of two Chinese characters, Ling and Xiu which originally denotes to collar and sleeve, indicating that the person who can give guidance and help to others and set an example to others. As the lingXiu of a country, his high responsibility is to administer the country.

The Tao of Rule was always stressed in Chinese traditional political culture in which stability occupies a very important place. Therefore, there was a dividing line between Zhi (order) and luan (turbulence). Zhi indicates the honest and upright politics and a society of peace and safety, whilst Luan, corrupted politics and a society of turbulence and danger. In Chinese history, the well reputed Times of Zhi were like The Reign of Wenjin (179B.C.---141B.C.) in the Han Dynasty, The Reign of Zhenguan (627A.D.--- 649A.D.) in the Tang Dynasty and The Millennium of Qianlong (1661A.D. --- 1795A.D.) in the Qin Dynasty. The essence of Chinese Tao of Rule is actually the leadersí choice-making between order and unrest, stability and upheaval. The ancient Chinese principle of state administration is fear not less population but inequality, fear not poverty but intranquility.

And therefore, stability means enjoying popular support, going toward the will of the people. Chinese national psychology of seeking stability and being afraid of turbulence has been long standing. The Chinese proverb Rather be a dog in the peaceful world, not be a man in turbulent days is a true reflection of this kind of mentality. Stability, unity, long-lasting peace and sensible politics and amiable relationship among people are ordinary Chinese peopleís everlasting ideals as well as what Chinese leaders of all times have craved for. With a history of thousands of years having experienced all kinds of hardships and suffered tribulations more than any other country in the world, Chinaís longing for stability is thus stronger than any of them.

Zhougong once said: The desire of the people, heaven must satisfy. The peopleís desire was regarded as the foundation of establishing a country and its prosperity. In the political philosophy of China, the idea of regarding people as foundation is of long standing and well established. The ruling classes always promoted the idea of regarding people as the foundation of a country. Dayu said that The key of morality (of a king) is to improve governmental system, and goal of a government is to maintain the people , while "Shangshu" pointed out that people are the foundation of a country and a solid foundation will make a peaceful country . The great thinker Confucius believed that The life or death of a monarch depends on the people . Mencius, the saint of Confucianism next only to Confucius took a further step to elevate the theory. He said: Precious are the people, second the state, minor the monarch . The emperor of the Tang Dynasty Tang Taizong said to his ministers The principle of a king is to place the interests of the people in priority. To infringe on common people for the interests of himself is just as to cut off a piece from his leg to feed the stomach, which will result in making a full belly in a dead body . The founder of the Ming Dynasty, Emperor Zhu Yuanzhang even claimed: The winner of the world is actually the winner of the heart of people. Kangxi, one of the emperors of Qin Dynasty stated: It is the people that affords the supreme key to the principle of achieving great order. Whatever is beneficial to the people, it should be done.

Since stability, security and order are the will of the people. How to achieve order? In Chinese culture it is believed that make the people rich and live in peace is of primary importance. As Zhang Juzheng, the cabinet minister of Emperor Ming Shenzong pointed out, in principles of administering a country, nothing is more important than setting peopleís mind at rest, so as to make people in peace and contentment. Shangyang, the famous politician in the time of Warring States (475-221 B.C.) considered Power must be in order because that makes power, the rich country must be in order because that is where wealth comes from and the power must possess wealth because that creates power. Guanzhong, the minister of the State of Qi in the Spring and Autumn Period (770 ---476 B.C.) pointed out that The understanding concerning giving benefits to the people will make benefits in turn a magic weapon of a ruler, he said Itís easy to rule the rich, but what to do with the poor, difficult. Thus the state in order is often rich whilst the one in turmoil often poor. Hence those who are good at ruling must make the people rich first and then rule them. He laid down the famous maxim A full loaded granary brings up men of courtesy, a life of plenty creates people distinguishing sense of honour from disgrace. Therefore, the well being of the people is the most important issue facing any regime in administering a country at all times.

Such a concept of state administration has come down in one continuous line. The present Chinese leaders have put Stability in a very important position as well, regarding political stability as a prerequisite for reform modernization. The General Designer of the policy of reform and openness of China, Mr. Den Xiaoping said in 1987 when receiving the former US president Mr. Jimmy Carter: The chief aim of China is to attain high development in order to have our people be lifted out of poverty and the country, backwardness, and to increase our national strength and raise the standard of living of the people gradually. To do this, there must be a stable political environment. Without a stable political environment, nothing could be done.

In 1989 when meeting with the former US president Mr. George Bush, once again he pointed out Of all the issues in China, the overwhelming one is stability. Without stable environment, nothing could be done; even what had been achieved in the past would be lost. China must hold on the policy of reform and openness, which is the hope to solve all the problems in China. To effect reforms, however, a stable political environment is indispensable , he stated at the same time Democracy is our goal, but the state must be maintained in stability .

The Freedom of Expression in China

It has been a misunderstanding that in the system of oriental value there is a lack of democratic consciousness and concept of freedom of expression. Actually that is not the case. As a matter of fact, in Chinese culture there exists great tradition of democracy. When the West was still under the rule of feudal nobles, China had already been practicing the system of prefectures and counties for a thousand years. The emperor of the Qin Dynasty was pursuing a legal system, advocating the idea of The committal of a crime by a prince will be equally judged as that of common people . The strict imperial examinations were open to all social stratums, which had ensured equality of opportunity and mobility of society. The powerful imperial supervisors could impose restrictions on the emperorsí mistakes and the officialsí abuse of power. As far as the freedom of expression is concerned, people understood that the future of a country depended on an open channel of expression. Being educated in such a way, the Confucianists regarded criticizing monarchsí faults frankly as a sacred duty.

The Spring and Autumn and Warring States Periods (770-221B.C.) witnessed the popularity of free expression, well known as the Contention of a hundred schools of thought . It was such a great flourishing age of Chinese culture that countless schools of thought such as the Confucianists, the Taoists, the Mohists, the Legalists and the Yin-yang School all emerged to express their own opinions on state affairs. In the powerful and prosperous Tang Dynasty, the emperor Tang Taizong paid great attention to the Free airing of views , encouraging Direct criticism . Tang Taizong once asked his prim minister Weizheng How do a wise ruler and a fatuous ruler behave? Weizheng replied, A ruler hearing all opinions becomes wise, a ruler who listens only to one side becomes fatuous. Being a wise ruler , Tang Taizong left the deservedly famous legacy of The reign of Zhengguan .

Nevertheless, the majority of Chinese, regardless of emperors or the common people thought that social stability and national unity was after all paramount to all other things. The monarch might be tolerant of some improper expressions when not endangering stability and unity; the freedom of expression must be suppressed once it created turbulence in the society. It may be said that in China consciousness freedom of expression is congenitally deficient since the belief in the great uniformity is deeply rooted. In 221 B.C the first ever-unified empire in Chinese history, the Qin Dynasty, was established. To strengthen its regime, Emperor Qin Shihuang attempted to unify cultures and ideologies. On uniformity of The Luís Annal s has the following to say: Ruling a state by listening to opinions of many people will lead to collapse of the state in no time , Thus uniformity makes order, whilst diversity, turbulence. And uniformity makes peace, whilst diversity, danger , thus putting the uniformity of thought on a very high plane.

In the shadow of The Great Uniformity , most part of Chinese history was dominated by the system of centralized autocratic monarch, where freedom of expression was suppressed to varying degrees. In the regime of The Emperor Qin Shihuang, suppression of ideological and cultural dissidence reached the full extreme when books were burned and Confucianists buried , the decree to burn books were issued and intellectuals advocating free expression were persecuted , the state affairs regardless of major or minor were exclusively decided on by his majesty . This deeply rooted tradition was carried on for thousands of years, and that led to another peak of suppression of dissident culture and ideology in the Ming and Qing Dynasties. The Ming emperor Zhu Yuanzhang carried out enormous executions for the so-call faults in publications. Jails were specially established for Confucian scholars punished faultyí publications. They were seriously punished simply because of their views.

The Qing Emperor Kangxi proclaimed that the current affairs whether big or small will all be managed by me in person singularly. It is definitely not allowed to have the authority shared with others . In a book banning campaign, he operated in person singularly for an extended period of as long as 19 years. A total of 15100 volumes of books had been burned and over 80000 printing plates destroyed.

On the cultural aspect, the Chinese national character has a tendency of advocating action and despising speech. Confucius said, Gentlemen should be slow in speaking but quick in action, cunning words show no benevolence, putting action ahead of speaking. In the world where order is achieved, people surely advocate action, whereas in a situation of turbulence, speech is necessary, stated the *The Imperial Wisdom* **The Siku Encyclopaedia**, The advocating of action creates the habit of sincerity, whereas the advocating of speech breeds habit of treachery, associating speech with turbulence. Therefore, in order to prevent social turbulence, people's speech must be controlled effectively.

The rulers of China had, since very early time, understood that taking precautions against people's mouths is more crucial than those against flood. People were educated to be cautious in speaking. Confucius said, Hearing rumours in streets and spreading them openly is a departure from morality, There shouldn't be more words, which would lead to much loss, emphasizing less speaking, more doing. With regard to relations between individuals and the collective, the traditional culture of China utterly stress interpersonal harmony and concord between human-beings and nature, incorporating personal value into the family, the collective and the country to become a stable structure. Only within the collective would an individual acquire his / her value.

This is completely different from the western tradition of individualism. With this complete difference in value, the interests of the collective were usually considered much more important than those of individuals. At times, the individual interests would be sacrificed to those of the collective. So was the case with freedom of expression. For the sake of collective stability and interests, usually personal freedom of expression could be restricted.

Nevertheless in the late 19th and early 20th centuries, some revolutionaries influenced by western democratic thought were attempting to bring China from a feudal state into modern society and they had introduced the concepts of democracy, liberty and human rights into their revolutionary thought. If we wish our country enjoying lasting order and stability, and our people in peace and happiness to conform to the trends of the world, civil rights must be applied, stated the great revolutionary pioneer Dr. Sun Yat-sen in his political programme The Three Peopleís Principles, In China we have two ancient idioms: He who is not in the position shall not manage the affairs and Common people make no comments (on politics)í, indicating that in the past the political power was completely in the grasp of the emperor, having no connection with the people. Today we are in favour of civil rights to put political power into the hands of the people.

Though a military dictator having said that Using foreign ways to do Chinese things is just like scratch an itch from outside oneís bootí, Dr. Sun Yat -senís successor Mr. Chang Kai-Shek admired the western style of democracy, particularly after he married Madam Song Meiling who was educated in the US. During the long-term of struggle against the Kuomintang, the Communist Party of China had been holding the banner of democracy and human rights. On the eve of the founding of the Peopleís Republic of China, when answering the question of the democratic leader Mr. Huang

Yanpei about how to jump out of the cycle of rise and decline of the previous dynasties and regimes, Mao Zedong pointed out that democracy is a key to the matter.

Deng Xiaoping said in 1978 For a revolutionary party, what it fears most is the inability to hear people's voice and the most terrible thing is that silence reigns , and he pointed out at the same time, that efforts should be made to create a lively political environment practicing centralism as well as democracy, discipline and also freedom, unified will and also individual ease of mind .

Since the founding of New China, great progress has been made with people's freedom of expression, which is guaranteed by The Constitution. In order to create the necessary conditions for the implementation of freedom of expression of the people, the state makes enormous efforts to promote the course of press and publication. In 1998, throughout the country a total of 30.04 billion copies, 2053 kinds of newspapers, 2.45 billion, 7999 kinds of magazines and 7.24 billion, 130000 kinds of books were published. As far as electronic media is concerned, there are 294 radio stations, 560 national, provincial and municipal television stations, and 1287 county radio and TV stations nationwide, with a TV coverage on 89% of the population and one billion viewers. Until June 1999, there were 1.46 million on-web computers with 4 million web users.

What is The First Choice that Today s Chinese People Make: Social Stability or Expression of Freedom?

What are the issues the Chinese people are most concerned about? Social stability or freedom of expression?

As the 1999ís New Year bells were ringing across the starry midnight, the Investigation Centre of Beijing Xinhua Information Advisory Company, commissioned by Beijing Youth Daily , interviewed 609 families in Beijing in order to find out the top 10 issues the inhabitants of Beijing were most concerned about in 1999. The result turned out to be as follows:

1. Public Order
2. Environment
3. Education of the next generation
4. Prices
5. Corruption
6. Social Security
7. Job (Unemployment/Promotion)
8. Transport Facilities
9. Policy /Law/Regulation
10. Health

The survey indicates that the No.1 issue people were concerned about in 1999 was social environment, paying close attention to social security.

How do common people evaluate the present situation and development in China? On 26th September 1997, The South Weekend published a social investigation report about the general attitude toward the issue. The survey conducted among 289 inhabitants of Beijing by the Beijing Century Blueprint Investigation Company indicated that the majority of the residents thought their living standard had been improved in the past five years, whilst 65% 0f the interviewees thought that the social life would change for the better. The diversity of social classes featuring income difference was increasingly distinct, and the people having low income felt particularly heavy pressure of livelihood. In addition, these are the responses to the various issues raised:

Evaluation of living standard in the recent five years
Increased remarkably 23.2%
Increased in some degree 67.0%
Unchanged 8.0%
Dropped 1.7%

Comments on the change of social life in the recent five years
Better 66.1%
Worse 3.5%
Unchanged 10.4%
Do not know how to make assessment 19.8%

The related analysis indicated that the majority of Chinese people held a positive attitude toward social changes brought about through the reform.

In the minds of the people, what was the greatest change after the 20 years implementation of reform and openness policy? The survey indicated that 45.7% of them considered that the income has risen, 21.8% interpersonal relations have become more complex, 18.3% cultural life becomes richer. Corruption, unemployment and reform of the state-run enterprises were the focus of the public.

The biggest problems in our society
Corruption 28.0%
Unemployment 20.2%
The state-run enterprises 18.2%
Social order 8.9%
Social security system 8.3%

Economic order 6.2%
Social Justice 5.1%
Housing System 4.3%

The Issues that the 15th National Conference of the Communist Party of China was expected to deal with

Anti-Corruption 25.1%
Unemployment 16.6%
Reform of the state-run enterprises 15.7%
Increasing Income 11.0%
Reform of the political system 7.7%
Education6.6%
Social order 5.6%
Housing 5.2%
Construction of Spiritual Civilization 5.2%

The rating of the first two issues indicated that people were concerned with the governmentís political future and societyís economic future and reflected their hope for a stable and well-ordered environment for living and development.

To summarize the two surveys, it can be concluded that what todayís Chinese people are mostly concerned about is social stability, which is therefore the first choice of the people.

Understand China: Take Your Own Path

Seek common ground while reserving differences is the consistent stand of contemporary Chinese leaders in dealing with international relations. On the issue of human right, the Chinese government has signed almost all related international treaties, clearly indicating the stand to seek common ground with the international community. As for the attitude toward these treaties, one may say that the Chinese government is positive and sincere, particularly from the second generation of leaders, namely Deng Xiaoping. The reform and openness policy that the Chinese leaders have been practicing since the mid-80ís of twentieth century is aimed at bringing the backward and sealed-off China to modernization by learning from the outside world and meeting the world standards.

The third generation of Chinese leaders with Jiang Zeming, because of their own education, background, experiences, and the alienation of the extra leftist ideology along with the change of times, hold an even more positive attitude toward constructing a society of democracy, human right and law in China. Democracy is the essence and property of socialism. said Jiang Zemin at the 14th National Conference of the Communist Party of China, Should there be no democracy and legal system, there would be no socialism, no socialist modernization. We should make remarkable advance in the fields of developing socialist democracy and strengthening socialist legal system .

On 19th March 1998 when meeting with the press circle, the newly inaugurated premier Mr. Zhu Rongji said, on the construction of democracy Please donít be too impatient. I am even more impatient than you all . Nevertheless, why has a government like ours even more impatient with democratic reform not as yet carried out the overall political reform as rapidly as people have expected? Why does it have reservations about some articles of international human right documents it has signed? It is because that the Chinese government considers there is a necessity of reserving difference on the issue of human right. And the necessity of reserving the difference is on account of China's national conditions and the present international environment.

Deng Xiaoping described China's national conditions as having a large population, poor economic base, unbalanced regional development and undeveloped productive forces. On the level of economic development in the current stage of China, the Chinese government has to focus on and gives priority to the most fundamental one of human rights --- the right to live, which is defined Article Three in the UN Universal Human Right Declaration. The Chinese leaders believe in the social developing principle that economic base determines the superstructure. Only when economy has been developed, the people become wealthy and the country powerful, can we have the capability to tackle the social turbulence caused by democratic politics. Only in the soil of developed economy can democracy and freedom of expression grow healthily. Economic development demands a stable social environment --- this is the reason why Chinese leaders have been repeatedly emphasizing that stability overrides all other things.

Stability is, as well, an important prerequisite for realizing democracy. Without stable social environment, not only could democracy be spoiled in the process of its development, but may also evolve into chaos causing social anarchy, the nightmare of which the Chinese people had suffered sorrowfully in the notorious Cultural Revolution, also known as the Ten-year Catastrophe.

From 1966 to 1976, China, one of the poorest developing countries at that time, experienced a turbulent period unprecedented in Chinese history when absolute freedom of expression were pursued by means of practicing the Great Democracy featuring speaking freely, airing views fully, holding great debates and writing big-character posters resulting in production stoppage, suspension of classes, masses led by different factions resorting to all sorts of violence. After the Culture Revolution that had left such a bitter memory with the Chinese people, restoration of social stability and economic development has become the will of the whole nation.

The case has from a negative side proved the celebrated dictum by Mencius a full loaded granary brings up men of courtesy, a life of plenty creates people distinguishing sense of honour from disgrace . As the fa mous Psychologist Mr. Marlos pointed out, Human beingsí desires are on different levels. Only after the desires on the lower level being satisfied, can people pursue higher ones.

According to the principle of Economic base determines the superstructure , The accomplishment of democracy is based on a certain level of economic development. This is a proposition that has been proved in the development of countries or regions throughout the world. In the book Democracy in Developing Countries , the senior research fellow at the Hoover Institution Mr. Larry Diamond wrote, As a countryís national economy has reached the level of GDP $2500/person, it will have stepped into the door of democracy. The economic development will surely lead to consistently increasing possibility for democracy.

Mr. Seymour Martin Lipset, a senior fellow at the Hoover Institution and the Hazel Professor of Public Policy at George Mason University, compared the Anglo-Saxon, European and Latin-American countries on different levels of democracy in his book Political Man , and found that The wealthier a country is, the more possibilities it has for democracy. In the book Is China Becoming More

Democratic? by Mr. Henry S. Rowen, a senior fellow at the Hoover Institution and a professor of public policy and management emeritus at the Graduate School of Business at Stanford University, he stated that The historical pattern is clear: As countries get richer, they become more democratic.

According to the above views and that of Mr. Larry Diamond in particular, China, with a level of GDP merely less than $1000/person has therefore not yet stepped into the door of democracy. By comprehending this, it will be easily understandable why Chinese government had severely penalized the Falungong organization if its activities were merely within the range of religion, the government would not have interfered. It was because of its massive and organized protest rallies threatened the social stability that the government decided to ban it. The former Soviet Unionís storm of political reform erupted since 1989 has caused economic recession, national split and a series of crises, while Chinaís economic reform begun in the 80ís in the 20th century has brought about rapid development of national economy, consistent growth of national strength with a consecutive growth of GDP as 9%(1997), 8%(1998), 7%(1999) and the return of Hong Kong and Macao as scheduled. This has from positive and negative perspectives proved that Chinese leaders made a wise decision to maintain social stability and to develop the economy firstly.

On the international side, one may say that China is still in a perilous position in the international environment. In 1993, Samuel. P. Huntington, the famous political scientist, professor at the Harvard University published an paper entitled The Clash of Civilizations and the Remaking of World Order in the US journal Diplomacy , claiming that the conflicts in todayís world are, in the final analysis, conflicts between western and none-western civilizations. In the paper, he described China as No. 1 antagonist resisting the western civilization, and hence he designed nine strategies to contain and isolate China. Since the research result of the paper is provided to the US government as reference in its policymaking, it virtually reflects the point of view of the government.

The argument of Clash of Civilizations raised in the paper has evoked strong repercussions worldwide, and in particular, aroused the vigilance of Chinese government and people. The US-led western forces have been attempting to contain and isolate China in the areas of politics, economy and military. Politically, some western forces have been adopting a hostile attitude toward China. In an attempt to split and weaken China, they support the independence of Taiwan and Tibet and use the issues of democracy and human rights to demonise Chinaís image in the international media including satellite television, short wave broadcast and Internet. In the economic area, the US Congress has been obstructing China from acceding to GATT and WTO. In the military field, the US, joining forces with Japan (and Taiwan, potentially), is planning to construct the TMD system, in an attempt to complete the encirclement to China.

On 8th May 1999, the US led Nato bombed the Chinese embassy in Yugoslavia, killing two Chinese journalists. All of these have given Chinese leaders serious warnings that China is facing a dangerous international environment and Chinese people must unite as one and develop the national strength in order to safeguard the state sovereignty, territorial integrity and peopleís lives. On 6th February 2000, the deputy foreign minister of China Mr. Wang Guangya, when attending the 36th International Security Policy Convention in Munich once again expressed the anxiety of Chinese government toward the international security environment. To counter some countriesí arms sales to Taiwan, he said, this is not only in violation of principles of basic international law, but also a direct threat to the safety of China and regional peace and stability . He pointed out that the USí development of NMD will seriously damage the global strategic balance and stability, destroy the world security environment, and may even initiate a new round of armament race.

He strongly condemned the acts of some countries that placed regional organizations above the UN Security Council, and even bypass the Security Council to conduct military intervention against a sovereign state, pointing out that the practices have seriously damaged the present mechanism of international collective security, and entailed very dangerous consequences. Under this circumstance, any state leader will come to an incontestable conclusion that social stability is much more important than freedom of expression. In this way, it is understandable why Chinese government impose restrictions on some international media such as satellite television and Internet, which sometimes only pursue sensational effect, but ignore the peopleís basic interests.

In the 80ís of the 20th century when China began to carry out its opening to the outside world policy, Chinese people, with their traditional character of modesty, were well prepared to learn from the west, and they, with their simple belief in credit, trusted what the West said. On 8th July 1983, Deng Xiaoping said to his colleagues Donít be afraid of spending a bit more money on inviting foreigners. In the past, we had learned from them less and had offered less opportunity to them to help with our work. They would like to help us with our work. Later on however, some Western leadersí and politiciansí pursuit of their national interests surprised the Chinese people.

For instance, as a permanent member of the UN Security Council, the US, without the authorization of the Security Council, expanded the scope of operation to enter the Iraqi territory in the last stage of the Gulf War 1991, having violated the Charter of the United Nations it had signed. In 1999, the US-led NATO, without the authorization of the Security Council at all, launched the Kosovo War in Yugoslavia, having once again violated the Charter of the UN, which they are under obligation to respect and implement. The US frequently accuses other countries of failure to meet international standards in human right protection, but the US itself is reluctant to comply with international standards.

The US does not recognize the priority of international laws, and the federal government takes no obligation to execute international conventions in each state. The freedom of expression in the US is merely a myth. According to an investigation conducted in 1998 by the American Press Editorsí Association, 78% of American people thought the press took a partial stand, 80% of them thought some reports had been dramatized for the purpose of sales, while over 75% took a sceptical attitude toward reports whose sources were hidden. In recent years, the random shootings took place in US schoolyards, killing many children. Although the public was strongly in favour of gun control, no effective measures of gun control have been taken due to the objection of the gun industry and their powerful lobby the American Rife Association. The innocent American childrenís most basic human right right to live is not effectively protected.

On the 4th February 2000, Clinton made another appeal to the Congress for approval of his new gun control measures. The 8th January 2000 edition of Washington Post released an inside story: in the investigation of the alleged Wen Ho Lee Spying case, the FBI agents even tried to extort a confession by means of threatening Mr. Lee with putting him to death in an electric chair. They lied to him by hiding from him the fact that he had passed the loyalty test. Alberta Lee, his 26-year old daughter said in an interview with ABC, I have never dreamed of the United States which keeps on talking about humanism to be so inhuman.

The US and other western countries, by taking egoistic attitude toward international conventions and adopting double standards on the issue of human rights, have set a bad example to the world. Originally an idealistic learner, China has to become more realistic, and the attitude of reservation that China has taken toward some articles of international conventions is therefore understandable.

The Chinese leaders believe that freedom of expression is a process of gradual advance. When meeting with members of the Drafting Committee of the Basic Law of the Hong Kong Special Administrative Region on the 16th April 1987, Deng Xiaoping said: Even if general election were to be practiced, there should be a progressive transition. Things should be carried out step by step. After 50 years in the next century, general election may be carried out in the mainland. Since we have a population of one billion, and meanwhile peopleís cultural and education levels are not adequate, the condition has not been mature for practicing direct general election. Jiang Zemin once said: Neither in this world have there been any abstract democracy of supra-class, nor absolute one. The development of democracy is always related to definite class interests, economic base and historical background of a society. Every country has its own history, tradition and real situation of economic and social development. Democracy should fit-in with the conditions of a country . Our socialist democracy will, too, be developed and improved in practice along with the progress of economy, culture and society .

In fact, democracy and liberty, including freedom of expression, are the common ideals and goals of mankind as a whole. However, owing to different backgrounds of society, economy and culture, the ways to achieve the goal vary. Each country should choose a way of development suitable path for itself and every country should respect each other's own choice. Every road leads to Rome should be a global consensus. China is a large country with a population of 1.2 billion, whose culture is the most influential worldwide, particularly in Asia. Once China's exploration on the way to a democracy consistent with its specific characteristics succeeds, it will be significant in setting an example for countries of non-Christian culture, especially of Confucian culture. Such an example can help them advance to a high degree of democracy, beneficial for peace, stability and development worldwide.

To that end, the West should treat China's course of reform with more help and understanding, but less intervention and censure. This will not only be consistent with the interests of the people of China, but also with the interest of the international community, including the West.

Bibliography

The Great Learning *The Book of Rites*
Sidney Hook: The hero of History: A Study in Limit ation and Possibilities
Xunzi
The Origin of Chinese Words (Ciyuan)
Taishi *Zuozhuan*
Dayumuo *Shangshu*
Chant of Five Scholars *Shangshu*
Black Gown *The Book of Rites*
Annotation on Mencius by *Yang Buojun*
Politics of Zhenguan by *Wu Jin*
The Annals of the Monarch
The Annals of the Emperors of the Great Qing (Kangzhi)
The Collected Works of Zhang Wenzhong
Shepherding the People *Guanzi*
Selections of Deng Xiaoping
An Introduction to the Culture of China
The Imperial Wisdom *The Siku Encyclopaedia*
Guoyu
Annotation on Yanís Admonition by *Wang Liqi*
The Collected Works of San Yat-sen
The Human Right Record of US by *Ren Ranshi*
The Speeches of Jiang Zemin
The White Paper on the Development of Human Right in China

Leadership for Creativity: The Case of Mughal Emperor Akbar

Hafiza Golandaz

Prof. Hafiza Golandaz is Professor, International Leadership and Management Alliance (ILMA) Mumbai, India.

Introduction

There are so many studies done on leadership and yet when it comes to understanding leadership one feels that it is still more like an elephant being defined by blind men. The fault does not, however, lie on 4725 and odd studies on leadership (Bass) because a way of seeing becomes a way of not seeing also. Pun notwithstanding, the review of studies on leadership points different approaches to leadership:

1. Traits/ Characteristics/ Qualities; (Inter-War-Period Studies)
2. Leadership Behaviour Employee-centered Vs Production-centered. (The Early Michigan Studies);
3. People-Orientation Vs Task-Orientation (The Ohio State Studies);
4. Flexible Leadership Styles based on A. Situation; B. Type of Followers and C. Time Available (Fiedler);

1. Transformational Leader (Bass);
2. The Situational Leadership (Hersy and Blanchard);
3. Multi-disciplinary Approach (Burns);
4. Knowledge Approach (Cleveland);
5. Cognitive Approach (Gardner);
6. Multi-dimensional Approach (Safty); and
7. Results-based Approach (Ulrich, Zenger & Smallwood).

While all these approaches do throw light on different dimensions of Leadership, one still misses the wood for the trees, though Safty is hopeful that his Multi-dimensional view of Leadership will provide the broad and holistic picture of leadership.

All the above stated approaches can be further categorized as :

Behavioral Approach: Overt Actions
Psychological Approach: Personality Traits
Cognitive Approach: Observations from Leaders
Normative Approach   Expectations from Leaders
Result Approach   What is achieved

Out of the five approaches, it is the last approach, which combines all the other four in terms of

1. Who leaders Are (Values, Motives, Personal Traits, Character);
2. What leaders Know (Skills, Abilities, Traits); and
3. What leaders Do (Behaviour, Habits, Styles and Competencies) (Ulrich, P.4)

One is tempted to add to this ARE-KNOW-DO approach, the fourth dimension of How. How it improves the bottom line for all concerned, be it at macro or micro levels, from international to family, as a single unit.

One main reason, among many, which led to many studies on leadership failing in providing a broad picture is the emphasis on understanding leadership per se, in isolation of equally important other concepts like Group/Team and Creativity.

Rost is right when he takes a view of leadership, which not only recognizes relationship between leader and follower but its types and mutual purpose between them (P.127). In essence, it boils down to the role of leadership and the effectiveness of any role cannot be gauged without relating it to other roles in a group and in a given context/situation.

While taking this Multi-concepts view, a new addition to many prevailing approaches to leadership by yours truly, it is stressed that leadership as a concept be treated at par with other equally important concepts of Team and Creativity because effectiveness of result hinges on interaction of all the three sets (SEE EXHIBIT-1). Hence, to understand leadership, it is important to assess its role in group vis- -vis other roles, and more importantly the role of creativity.

The purpose of this paper, however, is restricted to assessing the role of leadership vis- -vis creativity by using a cognitive approach and assessing the role of Akbar, a Mughal Emperor in India (1556-1606), as a leader for creativity.

A moot question to be asked here is to why bring Akbar out of the cobwebs of history. The reasons are mainly two:

1. Examples from contemporary history would have meant that the environment might have also contributed to their success   present-day democracies etc; and

2. To prove that even an autocrat or monarch could create the environment necessary for creative search if he, as a leader, has vision and perspective.

But before discussing Akbarís contribution to creativity, a few observations on Group and Creativity will be in order.

Role of Leader in Group

A collection of people is clearly a group when it exhibits most, if not all, of these characteristics:

1. A definable membership   a collection of two or more people identifiable by name or type;

2. Group Consciousness - the members think of themselves as a group, have a collective perspective of unity, and a conscious identification with each other;

3. A sense of shared purpose   the members have the same common task, or goals or interests.

4. Inter-dependence   the members need the help of one another to accomplish the purposes for which they joined the group;

5. Interaction   the members communicate with one another, influence one another, and react to one another; and

6. Ability to act in a unitary manner — the group can work as a single organism.

Groups change and grow because they exist in time as well as space. Not only is the group moving as a unit, but also the various elements within it are constantly interacting. A change in leader may bring change in procedure, which may affect the atmosphere, which, in turn, may influence participation pattern, which, in turn, may affect cohesion, which may have bearing on morale etc.

In all this, group goes through four stages of:

1. Forming:
   The very coming together.
2. Storming:
   Authority and/or competence of the leader is tested and even challenged.
3. Norming:
   The group begins to harmonise.
4. Performing:
   Roles are seen as functional to the task and flexibility between them develops.

While 2 and 3 stages deal with Maintenance Role, the last one is clearly Developmental in nature, without which, there is no meaning to the very creation of group.

Maintaining group cohesiveness and using it as a means towards achieving the purpose for which group is created are two roles of leadership. Whether in a given group these are performed by one leader or two different leaders is immaterial.

Group's effectiveness depends on growing to survive and surviving to grow and this, in turn, depends not only on different roles in a group but achieving a right balance among them.

R.M. Belbin has made a long study of the best mix of characteristics in a team. He ended up with a list of eight roles that are needed for a fully effective group.

Out of the eight roles, two The Chairman and the Team Worker relate to maintenance and the rest deal with development. However, on the development side, the role, which is steering every other role towards accomplishing the task, is that of Shaper, which can be called another leadership role.

In short, in a group, leadership roles are people-cantered and task-cantered and can be performed theoretically by one person. This is by far well known through Managerial Grid. What is less known is the role of leader vis- -vis creativity in a group?

Creativity in a Group and the Role of Leader

Creativity owes its origin to the Sanskrit word Kar, meaning to make, to originate, to bring into existence (Kyle, P.118). Development or doing something better than existing depends solely on new ideas and it is the role of creative person(s) to provide it. But like any other role, the creative role is dependent on other roles.

Merely generation of ideas itself does not lead to the success of the group. The ideas so generated need to undergo the acid test of efficacy — whether it is worthwhile to implement the idea or not. This is the job of the Monitor-Evaluator in a group. After he declares the idea viable, it is the Resource Investigator who offers or arranges resources for putting the idea into action. Then it is the work of the Implementer to implement and the Finisher to monitor the schedules. Thus, there is a clear cut backward and forward integration of creativity role with other roles in a group:

1. Backward Integration — with the Chairman and the Shaper, basically-leadership roles; and

2. Forward Integration — With other five roles.

However, achieving of this integration is not done by the person(s) performing creative role as they, like mother, fall in love with their ideas the moment they take birth. It is the leadership function to achieve the same and which can be achieved in full if leader:

1. Himself is development oriented;

2. has an eye to spot creative potential in others;

3. Gets potentially creative persons in a group;

4. creates creative atmosphere and encourages creative persons to give their best;

5. recognizes and rewards creative ideas and, above all;

6. creates cordial, cooperative and collaborative atmosphere not only between creative and other roles but also between two and more creative roles in a group.

From whom can one learn better from history than an Emperor who identified, brought together, encouraged, recognized and rewarded not one or two but nine creative persons who were gems in their chosen respective fields. No doubt, they were called Navratnas, nine Jewels in the Kingís Crown.

But before discussing the case of Akbar as Leader responsive to creativity, it will be only apt to lay down the principles on which Akbarís contribution as Leader to creativity could be assessed.

Development function of leader is very delicate, variable, and complex. It requires creating, absorbing and marketing new knowledge and skills. To encourage learning and adaptivity, effective leaders initiate and support the following special conditions as suggested by Zand:

1. Creative Deviance
2. Mastery of Existing Knowledge.
3. Unstructured Time.
4. New Perspectives.

To this should be added a few more principles:

5. Leader not competing with those performing creative roles in the team on creativity;
6. Leader desisting from acting as Monitor-Evaluator to creative personís ideas; and
7. Between the Chairman and the Shaper role, considering the sensitive nature, which generally creative persons exhibit, leader giving preference to the chairman role while interacting with creative persons in the group.

Leader Responsible To Creativity: The Case of Akbar

Mohammed Jalaluddin Akbar was the third king of Mughal Empire, founded by his grandfather King Babur in 1526. Because of his father's untimely demise, Akbar had to take the reins of Power at the tender age of 13, in 1556, but he ruled India for 50 years till 1605 and laid the solid foundations of the Mughal Empire through his strong tenets of effective leadership. His open-mindedness and tolerance for diverse views held the Mughal Empire together for long after he breathed his last.

His own creativity and his encouragement to others' creativity are analysed under the rubric of the following principles:

1. **To Create New, Often Radical, Leaders Have To Show Courage And Take Risk :** Akbar during his rule introduced many radical reforms/ changes which are commendable because he did not inherit from his father a very stable empire, and add to that his tender age and no formal education of any sort compounded the problem. Some changes introduced by Akbar worth sharing are :
(a).Affirmed his independence from the Islamic principles of sovereignty by putting in place political, military and religious systems that he controlled **(Beristain)**.
(b) Introduced Persian as the Court's official language.
(c) Abolished Islam as the State Religion.
(d)Made the tax levies corresponding to India's seasons. (e) Replaced the Muslim era of Hejra with the Ilahi era, of Persian type, whose months bore Zoroastrian names.
(f) Decentralized the power by distributing the responsibilities of administration among four different

ministers instead of keeping it under the charge of **Vakil** (Prime Minister) Finance, Army, Justice and Religion and Royal Household.

2. Effective Leaders Are Not Perturbed By False Starts Or Failures Of Their Ideas: Though not formally educated, Akbar learnt by holding discourses with the learned persons belonging to different religions about the finer aspects of each religion. During his period, there was a great deal of discord in the religious life of India, which troubled him as it affected the national progress and unity. He hit upon an idea of assimilating finer points of all religions and creating an ideal religion. In fact, it was supposed to act as a forum **(DIN-E-ILAHI)** on the model of a Sufi order.

What was the most applauding fact of this idea was that people joining this forum were free to retain their diverse religious beliefs and practices. Amber devised it with the noble intention of forging the diverse communities in the countryís population into one people. But many opposed this idea and Akbar gave it up from pursuing it to its logical conclusion.

What is worth praising here is that a) Akbar did this experiment at the age of **20**, just seven years after becoming the King and b) he did not use his power of the Kingship to thrust his ideas on others.

3. Effective Leaders Understand That The Creative Process Differs From Its Output, The Creative Product. The Process Flourishes In A Climate That Encourages Deviant Ideas: During his rule, the Mughal empire was rightly been called a Cultural State. It encouraged cultural endeavour through lavish patronage. It produced a galaxy of poets, historians, scholars, painters, calligraphers, architects,

musicians and craftsmen. Akbar also sent a special envoy to the Portuguese to find out what new articles of arms were available with them. He also encouraged the import of European paintings and their imitation.

Akbar is reported to have said **Kingship is in fact the understanding of men s worth** (Abu-I-Fadl) Akbar proved it right in not only identifying genius in nine persons but bringing them together in his government and forming a Council of Nine Jewels **(Nav Ratnas)**. They were 1. Bairam Khan; 2. Abu-I-Fadl; 3. Raja Mansingh; 4. Mulla Do Pyaza; 5. Raja Birbal; 6. Raja Todarmal; 7. Raja Tansen; 8. Hakim Hoomam; and 9. Abdul Qadir Badauni. Each one was expert in one′s field.

Records show that Akbar encouraged deliberations and discussions not only with his nine jewels but score of other experts. Although he did not agree with many of his counsels, he respected their views based on their knowledge and their experience. Akbar was always willing to listen to new ideas and to try them out. No doubt, the regime of Akbar was rightly called a citadel of renaissance in which, helped by good government and patronage, geniuses blossomed into masterpieces. This practice did not remain confined only to the Court and the Nobles but also percolated down to the grass-root levels.

4. Because Insight, New Ideas, And Consensus Building Follow An Irregular Disjoined Path, Effective Leaders Give Their People Unstructured Time To Pursue Creative Activity, Freeing Them From Routines, Repetitive Activities That Dull The Senses.

Creativity generates and flourishes in an environment where information flows are unrestricted, can only arise in an atmosphere of tolerance towards risk taking and experimentation and benefits from partnership where leaders also learn from others.

Record shows that Akbar not only provided patronage to nine jewels but also to persons having diverse interests, specialization and experience. They were kept free from any official routine. They were also assigned the tasks that did not remotely relate to their areas of specialization. For instance Hakim Hoomam, one of the Nine Jewels, was sent as an envoy to negotiate in the areas beyond the present Afghanistan. Raja Birbal, who was an intellectual, was sent to Rajputs to negotiate on various issues including establishing marital relations with the Mughals **(Sardesai)**. Raja Birbal was also sent to control Afghan attacks **(Sardesai)**. By encouraging undertaking diverse nature of tasks, Akbar had helped them to develop serendipity and their creative productivity.

5. Effective Leaders Understand That When People View A Situation From New Perspectives, They Learn And Discover New Knowledge.

Akbar had succeeded in bringing about the political, administrative, economic and, to some extent, the cultural unification of northern India by introducing Persian as the only official language, by bringing about the fusion of Hindu and Muslim architecture, painting, music and providing a common religious and secular literature. By introducing several social reforms, he attempted to make social unification a reality. But he believed that for this unification to be effective and permanent, it must be based on some kind of mutual religious-cum-cultural understanding and appreciation. In short, he wanted a common religious forum for at least the elites of various sections of the Indian society.

Every week, on Thursday, Akbar used to attend religious debates and involve 38 **Shaikhs**, 69 **Pandits (HinduScholars)**, 15 **Hakims** and 153 **Poets**. Whether in religious debates or any other deliberation, by listening, participating and by involving people with relevant or irrelevant background, Akbar tried to understand issues from different perspectives and also helped others to change their mind-set based on new knowledge. **(Sardesai)**

6. Leaders Usually Lag Behind Their People As Specialized Knowledge Advances. If They Do Not, Then They Are Probably Settling For Mediocre Subordinates Or In Some Way Inhibiting Their Growth. Effective Leaders, However, Continue Their Learning, Keeping The Knowledge Gap Between Themselves And Their People Within Workable Bound. They Do Not Expect To Be Experts But They Continually Acquire New Knowledge And Problem Solving Skill In Order To Understand The Advise They Receive And To Project Its Implications.

Having had turbulent childhood in the war-ridden Central Asia, Akbar could not gain formal education. But what he missed in formal education, he made up subsequently through his association with men of learning, Record shows that besides Nine Jewels there were hundreds of scholars, creative thinkers and artists, religious leaders who were patronized and Akbar used to have consultations with them. Akbar benefited from his battery of able advisors, experts, poets, and artists and like a confident and secure leader gave due credit to them for their contribution.

He probably was the first king who bestowed the title of **Raja** (King) to his nine jewels. The most important aspect to note here is that while learning about many fields from nine his Jewels and other experts, Akbar never ever competed with them. **The hall-mark of a true and effective leader is when he has in his team members who know more than him.** Akbar proved this dictum more than amply.

7. Effective Leaders Have Very Personal Style Of Working Through Difficult And Conflict Ridden Issues, Dispensing Justice And Honouring Merit.

Akbar possessed a high sense of responsibility. He looked upon a proper discharge of his duties as worship. Akbarís Courts were expected to dispense justice without fear or favour **(Abu-I-Fadl)** and he himself was available for hearing the complaints of his subjects. Akbar knew it well that his power could be sustained only through the satisfaction of his subjects. Akbar firmly believed in the text book maxim found in all the treaties on Muslim Statecraft that A polity can endure despite disbelief but it cannot last without justice . **(Qureshi)**

Akbar was also a great believer in merit. Recruitment to the services was strictly on the basis of merit. Even friendship with Emperor did not result in rapid promotion. Akbar did not permit his personal likes and dislikes to affect the prospects of a public servant. He was even willing to ignore lapses in loyalty on the part of his able generals and administrators.

8. Competent Leaders Do Not Waste Resources Reinventing The Wheel. Creating New Knowledge Builds On What Is Known. So Effective Leaders Encourage Their People To Master Existing Knowledge.

Akbar appointed Raja Todarmal (who introduced effective land reforms and revenue administration in the kingdom of Shershah Sur) as one of the nine jewels and allowed him to introduce a series of administrative and land reforms, the main aim of which was to increase revenue of the empire.

He divided the Empire into 12 provinces (**Suba**) and appointed as the Head of each a Governor, where duty was to administer its territory, with the help of a **Diwan** to collect taxes and a **Sadr** to look after religion. The governor no longer collected taxes directly but was remunerated by the central authority according to his rank and his responsibilities (**Mansab**), which was not hereditary (not were the titles). In the event of death or dismissal of this officer the Suba was returned to the Emperor who appointed someone else as its Head. When the Emperor felt that a single person was not adequate for the responsibilities of the office, another expert was associated with him. Sometimes the office was put into commission and two persons with equal authority were given charge of it. In order to ensure impartiality of such officers they were regularly transferred. Thus, Akbar was the exponent of merit system in India and the System prevails, with some modifications, even today.

Akbarí Diwans were responsible for many reforms in the administration and its procedures. These brought about efficiency in place of chaos, which had prevailed because of wars and disorders immediately preceding Akbarís reigns. Akbarís approach in personal and official interactions reveal a balance among three factors: Crisis, Creativity and Order. His constant struggle to defend, expand and maintain borders of his vast Empire, making the defeated kings in-charge of the areas won, establishing marital ties with non-Muslim kingsí relatives, patronizing fine arts, education, and their spread, and general satisfaction of people about land reforms, administrative reforms and system of judiciary are some of the examples to this effect.

CONCLUSION

A close look at Akbarís leadership style provides fresh vindication for the basic axiom of synergy that the whole is greater than the sum of its parts. Indeed, Akbar himself often suggested that the genius of a great leader consisted in the **constant harmony of holding variety of great purposes in mind all at once.**

It was his imagination, which, by necessity, was fuelled with experience that enabled Akbar to range across the large mass of detail that confronted a war leader. Candour and plain speaking, decisiveness, imagination and vision, the ability to balance a view of the whole scene with attention to details, ability to take bold new initiatives, ability to delegate, flexibility in problem solving approach, tolerance for heterogeneity and accepting dissent, are the qualities that contemporary leaders, both at macro and micro levels at international and local levels, can emulate well from him.

If one accepts the fundamental patterns of leadership behaviour as given by **Kouzes** and **Posner,** based on their study of people who accomplished extra-ordinary things in organisations, and apply the same to Akbar, he more than fits the bill. The fundamental principles, with two basic strategies for each, are:

1. **Challenging the process**
    a) Search for opportunities
    b) Experiment and take risks.

2. **Inspiring a shared vision**
    a) Envision the future.
    b) Enlist others.

3. **Enabling others to act**
    a) Foster collaboration
    b) Strengthen others.

4. **Modelling the way**
    a) Set the example.
    b) Plan small wins.

5. **Encouraging the heart.**
    a) Recognise contributions.
    b) Celebrate accomplishments.

What is generally observed is that most people fulfill some of the principles outlined above. It should be noted that following one or two principles well is no substitute/excuse for not doing well on others. An effective leader is not only good in the performance of all the five principles and ten strategies but by sequencing them well in his behaviour he also achieves the much needed synergy.

Akbar fulfilled this to a tee and at a time when circumstances, his age and his lack of any formal education were on his wrong side. Need one say more?

References

Abu-I-Fadl, Aine-I-Akbari (Part V), as quoted in Qureshi.

Bass, B.M. (1981), Stogdillís Handbook of Leadership (Re v. Ed.), New York, The Free Press. Joseph Rost also examined 312 books and journal articles on leadership written during the eighties and arrived at more or less the same conclusion. See Rost cited below.

Beristain, Valerie, (1998) Mughal India : Splendours of the Peacock Throne, London, Thomas and Hudson.

Belbin, R.M., (1981), Management Teams: Why They Succeed or Fail, Heinemann.

Burns, J.M. (1978), Leadership, New York, Harper & Raw.

Cleveland, Harland (1985), The Knowledge Executive, New York, Dutton.

Fiedler, F.E., Chemers, M.M. & Mahar, L. (1976), Improving Leadership Effectiveness, New York, John Wiley.

Gardner, Howard (1955), Leading Minds, New York, Basic Books.

Hersy, P. and Blanchard K. (1988), Management of Organisational Behaviour: Utilizing Human Resources, Englewood Cliffs, NJ, and Prentice Hall.

Kouzes James M. and Posner Barry Z., (1987), The Leadership Challenge, San Francisco, Jossey Bass Inc.

Kyle, David, T. (1998), The Four Powers of Leadership, Florida, Health Communications Inc.

Qureshi, Ishtiaq Hussain, (1990), The Administration of the Mughal Empire, New Delhi, Low Price Publications.

Rost, Joseph, C. (1991), Leadership for the Twenty-First Century, New York, Praeger.

Safty Adel (1996), Leadership; A Programmatic and Theoretical Inquiry, Extract from the Report submitted to United Nations University Council, Santiago, Chile.

Sardesai, G.S., (1993) Musalmani Riyasat (Vol.2), Mumbai, Popular Prakashan.

Ulrich Dave, Zenger Jark, Smallwood Norm, (1999) Results-based Leadership, Boston, Massachusetts, Harvard Business School Press.

A Clash of Civilisations: A Muslim Perspective

M. Fathi El Shazly

Ambassador El Shazly is Egyptís ambassador to Turkey.

Islam is a greater threat to Europe than communism. The author of this statement is Willy Claes, former Secretary General of NATO. He volunteered to make this erroneous judgment two years before he lost his position in 1996 in a shortsighted attempt to create a new enemy for the Western Alliance, at a time when many people were wondering whether by the disappearance of Warsaw Pact, NATO had lost its raison dí tre. The announcement by Willy Claes of his bid to depict Islam as the new enemy of the West coincided with the debate triggered by the publishing in mid 1993 of an article by Samuel Huntington about the inevitability of clashes between civilizations. Afterwards, reflecting on the future relationship between civilizations became the fashion of the nineties for academics and politicians alike.

In the West as well as in the East many prominent personalities stood up to condemn the dangerously misleading talk about clashes of civilizations. Crown Prince Charles of the U.K. and former American President Bill

Clinton were salient names among those who paid tribute to Islam while refuting the eventuality of clashes between Islamic and Western civilizations.

Outstanding scholars repudiated the New Darwinism proposed by Huntington, arguing that he was actually pretending that cultural specificities had not existed since time immemorial, not only between groups belonging to different civilizations, but also between individuals belonging to the same culture. He was pretending as if cultural impact of social and physical environments could be neutralized: desert versus jungle and nomadism versus urbanism, as if it were possible to delineate civilisational and cultural clusters, according to latitudes and longitudes.

Last September terrorist attacks committed by Moslem individuals on the United States, the leader of the western nations, have vigorously given new momentum to the ongoing investigation about the nature and direction of the relationship between the so called Western Civilization and Islam. Even before the debris of the World Trade Centre was removed, the mongers of the devilish theory preaching for the inevitability of clashes between civilizations resumed spitting out their poison. In an article for the special Davos Edition of Newsweek in December 2001, Huntington contended that the world has entered since 1980 an age of Moslem wars, which could yet spiral into a clash of civilizations. Francis Fukuyama of the End of History maintained that history has been moving inexorably toward universal democracy, but Islamofascism was the latest obstacle. For me the two were again mistaken and ill intentioned.

1) The wars and the resort to violence in the indicated period were not exclusive of Moslems. Latin America, Asia,

Africa were theatres of wars in which Moslems were not involved. On European soil, one of the bloodiest chapters of the war in Yugoslavia was between Serbs and Croats, both Christian. The separatist ETA movement in Spain killed 835 civilians in acts of terror committed since 1968. More than 3500 persons were killed in the terrorist operations of the Irish Republican Army since the sixties of last century. In Japan, the extremist organization Um Shenry Quo conducted in March 1995, a chemical weapon attack in a metro station that left 10 dead and about 5000 injured. USA itself experienced several violent terrorist attacks such as Oklahoma City bombing in 1995.

2) Huntington included in his list, wars in which Moslems were the victims. The American Administration itself officially referred to Bosnia Herzegovina and to Kosovo as instances in which America used force to repel aggression against Moslems.

3) In the other wars listed by Huntington, Moslems were fighting not in their religious capacity but for nationalistic or other motives such as the wars between Iraq and both Iran and Kuwait.

4) As for Fukuyama, he obviously needed to attend a course in basic information about Islam to properly understand the Islamic reality and not confuse it with the distorted image collected from terrorist propaganda.

The real irony lied in the fact that the talk about clash of civilizations was being propagated in a constantly shrinking world, whose different peoples were supposedly being brought culturally closer to each other thanks to the new Information Technology.

Before pursuing further my thesis to explain how Islam perceives the issue, I will make some remarks of general nature:

1- My first remark is to state that the revival of religious feelings is a recurrent phenomenon that manifests itself in all societies regardless of their creed, in a cyclical pattern.

2- The genius of the religion Islam, being a universal call for the entire human race, lies in its adaptability in ever changing space and time. This results in two consequences:
a) The emphasis and priorities vary from a Moslem society to another according to local circumstances, physically, socially, and culturally in a way that does not jeopardize the attachment by all to the basic principles of the religion.
b) That keeping updated the interpretation of Islamic teachings should be confined to those who master the theological and Islamic sciences in close and constant collaboration with experts in worldly sciences.

3- Consequently, no uniform prescription is available to understand and approach problems facing different Islamic societies including the phenomenon of violence arbitrarily and mistakenly attributed to Islam by politically or criminally motivated terrorists.

After these preliminary remarks, I wish to claim that three main factors contributed to the making of the perception of the other by both Islam and the West: the religion Scope , The implications of European colonialism and the believersí factor :

The Religion Scope

Both Islam and Christianity, unlike Judaism, have had a universal vocation. Both have been actively preaching, competing for the hearts and minds of the people around the World. According to some contemporary Western scholars, i.e. Prof. Alexander Bausani of the Italian National Academy in a dissertation published in 1983, Christian Churches played a very important role in changing the Christian curious interest in knowing more about Islam, often with admiration, to hatred and repulsion. He attributed this role mainly to political motives but also to financial egoistic interests. He cited as an example the abolition by the Abbasside Caliph Abou Jaafar Al-Mansour in the Eighth century of the taxation benefits and exemptions that churches and Christian clergymen used to enjoy within the territories of the Abbasside Empire.

The implications of European colonialism

With the advent of the industrial revolution and the era of great geographic discoveries the West turned aggressively to the East. Many Islamic countries felt victims to Western colonialism. To sustain its hegemony and control on its colonies, Western powers tried hard to alienate and even oppress and destroy the cultural identity of Islamic peoples in their colonies. This process mostly resulted in one of two reactions among Moslems:

a) Feeling mistrust in the West and absolute repulsion of the western civilization as an aggressive, materialistic civilization that exhibited low morality, while at the same time resorting to conventional salafy texts with its old and

outdated explanations as a way of protecting oneís identity.
b) Accepting the full defeat in front of the invading West and trying to fully adopt its approaches believing that modernization required westernization. Willing to neutralize the military supremacy enjoyed by the invading western armies, some Moslem Leaders decided to adopt the organizational and technological traits of those armies. Soon after, the leaders realized that their decision meant conscription that required conducting census and imposing taxes. It also entailed the building of factories and the establishment of modern Academies and training centres and the employment of foreign instructors. This process which in time developed into a modernization process, considered by some a westernizing drive of Islamic societies concerned, led to aggravating the burden of the state on the society, which in turn prompted resistance and encouraged some to escape from the reach of the state.

At the same time, while trying to eliminate the cultural identity of their Moslem colonies, Western nations came to believe that Islam was an enemy to the Western civilization and that Moslems were backward peoples that had nothing worthy respect. This negative understanding was underlined by the malicious addition crafted and inflated by the Zionists throughout the decades of the 20th century about the so called Judeo-Christian heritage building on the fact that Judaism preceded Christianity and that Old Testament is a part of the Christians Holy Book, the Zionist propaganda portrayed Christians and Jews as one sum while Moslems were considered among the others. This claim ignored that we Arabs have always had genuine Arab Christians, Orthodox in Egypt and Maronites in Lebanon and Syria and that all three monotheistic religions were in fact born, nourished and came to adulthood in our part of the world.

The believers factor

The third factor could be what the Egyptian famous reformist Mohamed Abdou; who lived at the end of the 19th century; meant when he claimed that Islam was hidden from the world by Moslems. It is true that the soul and real teachings of any religion could be confused and misunderstood by the behaviour and the image projected by its followers. In the case of Islam, the information world order, currently under the control of Western circles used a highly selective approach concentrating on negative aspects of Islam as projected by the behavior of some of its followers.

Terrorist groups such as the one led by Osama Bin Laden that have been practicing their terror in Islamic countries, that were being chased by Governments of Islamic Nations, condemned by Moslem public and challenged by Moslem scholars and that have been given indirect and overt support as well as safe haven by western capitals, are now taken by some western intellectuals as legitimate representatives of Islamic thinking and Civilization.

In the same vein, Western Media have been persistent in projecting a very negative image about Islam and Moslems. Mr. Jaques Shahin a Christian American of Lebanese origin who had never met a Moslem until he was forty when he was sent to teach in Beirut during the civil war of the seventies published recently, a significant work that took him two decades to compile. He went through the American film industry since 1980. He found out that the prototype of Arabs and Moslems depicted in films produced by Hollywood systematically portrayed a linkage between Islam and mistreatment of women, violation of human rights, violence, terrorism and all other evil doings. From hundreds of films produced between 1980 and 2000, Shahin was able to only single out 12 films that attributed positive qualities to Arabs and Moslems, including Robin Hood, the Prince of thieves of 1990, the thirteenth Warrior of 1999 and Three Kings also of 1999.

Unfortunately, Moslems themselves produced most of the ingredients for the defamation of Islam. Earlier, I made reference to the protective attitude of withdrawal of some Moslems in front of the victorious Western civilization. A few of us have chosen to escape into the past by highlighting old texts, refusing any contemporary discussion or interpretation thereof and attaching exaggerated importance to appearances and clothing code, often disputed , and adopting a very rigid attitude against non Moslems and against other Moslems. Some went to the extreme of boycotting their own Moslem societies and deserting them to remote localities. Needless to say that this withdrawal attitude engulfed in extremism is contrary to the teachings of Islam, and to the instruction of the Holy Quran itself. In Surat Al Bakara, verse no.256 says:

Let there be no compulsion in religion: Truth stands out clear from error: Whoever rejects evil and believes in Allah has grasped the most trustworthy handhold that never breaks and Allah is all-hearing, all-knowing

In spite of the negative position adopted by Christian world vis- -vis Islam and Moslems reaching its climax during the Crusades era, Christians` interest in Islam continued and even showed glimpses of fairness from time to time. In 1134 the outstanding French Abbot of Cluny Peter the Venerable ordered the first translation of the Holy Quran into Latin. In the thirteenth and fourteenth centuries, European

Universities witnessed the establishment of Arabic language chairs and the first book on the Arabic Grammar was published in 1613 by the Dutch Thomas Arbinius. The second half of the nineteenth century saw unprecedented flourishment of Orientalist studies especially in the Netherlands, France, Germany and the United Kingdom.

The withdrawing, rigid, suspicious mind displayed by terrorists disguising their ugly faces behind Islamic banners, is completely different from the tolerant, investigative and practical mind taught by the Holy Quran. The experimental approach established by Moslem scientists was in fact dictated by the Quranic order to Moslems to pursue the path of God through reflecting on Man and Universe. In Surat Fosíselat, verse 53 reads.

We will show them our signs in the furthest regions in the universe and within own souls until it becomes manifest to them that this is the truth .

In this context, it is worth mentioning that the founder in the 13th century of the Experimental Method in the West Roger Bacon invited everybody concerned to learn Arabic as the key for real knowledge. The great historian of science George Alfred Sarton of the 20th century followed the methodology of naming every chapter in the history of science in 50 years spans after the most important figure in that period. For instance, he considered the period 450 BC to 400 BC the era of Plato followed by the era of Aristotle. From the year 750 to the year 1100 , Sarton gave to the consecutive scientific poques the names of an uninterrupted glowing chain of Moslem scientists such as Gaber Ibn Hayyan, Al-khawarizmi, Ibn Sina and Ibn-ul-Haytham. Only after those 350 glorious years, names of European scientists started to appear again but together with

Moslem names such as Averroes or Ibn Rushd and Ibn-ul-nafis. Not only in applied sciences Islamic civilization led the development of the human race for several centuries, but also in philosophy and fiction. The great philosopher Saint Thomas Aquinas was deeply influenced by Averroes. The famous work of fiction Robinson Crusoe of Daniel Defoe can easily be traced to Hay Beni Yakhzan of Ibn Al Tofayel. Dante Alighieriís Divine Comedy finds its origin in Al Israa and Al Miraj accounts and Al Maariís Rissalat Alghofran.

I now turn to the principles to govern the conduct of the relations between Moslems and the followers of both Christianity and Judaism as taught by the Holy Quran:

1) Islam regards all peoples as one single nation descending from one single father and one single mother. In Surat Al Hogorat, verse 13, the Holy Quran says:
O mankind! We created you from a single pair of a male and a female and made you into Nations and tribes, that ye may know each other, the most honoured of you in the sight of God is the most righteous of you .

2) Moslems believe that all the three Monotheistic Religions: Judaism, Christianity and Islam came from the same source that is GOD. A true Moslem should equally believe in the prophets and holy books of both other religions. Those who donít are not true Moslems even though they believe in Prophet Mohamed. Therefore Islamís perception of the other two religions of the Book, and regardless of their repulsion and negative position *vis a vis* Islam and Moslems, goes beyond mere tolerance to accepting and believing in the Prophets and Books of Christianity and Judaism as integral parts of its own beliefs.

In the verse 84 of Surat Al Imran the Holy Quran says:

We believe in Allah and in what has been revealed to us and what was revealed to Abraham, Ismail, Isaac, Jacob, and the tribes and in the books given to Moses, Jesus and the Prophets from their Lord. We make no distinction between one and another among them and to Allah we do bow our will

3) The original state of the relations between Moslems and non-Moslems is peace. War is an exception that should not be resorted to unless in extreme cases and to repel aggression. Preaching should be made peacefully and with politeness. In Surat Al Ankabut, verse no.46 the Holy Quran says:
Ö.and dispute ye not with the people of the Book except with means better than mere disputation, unless it be with those of them who inflict wrong and injury, but say: we believe in the revelation which has come down to us and in that which came down to you, our God and your God is one, and it is to Him we bow.

And in Surat Al Nahl verse 125 the Holy Quran says: Invite all to the way of the Lord with wisdom and beautiful preaching, and argue with them in ways that are best and most gracious.

4) In the exceptional case of war, Moslems are ordered to immediately stop hostilities and resort to peace if the enemy stops fighting. In Surat Al Anfal, verse 61, the Holy Quran orders Moslems *But if the enemy inclines towards peace, do thou also incline towards peace and trust in God*.

5) Another rule for the conduct of the relations between Moslems and non-Moslems is the obligation of Moslems to

honour the pacts and accords concluded between them and others. Islam does not allow Moslems under any circumstances to breach their commitments. In Surat Al Nahl, verse 91, the Holy Quran says *fulfill the covenant of Allah when ye have entered into it and break not your oath after ye have confirmed them. Indeed ye have made Allah your surety, for Allah knows all that ye do*. The Quran prohibits breaking the commitment even if the breakage were for the sake of Islamic solidarity. Verse 72, of Surat Al Anfal says *But if they seek your aid in religion, it is your duty to help them except against a people with whom ye have a treaty, and Allah sees all that ye do*.

Conclusion

From the expos I just made, it becomes obvious that Trans-Civilization cultural interaction has always existed with differing intensity and different directions. Long before the post cold war attempts of theorization, London hosted at 1936 a joint session of dialogue between Al-Azhar and the Vatican. Al-Azhar hosted another session in Cairo in 1978.

Recently, especially after Huntingtonís article of 1993, a boom occurred in the dialogue between religions as well as in the wider sense between cultures and civilizations. If a compilation were made of the conferences held, lectures given, and articles and books published, we would be able to produce several huge volumes. Only in the years 1995, 1996, and 1997 I was able to count forty-five events around the subject that issued a great wealth of ideas and information.

The Barcelona Process for building a comprehensive partnership between the EU and twelve Mediterranean countries made a valuable contribution to the debate about the future relationships between cultures around the Mediterranean. The UNO declared the year 2001 as the year of dialogue between civilizations. What added a sense of urgency to the subject were obviously the terrorist attacks of last September on New York and Washington. I personally believe that Islam and Moslems stand to benefit of this outcome. Sales of the translations of the Holy Quran and of books about Islam in the US and most of the European countries have unprecedently soared up in the past few months.

This is a very healthy phenomenon as it prepares the grounds for a more serious dialogue between civilizations which is very beneficial to all in the light of the following reasons:

1) The growing tendency towards globalization in the trade of commodities and services requires a great deal of mutual understanding and cultural awareness and tolerance.

2) The appearance of new trance-boundary challenges and threats, indifferent to cultural diversities demand closer international cooperation and solidarity. Those include the degradation of the ecosystem, the attrition of natural resources, the proliferation of weapons of mass destruction, the growing dangers of organized crime and the emergence of new contagious diseases threatening humans, fauna, and flora.

3) The moral questions raised by certain scientific advances such as cloning and genetic engineering. The international consensus on protecting human rights and promoting democratic ideals, which are questions of great interest and varying connotations to different cultures, require a dialogue conducive to a better understanding

between groups belonging to different cultures. The growing involvement of religious institutions in the socio-political life of societies all over the world and across the cultural divides as well as the increasing universal dangers of terrorism and the relentless attempts by some of its mongers to disguise it under religious banners need a universal will to maximize the benefits, minimize the risks and combat the evil.

I personally believe that in order to have the best outcome possible of the dialogue some considerations should be made:

1- Culture dialogue should survey the images of one self and the other as projected by literature, arts, religious interpretations, and political position takings. It should also survey the relevant content of information material and school textbooks.

2- Dialogue should not be limited to contemporary cultural products, but should also address inherited stereotypes contained in folklore.

3- The involved partners in the dialogue should not only be the intelligentsia and specialized circles. Its impact should also filter down to the grass roots and the recipients and consumers of cultural products and media messages.

4- The checklist of the above mentioned survey should include subjects frequently used to foment misunderstanding, for example: Islam, violence, and terrorism - The Crusades - The Immigration - Human Rights - The status of Women - Civil Society - Democracy and the Rule of Law.

Civilizational dimensions are now being politicised in order to promote national interests and serve strategic objectives. When we look back to the major events that occurred during the 20th century, we´ill easily find out that most of the combating parties to the two World Wars that left tens of millions of victims and caused devastation and terrible sufferings, belonged to the same civilization. The driving force inspiring the parties was conflicting interests. When an alliance was formed in the 2nd World War between the two European axis powers and Japan, that alliance was not founded on a common civilization but simply on shared interests.

In the age of globalization, any attempt to impose universal cultural uniformity is against the thrust of history. A uniform global outfit, cut and trimmed according to the measurements dictated by the World Information Order will result in repulsion, resistance and withdrawal.

In the era of Information Technology, what could and should be done is to deploy technological innovations for the propagation of a multifaceted plural culture knitted around the moral system common to all civilizations.

The Clash of Civilizations a European perspective

Ingmar Karlsson

Ambassador Karlsson is Consul General of Sweden and Director of the Istanbul Centre for Turkish-Swedish Cooperation

When Friedrich Hegel saw Napoleon ride through Jena on the eve of the battle between the French and the Prussian armies in 1806 he thought he was about to witness the end of history. The victory of the French revolution over the Prussian monarchy was to signify the final victorious march of freedom and reason all over the world. We heard similar prophecies in 1989. An American diplomat, Francis Fukiyama, attracted much attention by claiming that we were standing at the threshold of the end of history. With the collapse of communism western liberal democracy would start a victorious march across the globe, and the world would finally become homogenous with liberalism both in economy and in politics as its prominent features.

It did not take long, though, before the tones changed. In an article entitled The Clash of Civilizations? which attracted considerable attention when it appeared in the journal

Foreign Affairs in 1993, Samuel Huntington claimed that the global political process was now entering a new era.

During the period of a century and half that followed the signing of the Peace of Westphalia in 1648 and the emergence of the modern international system, conflicts were, according to Huntington, largely between princes emperors, absolute monarchs and constitutional monarchs who were attempting to expand the influence of their bureaucracies, their armies, their mercantilist economic strength and, most important, the territories they ruled. An outcome of this process became the creation of the national state.

Beginning with the French Revolution, the conflicts were mainly between nations and people, rather than between princes, according to Huntington. This 19th century pattern lasted until the end of the World War I. Then, as a result of the Russian Revolution and the reaction against it, the conflicts between nations were superseded by conflicts between ideologies, first between communism, fascism-nazism and liberal democracy, and then between democracy and communism.

With the end of the Cold War, the Western phase in international politics came to an end with the focus shifting to the interaction between the Western and the non-Western civilizations.

According to Huntington, the clash of civilizations will occur on different levels. At the micro-level, various neighbouring groups will be getting into states of conflict, which can frequently become violent, along cultural fault lines, fighting over the control of territories and each other. At the macro-level, states with different cultural ties may struggle for military and political dominance, for control over international bodies, and for power over third parties.

Huntington s argumentation has seemingly been justified by the tragic events of September 11 and by the Bin Laden s rhetoric that followed the attacks on the World Trade Centre and the Pentagon, but it contains a number of weak points. Huntington divides the world into seven or eight major civilizations : Western, containing Western Europe and North America, Confucian, Japanese, Islamic, Hindu, Slav-Orthodox, Latin American and possibly an African civilization . Incidentally Huntington does not ascribe any distinctive status to Judaism or Jewishness. In his essay he describes Israel as a creation of the West .

Huntington s division is rather inconsistent. Some civilizations seem to be defined according to religious and cultural criteria while in other cases the key factor seems to be geography. What distinguishes the Western civilization from the Latin American? Both North and South America are inhabited by European immigrants who brought along values that they have retained ever since. While it is true that the American Indian element is much greater in certain Latin American countries like Mexico, Guatemala, Peru, and Ecuador than in the United States, it is equally true that Chile, Argentine and Costa Rica are more European than the United States, which is rapidly becoming more Hispanic. In fact both South and North America can be characterized as Western civilizations but with different degrees of other cultural elements.

Are the catholic Philippines Western or Asian? Huntington is speaking about a Buddhist Civilization but what unites a Thai, a Tibetan, a Mongol, and a Kalmuck living in the Russian Federation?

Where is the Confucian world that Huntington is talking about to be found? In spite of the shared Confucian heritage China and Vietnam have always been enemies. Vietnam deeply mistrusts China s intentions, irrespective of who is in power in Hanoi and Peking. Similarly, Peking s efforts to stress the common Confucian heritage to facilitate a reunification with Taiwan are watched with contempt by Taipei.

Huntington draws straight lines across the maps showing the beginnings and ends of the various civilizations. He acknowledges that the Islamic cultural sphere has an Arab, a Turkish, and a Malayan subdivision but for some reason he ignores the substantial Islamic contingent in Africa and he does not even touch upon the major differences that exist between the Islam in the Indonesian Archipelago, that is strongly permeated by Hinduism and Buddhism, the Islam in West Africa, influenced by animism, and the Islam in its Arab heartlands. Huntington also ignores the fact that the concept of Islamic unity hardly existed 50 years ago. In fact, the Islamic world has been divided ever since the death of the fourth caliph in 661, and this not merely between Sunnites and Shiites but along other lines as well. Islam is magma a reservoir containing quite distinct concepts and ideas, ranging from nostalgic-utopian doctrines of salvation to a secularised cultural identity like the one existing in Turkey.

Nevertheless, Huntington conjures up a picture of a green Islamic International which, as was the case with the Comintern, exerts control by applying a clear strategy. In reality the interests of the individual states have always gained the upper hand. The Iranian revolution has been regarded as a threat since its very beginning not only in Iraq

Saddam was the first to go to war against the Islamic fundamentalism - but also in the conservative Arab states. Therefore a Sunni International was to be created to stop the ideological bushfire spreading from Iran. But despite their oil resources, the Sunnite monarchies were not more successful than the ayatollahs in their attempts to establish a new political/ religious order.

Islam has become nationalized and, in the same way as the Arab front states built up their own Palestinian organizations in an attempt to control the Palestinian nationalism today we can see how the various Islamic organizations propagate a certain brand of Islam, be it Shiism, Wahabism or other in accordance with the national interests of the sponsor country. Thus, e. g. Saudi Arabia has financed all the Sunni organizations in Afghanistan as long as they were hostile towards Iran even the radical Hizb-I Islami group. Similarly the FLN regime in Algeria supported the Tunisian fundamentalists in An-Nahda while at home they were trying to crush the local Islamic organization FIS. This organization in its turn could rely on both secret and open support from Tunisia.

Today we can also see examples of the nationalization of Islam in the disintegrating Soviet Union where Islamic groups organize themselves within the framework of the new national states rather than in the form of a Central Asian Islamic International. Tajiks and Kazakhs have broken loose from the Tashkent muftiate created once by Stalin since it was considered to have been dominated by Uzbeki interests. The previous muftiate for the Caucasus region has split into five units, and the Islamic Renaissance Party, founded as recently as 1990, proved to be incapable of representing all Central Asian Muslims and quickly splintered into national fractions.

The specific Egyptian characteristics and the fact that the Egyptian identity is much older than Islam were some of the reasons why Sadat was able to break with the putative Arab-Islamic community and recognize Israel. Similarly, Turkey is not going to turn its back on secularism and align itself with Central Asia rather than Europe unless the West forces the Turks to make this choice. Ankara and Istanbul look to Brussels, Paris, London and Berlin, not to Ashkhabad, Alma Ata, or Bishkek.

Huntington defines the Gulf War as a war between civilizations. In fact, no other conflict has so clearly demonstrated how the interests of the state predominate over the religious sphere. Saddam did not justify his attack on Kuwait in religious terms - he did so only when he was forced to retreat by a coalition formed by Saudi Arabia, Turkey, Egypt and Syria, together with American, French and British forces. The Saudi Royal family even managed to mobilize Islamic authorities to proclaim in a fatwa that the fact that American infidel soldiers were defending Mecka was not in conflict with the teachings of Koran.

Iran was biding its time and despite all its anti-American rhetoric it had nothing against the Great Satan acting in the interest of the ayatollahs.

Hence, the frontiers of the Islamic fundamentalism have already been drawn up right from the start and there is no correlation between the strategic decisions taken by states and their domestic cultural opposition. Attacks on Christianity are a particularly prominent feature in Saudi Arabia, the primary ally of the United States, which does not permit existence of any Christian churches on its territory, whereas the Christian communities in Syria and Iraq can exercise their belief freely. Political Islam is not a geopolitical game but rather a social phenomenon. The North-South antagonism can of course further discontent which may put on Islamís green colour, nevertheless, the much discussed and publicised Islamic world revolution is a myth.

One of the main points Huntington makes is that we now witness the emergence of a Confucian-Islamic axis or connection : A c entral focus of conflict for the immediate future will be between the West and several Islamic-Confucian states .

The only concrete evidence Huntington produces as support for this remarkable thesis is North Korea s and China s arms exports to Libya, Iran, Iraq and Syria. These contacts between two Communist dictatorships and a Libya governed according to Qadhafi s bizarre green theories , which all Muslim clerics consider to be heresies, or with the two secular, rival Baath regimes in Damascus and Baghdad, are quite clearly neither expressions of any ideological affinity, nor an Islamic-Confucian plot. It is simply a question of money. Furthermore one of the major domestic problems faced by the Chinese government is the fear that Muslim fundamentalism could spread to the Uigur people in Sinkiang from their Turkic kin in Central Asia and this is the reason why Peking supports the attacks on Afghanistan.

It could be just as well argued that the American and French arms sales to Saudi Arabia indicate that a Christian-Islamic alliance is being built up.

Thus, Huntington s suggestion of a clash of cultures at the macro level is not soundly based. He seems to be on a firmer ground when he claims that conflicts at the micro level will run along the fault lines between cultural spheres. The civil war in Tajikistan and the conflicts in the Caucasus seem to support this thesis and even more so the civil wars in the former Yugoslavia where the front lines largely followed the traditional frontier between the Eastern and the Western Roman Empires and between the Ottoman and Hapsburg empires.

Even these arguments do not bear closer examination, though. Not a single war during the last century was provoked by a clash between civilizations, no matter how they are defined. In 1914 the protestant Berlin got allied with the catholic Vienna and Muslim Istanbul against the orthodox Moscow, the catholic Paris, and the protestant London. The orthodox Serbia did fight against the catholic Vienna but it was at the same time at war with the orthodox Bulgaria. The aggressors in the Second World War, Italy, Germany, the Soviet Union and Japan were able to co-operate in spite of their belonging to different cultural spheres and when Hitler attacked Stalin, Churchill and Roosevelt did not ask their new ally whether he was an orthodox Christian or a communist.

The majority of the wars that took place after 1945 have been fights within civilizations : Korea, Vietnam, Cambodia, Somalia, Iraq, Iran, and Kuwait. The longest and most blood-filled conflict in the Middle East in the eighties did not take place between the Arabs and the Jews but between Muslims in the war between Iran and Iraq. Poisonous gas has been used by Iraqi Arabs against Kurds and not against non-believers .

The wars in the former Yugoslavia with their ethnic cleansings were, contrary to Huntington s theories, no jihad but a fight for power and territories fought among atheist Orthodox, Catholics and Muslims in shifting unholy alliances. The nationalism coloured by religion had been consciously cultivated together with the social antagonisms and tensions. The conflicts in the former Yugoslavia demonstrate how easily nationalism can be instrumentalised, but they cannot be used as a proof for the thesis of a war between civilizations.

In Bosnia, the Serbs claimed to fight for Christianity against Islam. It is true that the wars in former Yugoslavia followed the cultural boundaries between the Eastern and the Western Roman Empires, and that they subsequently developed into a war between Orthodoxy and Catholicism, and between Orthodoxy, Catholicism and Islam. But this was primarily the result of the Serbian nationalism combined with the determination of the Communist Party bosses not to surrender their power. The Serbian offensive, aiming at establishing a Greater Serbia, was initially directed against their Christian neighbours, Slovenia and Croatia. In Bosnia the Muslims stood for a secular, civilized society while the Orthodox Serbs demonstrated a bigotry and narrow-mindedness comparable with that of the most fanatical exponents of Islamic fundamentalism and in Bosnia as well as in kosovo forces from the Western civilization intervened on the Muslim side.

Civilizations do not control states. On the contrary, states control civilizations and they intervene and defend their own civilization only if it is in the stateís interest to do so.

In the war between Azerbaijan and Armenia Teheran has tried to act as a mediator and tended to support the Christian Armenians rather than the Muslim Azeri out of fear that an Azeri victory might strengthen the separatist tendencies among the large Azeri minority in Iran.

What at the first glance can give an impression of a clash of civilizations turns when analysed out to be a rivalry among states concerning resources and territories, for strategic advantages and political prestige. The war against Saddam Hussein was not a war between civilizations — civilizations do not make wars — but a fight for oil and the strategic balance in the Middle East. The antagonism between Peking and Washington over Taiwan, pirate copies of CD-records, or export of arms is not a fight between Confucius and Thomas Jefferson but a conflict between two superpowers.

Huntington defines a civilization as the broadest level of identification a person can intensively identify with . Only very few persons can intensively identify with a notion as wide as the concept of civilization. They seek rather more narrow identities such as nations or ethnic or religious groups. Even though the European identity is nowadays being constantly conjured up nevertheless the investigations carried out by the EU Commission show that more than 70% of the populations in all EU countries see themselves primarily in national terms and that the European identity comes as second.

The civilizations Huntington talks about are not homogenous tectonic plates wearing out one another but syncretistic ones and this not only in the border regions but also in their cores. Even the Islamic fundamentalists make use of the Western technologies as was clearly demonstrated on September 11 and they thus show also a way of thinking which is considered to be alien to their culture. To take another example: in 1957 there were 1,7 million Christians in South Korea. At present the number is 14 — 17 million, that is 40 per cent of the population. The frequent strikes are said to be directed against the Confucian values that are considered to have been the basis for the Korean economic miracle, which has now faded.

Huntington s thesis is purely mono-causal. He does not at all take into consideration the effects that the free market economy exerts on the political systems and the forces that are set free by the processes of the economic integration. Therefore the assumption that future conflicts will be connected with distribution of wealth within and among the states has a higher credibility. The paradigm of the bi-polar world has not been substituted by Huntington s clash of civilizations but rather, to quo te J‚rgen Habermas , by a new incalculability . We can nevertheless wage a prophecy that the future neither will bring the end of history nor a clash of civilizations.

The real clash today is not between civilizations but within them between Muslims, Christians, Hindus, Buddhists and Jews with a modern and progressive outlook and those with a medieval one. Jerry Falwell, to take one example, told his television audience after the attack on the World Trade Centre that America deserved to be punished. Abortion providers, gay rights proponents and federal courts that banned school prayers had according to him made God mad .

According to Huntington Islam has got bloody borders. This statement is not only historically false, it is also dangerous. Islam and Christianity have lived side by side for almost 1400 years, always as neighbours, mostly as rivals and far too often as enemies. In fact, they may be regarded as co-religions since they share the same Jewish, Hellenistic and Oriental heritage. At one and the same time they have been old acquaintances and intimate hereditary enemies, and their conflicts have been particularly bitter precisely because of their common origins. Both sides have been divided more by their similarity than by their differences.

The Islamic culture is not as strange as it often appears in the light of our prejudices and clich s. One of the most widespread myths is that Charles Martel, the ruler of the Franks, saved the West from destruction by his victory over the Saracens at Po itiers in 732. The Saracens were driven back over the Pyren es and returned to southern Spain where a Muslim state then continued to flourish for almost 800 years. This Islamic presence on the European continent did not lead to a collapse of the Western civilization but to a unique and fruitful symbiosis between Islam, Christianity and Judaism which resulted in an
Unparalleled boom in science, philosophy, culture and art.

At the close of the Middle-Ages, both Islam and Judaism were constitutive elements in the formation of Europe. As a result, Islam is at the same time an alien, an original and due to growing migration a new element in Europe of today. A Europe that is getting increasingly populated by people who live in a no-manís land between the different cultures similarly as the enanciados in the Moorish Spain. There are already more than 20 million Muslims in Europe more than the number of Scandinavian Protestants not to speak - and their numbers will increase as a result of the continuing migration. Estimates speak of 60 millions in 25 years. The European Union is therefore no longer conceivable without the Islamic green component. Whether it will be possible to construct the European house based on the model of Alhambra the symbol of the multicultural Moorish Spain is therefore a decisive question for the future of Europe.

If we regard Huntington s reference to Islam s bloody borders as an indisputable fact we shall never be able to integrate our growing Muslim population. In that case Huntington s prophecies of a clash of civilizations might become a reality but not in the form of a military measuring of strength between the West and the rest and a new siege of Vienna but as a permanent guerrilla warfare in the suburbs of the big European cities turned into ghettos.

This is the real risk of a clash of civilizations. To prevent this from happening is the greatest challenge for the European politicians today.

Civilizations and Natural Laws: A positive sciences perspective

Halil Güven

Dr. Güven is President of the University of Bahçesehir. Istanbul, Turkey.

Introduction

Braudel (1995) defines civilization as *an ordered urban way of living which consists of integrated material, moral, intellectual and psychological components, and which has been set up and conserved by a certain group of people from generation to generation.*

- Every civilization is based on:

- a geographical area or system of areas;
- presupposes the existence of fully developed cities;
- is inseparable from its hierarchical society (Levi-Strauss, in Charbonnier 1961);
- survives through mobility, and also mutual impact with other societies;
- involves challenges and responses (Toynbee, 1946-57);
- depends on economic, technological, biological, and demographical circumstances;

- presupposes an underlying psychological structure with its own peculiar ritual practices.

Since the start of writing, that is, written history, and urban living, around 3500 to 3000 BC, the history of human development has seen the birth and death of many civilizations. According to Toynbee (2001) throughout history, world civilizations have gone through the following stages:

From slavery to faith, from faith to courage, from courage to liberty, from liberty to abundance, from abundance to individualism, from individualism to obedience, from obedience to indifference, and from indifference to the loss of liberty. Nineteen of 21 great civilizations collapsed because of internal threats. As we can see, civilizations start with slavery and end with slavery. This period goes on for 200 years and then history repeats itself.

The history of human development has ample proof of collapsed civilizations. The great ancient four valley-civilizations of Egypt, Indus, Mesopotamia and China withered away. The Hittite, Mycenaean, Phoenician, Mesoamerican, Ancient Greek and Roman civilizations/empires also collapsed and perished one after the other.

Approximately 5500 years after the start of human civilizationí adventure, today, we have just arrived at a techno-globalí stage of human development with numerous civilizations around the globe, some larger than others, some more advancedí than others, some younger, some older, etc. Moreover, the contemporary issues of the day are globalization , clash of civi lizations , etc.

The questions that come to one's mind under such circumstances can be put forth as follows:

1. Do we need a redefinition of the word civilization in a techno-global world?
2. If so, how do we define, characterize and/or classify contemporary civilizations?
3. Are we still living in a world which gives birth to new civilizations, and in which some older civilizations collapse and/or die?
4. If so, why do civilizations die? What are the internal threats?
5. Are civilizations against natural laws?

In this paper, a comparison of contemporary civilizations is attempted, along with an endeavor to seek answers to the above questions from the perspective of natural laws and positive sciences.

Civilizations and Positive Sciences

A law in positive sciences is simply defined as a dictation of nature (i.e., how nature works, what nature will allow, and what nature will not allow, etc.). These laws were discovered as a result of scientific curiosity, experimentation, and a search for the unknown or the truth. Having discovered these laws of nature and accepting them as such, and building on them, has resulted in an explosion of technological growth and progress on the way to our current techno-global civilization.

One can try to develop analogies, or draw parallels, between *civilizations* and *scientific laws* of different disciplines.

There could be numerous physical phenomena with their own laws,í such as Ohmís law, Newtonís law, Maxwellís law, laws of gravity, laws of thermodynamics, etc., which can be used to tentatively explore and explain certain developmental or operational aspects of civilizations.

For instance, in 1959, Levi-Strauss (Charbonnier, 1961), in his radio interviews broadcast by RTF, France, introduced an analogy between thermodynamic processes, which involve heat engines and entropy production, and modern civilizations:

Modern civilizations are not only societies where there are widespread use of heat engines[18], but they also display structural (operational) similarities to heat engines. This is because they possess various forms of societal hierarchical potentials (analogous to temperature difference potential-for heat engines), which makes them operate, in principle, as heat engines. If we step out of the context and look at the whole picture, it will serve no purpose to name this as a class difference, such as slavery and feudalism. Such (modern) societies, on the one hand create more order mechanical societies --, while on the other hand they succeed in producing a sort of instability, which they utilize in creating more disorder in human relations and creating entropy.

This relationship between civilizations and thermodynamic concepts involving heat engines and entropy, proposed by

---

[18] An engine (device) that converts heat to work is known as a **heat engine**. A heat engine works between two heat reservoirs (temperature potentialí): A hot reservoir (higher temperature source) and a cold reservoir (lower temperature sink). A heat engine will transfer heat from hot to cold reservoir, and result in work output.

Levi-Strauss, is quite fitting. In particular, the reference to entropy in the context of workings of modern civilizations or societies deserves an in-depth study.

Laws of Thermodynamics
Thermodynamics is the science through which the energy conversion and energy exchange processes are regulated. There are two major laws that govern all thermodynamic processes. The first law of thermodynamics is the conservation principle; it establishes that energy, when converted from one form to another, must be conserved.

The second law of thermodynamics establishes the limitations on energy exchange (conversion) in nature, and explains the inefficiency notion in natural processes. This law also establishes why nature will not allow for a perpetual motion machine .

To reveal some of the ramifications of the second law, we can take up the concept of heat engine, introduced by Levi-Strauss, and study it in some detail here. For simplicity, a familiar heat engine, an automobileís (heatí) engine, will be used as an example. An automobileís engine first converts the stored energy in a petroleum product to heat through a combustion process, and then converts this heat to work (rotational energy at the wheels) through a mechanical process. In doing this:

- A fixed percentage of energy is released (or rejected) to nature as nonconvertible (unusable) energy-- almost like a flat tax which nature imposes, and

- Some additional percentage is lost to such unavoidable natural phenomena like noise and friction in the moving parts of the engine.

The highest temperature achieved in the combustion process (Tsource or Thigh) and the temperature of the ambient air (Tsink or Tlow) establishes the higher and lower limits of temperature potential, respectively.

A simple calculation (100 x Tlow/Thigh) reveals the percentage of flat tax nature will impose on this transaction [19]. In addition to this, there will be additional reductions in efficiency (additional taxes) to such things as friction and noise, which cannot be avoided. However, the amount of efficiency lost to these unavoidable processes will depend on how well the mechanical device is built . In a well-built engine, these lossesí can be reduced to a minimum, but they cannot be totally eliminated[20]. One could also look at this as a *giv e and take* relationship with nature.

Entropy
Entropy is a product of the second law of thermodynamics, and it is defined as the measure of uncertainty, chaos, and randomness (Reynolds & Perkins, 1977). Entropy establishes the theoretical underpinnings of the flat tax and additional taxes imposed by nature on all energy

---

[19] This is known as the Carnot Cycle (ideal heat engine) efficiency calculation in thermodynamics. The word transactioní is used here metaphorically to depict the energy conversion process at hand, which is conversion of stored energy in the petroleum product to mechanical work at the wheels.
[20] Friction and noise are considered as lossesí or nuisancesí in design of most mechanical devices such as heat engines.

conversion processes. Some of the fundamentals of this theory are:

- Things in nature (natural processes) have a tendency to move towards a more disorderly state by default (increase in entropy).
- Nature will always work towards maximizing entropy: i.e., nature will work towards creating more disorder, chaos and uncertainty. Natural processes will choose the path that will maximize entropy.
- A process to create less entropy (negative entropy = negentropy), i.e., to create order and organization, is possible with constant work input.
- The amount of entropy generated in a heat engine will determine the amount of work output. More entropy generation will mean more inefficiency, and hence less work output.
- Friction is a natural phenomena, which creates entropy, and hence a reduction in work output.

The concept of entropy generationí is very interesting, and it can help explain a lot of simple natural happenings from our everyday life too. For example, a neatly piled stack of paper left unattended on a table in an empty room for a period of time can be found dispersed on the table or the floor. The possibility is there due to a number of random reasons (e.g., a breeze under the door blowing the papers off, etc.). However, the reverse is not possible. That is, a stack of paper dispersed on the floor of an empty room left unattended for a period of time, cannot be found neatly stacked on the table because of a random phenomena (such as a breeze under the door). Someone must physically pick up the papers and place them back on the table (work input is necessary), and create order (which is negentropy). This simple example of an everyday observation explains what nature will allow and what nature will not allow (what is possible and, what is impossible), and it can be explained and formulated scientifically through the second law and entropy concepts.

Civilizations and the Laws of Nature

In very simple terms (at the core), the concept of *Civilization* can be linked to creation of order (laws, rules and regulations), organization (political and social), and efficiency (minimizing loss of effort due to disorder and disorganization, time savings from good infrastructure and order, mass-production, etc.).

Once a civilization is underway, however, the order-organization-efficiency is already in place. Then one wonders as to what makes this mechanismí collapse or die ? According to Paul Kennedy (1989), all great empires collapsed because of internal conflicts and overstretching. As quoted above, Toynbee (2001) called it internal threats . We can attempt an explanation of this peculiarity of civilizations using the aforementioned thermodynamic laws.

The first law (conservation principle), for the purposes of this analysis, though relevant, does not present a striking significance such as the second law. One of the requirements of being a civilization is the characteristic of *conservation* (of knowledge, traditions, etc.) from generation to generation and the ability to survive mobility. In this sense, one can advance the notion that civilizations are in conformity with the first law. This can be a defensible position and can be articulated. However, in this discussion we will be focusing our attention more on the second law analysis instead.

The second law states that nature will strive to maximize entropy production (i.e., maximize disorder and uncertainty). In this regard, civilizations (creation of order and organization) will be on a path for head on crash with nature. Civilizations, by definition, are sources of negentropy. Of course, negentropy can be generated for a *specified period of time* by work input. But this cannot be sustained indefinitely. Hence, the second law can be used to explain why civilizations are bound to die.

Here one can draw an analogy between a perpetual motion machine and a civilization. The classic example of a simple perpetual motion machine is a well built and highly lubricated wheel start rotating after an *initial push*. Everyone knows that such an experiment will end with the eventual halting of the wheel. Simple reasons are: Loss of energy to air resistance (unless the wheel is rotating in a vacuum chamber), loss of energy due to friction at the mechanical parts (minimized but cannot be totally eliminated), vibration (minimized but cannot be totally eliminated), noise (minimized but cannot be totally eliminated), etc. Depending on the technology used and how well the mechanism is constructed, the wheel may seem like a perpetually rotating one, defying nature. *But* this will not change the eventuality. The wheel may take longer to stop, but we all know that it will eventually stop due to the taxation of the nature (friction, noise, vibration, etc.). All attempts to build perpetual motion machines throughout the history have failed. Entropy generated as a result of the taxation will explain, from the second law perspective, why the wheel cannot rotate indefinitely.

Coming to civilizations, having been built (set-up) by members of nature (human beings), it can be stipulated that civilizationsí should be subject to the laws of nature, as well. This is analogous to a heat engine (built by members of nature) being subject to laws of nature. Then one can further stipulate that the internal threats and internal conflicts in civilizations will be analogous to friction, noise and vibration in the rotating wheel. This will be natureís tax collection and it will halt the civilization from continuing indefinitely. Nature will allow a civilization (order) to start (the initial pushí in the case of the wheel), but at the same time it will halt it due to its own reasons (laws). The period from start to finish of the wheel will vary depending on how well the mechanism of the wheel is built (or how well the civilization wheelí is constructed and lubricated). Some will last longer than others. Toynbee (2001) stipulates that an advanced civilization will have an average of 200 years of life.

A civilization being *advanced* or *primitive* will not be a determining factor on the longevity of a civilization. A civilization must die eventually (just like wheel stop rotating). However, its ability to create prolonged conformity with the laws of nature and its resilience will be at issue. A civilization may sustain itself for long periods of time if it allows for gradual (or implicit) conformity with the laws of nature (i.e., entropy generation). This is possible by creating periods (pockets) of balance between order/organization and disorder/randomness/uncertainty, during the life of the civilization. One can call these pockets controlled disorder or chaos periods to release built-up pressure due to negatropy. This will be discussed further in the following sections, when different civilizations are compared.

Civilizations: Material versus Social

In previous sections, definition of a contemporary civilizationí was linked to creation of order, organization, and efficiency. As a consequence of this definition one could arrive at the following corollary: A better-organized society with higher efficiency in its political and social organizations (more ordered urban way of living) should be *more civilized*í or possess a *higher civilization*í.

This, however, will not be a correct conclusion. Some nations have more experience than others in organized living. On the other hand, some other nations have tribal beginnings, and have less experience in organized (established) cities and permanent settlements. This should not suggest that nations with tribal roots-- Bedouins of the Middle East, Turkic peoples of Central Asia, natives (red Indians) of the North American Continent, African tribes-- have *lower or lesser civilizations* (Diamond, 1996).

Therefore, we should search for a definition (or redefinition) of the word contemporary civilization . There is certainly no doubt that all civilizations have materialí and social and spirituali dimensions. At least two speakers, Professors Bruce Lloyd, and the late Professor Howard Berry, at the Global leadership forum[21] presented concepts referring to spiritual capital of a society, which is a fairly new concept.

For the purposes of this discussion, we will divide a civilization into two major complementary components: Material civilization and social civilization.

---

[21] Global Leadership Forum, University of Bah esehir, Istanbul, June 2001

Material Civilization
There is no doubt that a civilization requires a certain degree of organization at its onset. This organization has to have political and social nature, and should set up the necessary mechanisms for regulating political and social aspects of the society. Institutions must be in place for making laws, rules and regulations. The end products of which should be orderly functioning of the societyís everyday life, where its citizens live, work, produce, reproduce, entertain, and be properly compensated in harmony. All the needs must be satisfied to a great extent to create security and fair environment to allow for the pursuit of happiness for all. This has been the motto of most western civilizations that made enormous progress in setting up advanced democratic institutions resulting in what we term as advanced societies today. These civilizations have resulted in amassing enormous material wealth, and tremendous material civilization, which is readily visible. Moreover, these advanced societies, in pursuit of order, also endeavour to tame the nature, and minimize the impact of natural catastrophes.

As quoted above, for Toynbee(2001)[22], wealth/abundance (i.e., material civilization) and individualism are closely related. A smooth functioning advanced society, which creates an abundance of material wealth (thingsí), invariably results in (or gives birth to) individualism. Proper functioning of the rules, regulations, and laws of a well-lubricated civilization machine necessitates the weakening of

---

[22] Stages in the life of a civilization is given by Toynbee (2001) as: slavery to faith; faith to courage; courage to liberty, liberty to abundance; abundance to individualism; individualism to obedience; obedience to indifference; and indifference to the loss of liberty.

the social ties among its constituents. Hence, individualism is implicitly promoted. A society with an advanced stage of individualism will have less deviation from its rules, more order, rule of law, full organization i.e., proper implementation and enforcement of its rules and laws. This will then promote a rule-driven (dominated) society with a high level of obedience. Less uncertainty in implementation of rules, less uncertainty in social interactions will also mean less entropy. Then, the sought after civilization, which starts out to provide order, organization and efficiency in pursuit of happiness, results in the creation of citizens, who are like *small islands* cut-off from each other, lonely, robotizedí by rules, and may even be unhappy. Also the negatropy due to taming of the nature may result in unhappiness, since humans are essentially creatures of the nature itself.

Social Civilization
We can coin the term social civilization to describe the wealth and depthí a civilization has in its social and spiritual dimensions. This can also be looked at as a non-material component of a civilization. In the pursuit of happiness, certainly, order, organization, efficiency and taming of the nature are necessary, but not sufficient conditions. Obviously, role of religion (spiritual capital) in social civilization must also be studied and not overlooked.

If human beings live closer together in extended families with more random social interaction, and greater uncertainty in allocation of their time, this will create more entropy. Lack of (or weak) individualism, more social ties, extended family relations, friendships, etc., will most certainly lead to inefficiencies in implementation and enforcement of rules, regulations and laws. It may also lead to creation of lesser material civilizationí. However, it may also result in less urban crime, less homeless, and warmer people. Societies with higher social civilization should operate in greater conformity with natural laws (less negentropy!), and could be overall happier campersí.

Comparative civilizations
Though it may somewhat jeopardize the objectivity of the study, an attempt will be made at comparing the western civilizations with eastern civilizations. It will be very brief see the following graphic presentation.

Eastern Civillization
In the western civilizations, the excess negentropy generated due to the requirements of material civilization (order) can be detrimental to the well-being and happiness of human beings, who are products, and also part, of the nature itself. Therefore, attempts must be made for conformity with the second law of thermodynamics. Some uncertainty and disorder (at the expense of material civilization) should be tolerated, in order to make a civilization more humane and liveable . This will also provide a longer life to a civilization -- The internal threats and conflicts mentioned in the earlier sections are from nature itself, working through its disgruntled members (people).

On the other hand, eastern civilizations must work on developing better synchronization with the western civilizations, as they are lagging in material civilization at their own detriment. Some negentropy (at the expense of social civilization) should be tolerated in the eastern civilizations.

A case example: EU and Turkey

An aged civilization like the Western European civilization is first of all too wealthy and lacks the proper dynamics (governing!) to continue. It may collapse and die under its own weight. Plus the intolerant ways of the western civilization (rules, order, etc.) contributes to this problem. Taking in a country like Turkey into the EU can serve as a relaxation of this civilization negentropy and provide additional life (extended life) to this civilization. This will be an interesting infusion of young blood into this civilization. The U.S. does this in a controlled way by allowing limited immigration (e.g., diversity visa) and other means.

Concluding remarks

The industrialized western civilizations developed advanced material civilizations, amassing enormous amount of wealth and with it the potential to dominate other civilizations. It will be wrong to assume that civilizations can be rank ordered. That is, one is superior to another. We have to continue living on this planet together. In his now all too famous article, Huntington (1993) claimed that eastern and western civilizations are bound to clash. In light of the redefinition of contemporary civilizations, given in this discussion, I believe that a clash can be avoided through:

- proper diagnosis of the problems at hand (e.g., impact of globalization on civilizations and cultures);
- better balance between social and material civilizations;

- better dialog among civilizations on an equal footing, opposed to monologs and dictation from one to another;
- more sharing, understanding, respect, goodwill and tolerance.
- Civilizations have a lot to learn from each other. We need better inter-civilization education, similar to interdisciplinary educationí. We need to find a better recipe for coexistence, which must have elements of both easterní (easterní is used loosely) and westerní civilizations.

References

Braudel, F. *History Of Civilizations*, Penguin/Viking, 1995.

Charbonnier, G. *Entretiens Avec Claude L viStrauss*, Plon, 1961.

Diamond, J. *Guns, Germs, And Steel: The Fates Of Human Societies*, W.W. Norton, 1999.

Huntington, S. The Clash Of Civilizations,í *Foreign Affairs*, Summer 1993.

Kennedy, P. *The Rise And Fall Of Great Powers*, Fontana Press, 1989.

Reynolds, W & Perkins, H. *Engineering Thermodynamics*, 2nd Ed., Mcgraw-Hill, Inc., 1977.

Toynbee, A.J. (From Page 311 Of Polat, A., An Accumulation Of Three Thousand Years (*Bin Yillik Birikim*), Enes Matbaacilik, 2001--).

Toynbee, A.J. *A Study Of History*, Abr. By D.C. Somervell, 2vols., Oxford University Press, 1946-

Dialogue of Civilizations: Paradigms on Economic Development and Social Advancement

Halil Güven

Dr. Güven is President of the University of Bahçesehir. Istanbul, Turkey.

Introduction

In an earlier discussion (Güven, 2001) a redefinition of contemporary civilizations was given. Also, diagnoses of the problems related to civilizational disharmony in the world, in light of Huntington's (1993) claims of clash of civilizations, were attempted.

Firstly, it was argued that civilizations had both social and material components, and these two equally important aspects of civilizations should be kept in balance. A civilization with enormous material basis (rules, regulations, laws, order, and efficiency at all levels) without a balanced social component would make the end-users of that civilization (i.e., human beings) unhappy. Similarly, an enormous social civilization (social ties, family ties, warmth of individuals, spiritual capital, etc.) without a balanced material component would create the same effect on its constituents: unhappiness. It was therefore argued that a better balance should be sought between social and material components of civilizations.

Secondly, it was argued that the industrialized western civilizations had developed advanced material civilizations, amassing enormous amount of wealth and with it the potential to dominate other civilizations. It would be wrong to assume that civilizations could be rank ordered, that is, to consider one to be superior to the other. This would create accumulated civilizational disharmony, leading to a clash.

Thirdly, it was proposed that a clash (of civilizations) could be avoided through:
• Proper diagnosis of the problems at hand (e.g., impact of globalization on civilizations and cultures);
• Better **dialog among civilizations on an equal footing**, opposed to monologs and dictation from one to another;
• More sharing, understanding, respect, goodwill and tolerance among civilizations.

We all agree that civilizations have a lot to learn from each other. It will, therefore, be quite appropriate to coin a new word, *inter-civilizational education* , similar to interdisciplinary educationí. We need to find a better recipe for coexistence, which must have elements of both easterní (easterní is used loosely) and westerní civilizations.

Background

Currently there happens to be 189 countries in the world with a total population of more than 6 billion people. Among these countries, there goes on an endless redefinition of the Otherí whereby a number of countries or a whole civilization is targeted as the group to be left out of the photograph of the human family!í For instance, a poorer developing world,í once called the *Third World* and now referred to as the *South*, and in fact together with what is termed as the *Global South*, are readily molded into the otherí in the eyes of the richer *North*.

The term *Global South* has been introduced by Safty (2001). From what Iíve gathered, this global southí actually includes people who are living in the industrialized countries but at the same time have the characteristics of people of the developing countries, so they are being shunned out of the system of livingí peculiar to the developed countries. Accordingly, the industrialized countries of the North happen to have members of the global southí among them, usually the poor and the dispossessed.

It is an undisputed fact that such other worldsí are getting poorer and poorer, while the countries that have been termed as the *West* or the *North* have embarked upon a fast track moving onto a notion of *Advanced Society* where a lot of the simplerí human problems are readily solved and some of the more complex ones can be tackled with efficiency.

Whereas, in the other countries or civilizations,í the superimposing of the concepts directly borrowed from the countries of the *North* onto their own traditionally inherited norms usually ends up in scope for corruption or moral disintegration. Another sore eye the Otherí gets is the lack of initiative or funds in providing their people with an efficient and sufficient infrastructure. This, in turn, leads to health problems of gargantuan dimensions for the poor and the needy.

It has, for sometime now, been considered that the introduction of consumer economics and communication revolution with its internet and the satellite TV would bring about globalizatiorí and hopefully pave the way for solving such problems as have been defined above. However, under the name of *globalization*, the world has lately witnessed an unforeseen increase in nationalism leading to ethnic wars and divisiveness, the exact opposite of what the word globalizationí connotes!

Considering the state of affairs from the perspective of Advanced Societies will, of course, present us with a totally different picture. These are the societies whose progress has resulted in globalization as a natural outcome and for whom globalization stands as an undeniable achievement.

A brief survey of the underpinnings of Advanced Societies through the magnifying lens of the U.S., their incomparable example, will, therefore, be beneficial in reaching an understanding of the systemí of the North/West that has given birth to and has been harvesting the fruits of globalization.

The three pillars that have upheld U.S.A. since the very beginning happen to be

- Separation of the branches of government and checks and balance,

- Military Power, and

- Government for People by the People. .

Based on the firm foundation laid and maintained by the above,

The U.S. has managed to unleash its human potential, leading to technological discoveries, as can be deduced from the highest number of patents in the world being awarded in the U.S., which, in turn, brought about an unprecedented economic growth.

During this challenging process, U.S.A. learned how to efficiently organize diverse avenues of thought

- While coming up with such non-linear ways of thinking as the Game Theory and the Theory of Chaos,

- Then, based on these, it went on to setting up Think Tanks,

- And ultimately, topped it all with Social Engineering.

Inter-civilisational Dialogue

I think the establishment of **a common language, common values,** and **common goals** among countries and/or civilizations, say in a time-span of 15 to 20 years, will do away with the notion of the Otherí and create an understanding of *civilizations on equal footing* . Education has a role to play in preparing the future generations for this task. As somebody who set up a new university with such a philosophy in mind, I am confident that higher education has a valuable contribution to make in this area.

I suggest therefore that students be offered an **inter-civilizational education** that by the time they graduate, the idea of an **inter-civilizational dialogue** should become a crucial factor in their agenda for the future. So, it is through education that the potential leaders of the future can reach a level of mutual understanding whereby using **a common language** with the members of different civilizations, and basing their ideas and opinions on **common values** and, in fact, cherishing **common goals** become the norm.

In the year 2001, UNESCO clearly declared that:

Education is one of the essential foundations of both a culture of peace and a dialogue among civilizations. It advocates for the respect for universal values common to all civilizations... (UNESCO, 2001a)

Based on the above, UNESCO has already launched a *Non-Violence Educational Programme*

To enable individuals to become autonomous beings who can assert their points of view and take initiatives in conjunction with others. Passing on and awakening in others such values as tolerance, solidarity and peace is what education means, so that each may be given the ability to face up to conflict in a positive manner by transforming it. One of the main stakes of non-violent education is teaching human beings how to resolve conflicts from an early age. (UNESCO, 2001b)

COMMON LANGUAGE

What can the *common language* be based on, or derived from? As of today, only a number of points of departure, í which consist of the conceptions or norms of living peculiar to the two main groups of civilizations, can be listed.

East or South:

- Social duties & responsibilities regarded as sacred laws;
- An inner feeling of justice apart from Law itself;
- Various forms of tolerance among social groups;
- Society or groups being more important than the individual;
- Solidarity;
- Art: repeated patterns allowing for limited innovation.
- Traditions
- Overlapping of interests
- Considering all humanity as one
- Altruism

West or North:

- Individualism & autonomy;
- Secularism;
- Social contract;
- Competitiveness;
- Self-made man;

- The Law;
- Art: individual creativity craving for innovation.
- Change
- Conflict of interests
- Human rights

On the other hand, certain terminology dear to the Northern or the Western worldview does not even exist in the South or the East in any equivalent form:

- Planning
- Program
- Professionalism
- Challenge
- Competitiveness
- Checks and balances
- Equal opportunity
- Rule of law
- Balance of powers
- Innocent until proven guilty
- *Cost-benefit analysis*
- Rules Vs. Freedoms
- Where There Is A Will, There Is A Way
- Pragmatism

A good example can be given, in this instance from Turkey, concerning the need for developing a fully working sense out of such terminology and coming up with **a common language** if we want to get integrated with the world financial system to get out of the current financial crises.

Concepts like Conflict of Interests¡, or Corruption¡ (or Irregularities¡), or still Planning,¡ do not ring a bell in our country.

Let us take *Conflict of Interests* as the first example; it does not mean anything in Turkey. How will then international financial organizations or institutions like the IMF or the World Bank manage to explain to us that we should not conduct this bidding like this because of conflict of interests? One should not have a member of parliament vacationing for free in a businessmen¡s tourist village, because it may create a conflict of interest when this same businessman has a bill pending in the parliament affecting his business, or, similarly, one should not use the plane of such and such businessman to travel somewhere.

Moreover, although the notions of *Challenge* and *Competitiveness* are very important in the West, these are devoid of any sense in our civilization. Or consider the word *Professionalism* : It connotes an effort to attend meetings on time, to do A, B, C, D well, etc., but it just does not exist in this culture. This does not at all mean that we are not getting things done or that we are not progressing but the case is simply that the concept is not in our minds.

Innocent until proven guilty: In this case, the opposite conception seems to be valid in our culture. The Turkish proverb of *No smoke comes out unless there is a fire* points at the understanding that if somebody is accusing you of something, there must definitely be something you have done.

Anyway, why am I telling these things? These are again just food-for-thought type of things seen from an engineer¡s point of view, things that have to be tackled with, as in problem solving, if we are at all interested in creating **a common language**.

On the other hand, a corpus of terminology cherished by the South/East for millennia as concepts to be put into practice or realized in their lives are only looked upon by the North/West as items of curiosity:

- Dharma/Tˆre
- Tao
- Dreamtime
- Maya
- Nirvana
- Satori
- Mana/Kut
- Tawakkul
- Ahimsa

Social psychology, which looks at the behavior of people in small groups, or studies and compares the thought patterns or worldviews of people from different countries, may be considered as a scientific branch that can be quite helpful in the setting up of a foundation of understanding which embraces or sympathizes with most of the above-mentioned concepts or norms whereon **a common language** can be built.

So far so good but since one cannot think of anybody, even if duly educated, entering into an **inter-civilizational dialogue** or sharing a common language with the poorí and the wanting,í that is, people in need of bare essentials for existence, another aspect that has to be attended to with utmost care and attention happens to be **human development** itself.

Human Development

Human Development requires a holistic perspective based on economic development and social advancement going hand in hand. So, any country should have a strong economic side to their development; however, while it is keen on developing its economy, it should also pay utmost attention to its social advancement and nourish good citizenship.

> * This is needed so that a *social balance* is achieved;
> * This is needed so that a country can have an *integrated human development;*

? ?

> And to achieve a simultaneous economic development and social advancement, *education* plays a very important role;

So

> **HUMAN DEV = *I-C. EDUCA* ? ECON DEV + SOCIAL ADV**

Therefore, **inter-civilizational education** can and should become **the fulcrum** upon which both of the sub-fields of

Human Development and **Inter-Civilizational Dialogue** can rest in full balance to sustain **a common field of integration** where the potential for the creation of the otherí becomes nullified by itself, allowing the intrinsic energies of the field to be channeled into a productive interaction of the two.

Accordingly, the crucial issue that is at hand is how such a human development for members of the South or the Global South can be brought about and their standard of living can be raised. The answer that the world is coming up with nowadays is the magic word of globalizationí. We have been using this word for almost, I think, a decade now; has it solved anything so far? Is it going to solve the kinds of problems that we are faced with in Cyprus and in the Middle East, in the Balkans and Central America, in Latin America?

Actually, globalizationí appears to have resulted in fueling the very principle of consumer economics, which aims at selling more and making more money for the benefit of the north and loss of the south! So, I think it is only adding more problems to a growing list, rather than solving them.

Moreover, globalization and consumer economics are leading to corrupt subcultures in the cities of Southern or Eastern countries causing the social civilizations of the East or the South to rot from inside, like an apple.

A. Economic Development Models

One can talk about diverse economic development models currently offered by the World Bank, IMF, WHO, UNDP, etc., etc. All these organizations and institutions have vested interest in the economic welfare of the 189 countries making up the UN mosaic. However, there is something missing in the functioning of the models utilized by these institutions. Taking scholars to the countries of the north or sending delegations to those of the south to study the problems faced in such different sectors as health, finance, infrastructure, educational investments, etc., does not quite work either!

The West is trying to see its relation with eastern countries as one of meeting certain material indicators: economic development, human development, etc. There actually is something more than that; may be a soul indicatorí. Nonetheless, I had an experience dealing with Central Asian states, just at the time of the collapse of the Soviet Union. I visited three out of the five Turkic countries there. These countries overnight became developing countries. They were second world countries up until the collapse, and then they became third world countries. So all their indicators were that of a third world country. Yet the countries were sophisticated, but their system, the communist system, had collapsed, so they were totally devoid of free market ideas, exporting ideas/experience, etc. So, IMF came, World Bank came, WHO came, and provided some prescriptions for them, You should do ABCD! and left. They come back after 6 months and asked: *Have you done these*?

The answer was, *No!* You do not qualify for EFGH then, because you have not filled the ABCD prescription. Next step for the international organizations is to take a couple of high-level bureaucrats and officials from these countries to the U.S., and show them what they are supposed to be doing. Such taking of some high-level bureaucrats or some academics/researchers to the countries of the North or West takes two to three years of rushing back and forth to create a common language and common understanding between the institutions of the North/West and those countries of the

South which are trying to receive the kind of help they need to get out of their problems.

These countries need help in their endeavor to provide economic development for their population, which is of course linked to their social advancement, and eventually for the building up of their integrated human development. I see economic development and social advancement as an integral part of human development. I worked for four years trying to create a different economic development model using technology where the first phase should be a face-to-face meeting as mentioned above. Then, subsequently, satellites and videoconferencing can be used as follow-up. Therefore, after the members of a delegation pay a visit to the relevant country and come up with an ABCD prescription, having established the necessary human connection, the progress can then be monitored by weekly progress reports through technology.

The above method will facilitate faster development and professionalism. Taking scholars to the west is actually like taking fish out of water; normally, making such an arrangement for a short period only is fine. It is good to show around and offer ideas but for more than a week or ten days, I think, this does not work. It gets very confusing because then you are dealing with an inevitable culture shock both ways.

Social Advancement
As far as social advancement is concerned, every civilization presupposes a specific worldview which defines the way members of that civilization perceive and even dream of their own worldí as the setting for the state and process of their existence and being. This directly shapes the way people of diverse cultures and/or civilizations behave and/or

act. For instance, in the Eastern or Southern cultures, people are warm. They can sit together in close proximity or even walk around holding hands. For them friendship is very important, while individualism of the North creates *small islands*.

When I first went to the U.S. on a Fulbright Scholarship, as part of the orientation package, I was given an article to read about *privacy circles*. Each culture has its own privacy circle with a certain radius. In the West, this privacy circle radius is very big, maybe one meter. Depending on the country, this radius maybe fifty cm, ten cm, etc. You can get closer to someone from the Eastern culture both physically as well as privacy-wise. Whereas, if you start asking someone in the West such questions as, *What is your religion?* Or *How old are you?* You will quickly offend them since these are considered as private matters and you will be violating their *privacy*. In other words, when you sit in someoneís privacy circle, he will try to back off, and this will create discomfort.

Conclusion

So, these things are again proofs of the need for *a common language* eventually leading to *an inter-civilizational dialogue*, a challenging process which can be achieved through an *inter-civilizational education* that should also become instrumental in attaining *economic development* and *social advancement* simultaneously, eventually resulting in integrated *human development*.

References

G,ven, H. *Civilizations and Natural Laws: A positive sciences perspective*,í *Global Leadership Forum*, University of Bah esehir, Istanbul, June 2001.

Huntington, S. *The Clash Of Civilizations*,í *Foreign Affairs*, summer 1993.

Safty, Adel. Leadership for Human Development. *Global Leadership Forum*, University of Bah esehir, Istanbul, June 2001.

UNESCO
http://www.unesco.org/dialogue2001/en/education.htm
2001a.

UNESCO
http://www.unesco.org/education/nved/index.html
2001b.

Leadership in Education: An intercultural Model in Progress

Halil Güven

Introduction

In earlier discussions (Güven, 2002a and 2002b), a redefinition of contemporary civilizations was given. Also, diagnoses of the problems related to civilizational disharmony in the world, in light of Huntington's (1993) claims of clash of civilizations, were attempted. Firstly, it was argued that civilizations had both social and material components, and these two equally important aspects of civilizations should be kept in balance. A civilization with enormous material basis (rules, regulations, laws, order, and efficiency at all levels) without a balanced social component would make the end-users of that civilization (i.e., human beings) unhappy. Similarly, an enormous social civilization (social ties, family ties, spiritual capital, etc.) without a balanced material component would create the same effect on its constituents: unhappiness. It was therefore argued that a better balance should be sought between social and material components of civilizations.

Secondly, it was argued that the industrialized western civilizations had developed advanced material civilizations, amassing enormous amount of wealth and with it the potential to dominate other civilizations. It would be wrong to assume that civilizations could be rank ordered, that is, to consider one to be superior to the other. This would create accumulated civilizational disharmony, leading to a clash and prolonged conflict. Instead, civilizations should make every effort to learn from each other.

Thirdly, a new concept, *inter-civilizational education*, similar to interdisciplinary educationí was introduced, along with economic development and social advancement paradigms, in the context of human development.

In this chapter, educational paradigms and a case study are presented. The case study is a new university in Istanbul, Turkey, Bah esehir University. The vision, mission, and the foundation principles of the university are presented. University of Bah esehir is discussed as an intercultural education model in progress.

Background

I lived twenty years in the west. Having been educated in the west and having served in the western higher education system for over a decade, I believe I have gained invaluable experience and insight into the western educational system. Also, having raised three sons, I have gained some insight into how the kids are raised in the west. One of my sons finished his elementary education in the U.S., and the secondary education in this part of the world.

In the West, kids are raised with the basic understanding that "they should be self-reliant". Kids are raised with a lot of responsibility, a lot of individualism, and a lot of self-confidence. Kids are taught to grow up with MORE INDEPENDENCE / LESS DEPENDENCY. The basic *modus operandi* is INDEPENDENCE AND INDIVIDUALISM: Kids must be **independent and self-sufficient** as soon as possible, actually starting from the nursery school.

In the early 1980's, I was watching a TV news program in California, U.S.A. The reporter was complaining about the former USSRís very existence -- during the height of the Cold War. The topic of the complaint was: "How could we ever understand these people? while showing a *great siní* on the screen. The siní was actually that of a mother dressing her son aged 5-7, putting on his snow jacket, and tying his shoelaces. This was the great siní that the reporter was alluding to! From another personal experience, when I was living and working in California, my morning chores included taking my 4-year old son to kindergarten. It was very interesting for me (admittedly, sometimes annoying) to wait for my son trying to tie his shoelaces, refusing help, and insisting that I can do it myself dad . In my sonís kindergarten, one of the dominant messages was you can do it yourself! and "you should give a break to your parents!" When I tried to speed up the process of tying the shoelaces, my son always strongly objected. My son cannot imagine why I should tie his shoelaces (!)-- I believe, in his mind my son thought that I was interfering in his self-development (and self-reliance) path. Raising kids as individuals, independent and free is, of course, at the onset, an admirable project, and this suits and is needed in the Western way of living and norms.

On the other hand, the Eastern worldview requires kids to be raised under as much protection as possible, and that is, at *the expense* of their individualism. Lack of individualism in the kids and youth results in: Inability of expressing opinions, afraid of saying no, lack of self-confidence, dependency, less freedom, etc.

Kids are, by and large, raised with a lot of protection all the way to the doors of the university. So, the kids we get at the university are just off from their family homes. Their parents still decide about a lot of things concerning their lives. What I am saying to these students at the university is,

Stop seeking total protection and guidance from your parents! You should make your own decisions about your future, what you want to study, and what you want to do with your life.

Of course, this is easier said than done. There should be a better balance between dependence, independence, individualism and freedom of expression.

So, the norms or concepts of *Privacy Circle*[23], *I can do it myself*, *Self-Made Man* and, of course, *Individualism*, which

---

[23] When I first arrived in the United States with Fulbright Scholarship in 1979, as part of the orientation package they give me an article to read about *privacy circles*. Each culture has itís own privacy circle with a certain radius. In the west, this privacy circle radius is very big, maybe one meter. Depending on the country, this radius maybe fifty cm, ten cm, etc. You can get closer to someone from the eastern culture (both physically as well as privacy-wise). While if you go to talk to someone in the west about *what is your religion? How old are you?* You will quickly offend them, as these are considered as private matters, and you are violating their privacy. In other words, you are sitting in this

are peculiar to the Northern/Western worldview, and which have played a great role in the setting up of the Western way of living as we know of it today, happen to be totally absent in certain other civilizations including ours. And the Northern/Western mentality finds it difficult to allow for the absence of such concepts that are fundamental to its achievements.

A gap, a civilizational gap, is thereby formed, hindering the flow of human interaction between the members of different cultures or civilizations, and consequently setting up barriers against **human development** itself. Therefore, this is another issue to be tackled while creating **a common language** of good will; tolerance and equality to bridge any civilizational gaps and build up the much needed **intercivilizational** (or intercultural) **dialogue**.

I truly believe that education, and especially higher education have an important role to play in building the intellectual infrastructures necessary for the intercivilisational dialogue to flourish and take roots.

In the following section, an intercivilizational (or intercultural) higher education model in progress is given. This ambitious project aims at raising leaders that speak a *common language* of good will and tolerance, and equality.

---

personís privacy circle, and he will be trying to back off, and this will create discomfort, etc. I found the privacy circle concept to be quite useful in understanding and adapting to my life in the west.

A new University in Istanbul: Bah esehir University

There are 74 universities in Turkey. From these, 53 are state universities and 21 are foundation (trust) universities. In these universities a total of 1.5 million youth are educated. Every year, approximately 1.5 million new candidates for university education take a centrally administered exam. Only 10% of these students can be accommodated in the existing universities. Starting new universities, in order to increase the supply is encouraged by the Turkish Higher Educational Council (Y K), a state entity in charge of central coordination of the Turkish Universities.

In 1997, there were 15 foundation universities (there are 21 total in 2002). In early 1998, Y K issued permits to start three new foundation universities. One of these three universities was Bah esehir University. Bah esehir Ugur Education Foundation (Trust) was awarded the right to establish the Bah esehir University with the Turkish National Assemblyís (TBMM) resolution (Law No. 4324 dated Jan. 15, 1998) published through the Government Bulletin (Resmi Gazete Issue No. 23234, dated Jan. 18, 1998).

The Trust itself has been established by some of the most experienced people in the field of education in Turkey. Starting from nursery and primary schooling, through to high school and university entrance exams, the Board of Trustees for Bah esehir University have been involved in providing comprehensive education for all ages. It is upon this experience, knowledge and dynamism that Bah esehir University was founded. The University has a vision to educate students who are able to become leaders anywhere in the world in their respective fields.

The University is named after the town in which it is founded Bah esehir. In 1996 the town was awarded The Best Satellite Town Award by the UN Habitat for Humanity Conference. Today Bah esehir-Istanbul is regarded as one of the best examples of a satellite town in the world.

In the New Millennium, the combined knowledge, experience and determination of the University founders together with a modern infrastructure and well-equipped staff provided the necessary ingredients for Bah esehir University to play a prominent role in higher education not only in Turkey, but also around the world. In a short time, Bah esehir University set itself apart from its kinds in Turkey and started making headway internationally as well.

Since enrolment of ís first students in 1999-2000 academic years, the Universityís enrolment this year has grown to 1200 students. It currently has six different faculties and 18 different degree programs. The University also has graduate programs in Business and Sciences. In the following section, the steps in the formation of this University are given along with its mission and vision.

Steps in Setting up the University

I joined the Bah esehir University project at its onset in January 1998 as the International Programs facilitator. At the time, I was working for the San Diego State Universityís self-support unit, College of Extended Studies, as International Development Director, and I have had over 10 years of experience as a faculty member in the same university's Mechanical Engineering Department. In this 10-year period, I spent a year of sabbatical leave at Eastern Mediterranean University in Magosa, North Cyprus. I had been travelling to the region (Turkey, Cyprus, Turkmenistan, Kazakhstan, Uzbekistan, Israel, Egypt, Saudi Arabia) as the International (Project) Development Director for almost 5 years before getting on board the Bahcesehir project. After accepting a post as the International Programs facilitator at Bah esehir, over the course of next 11 months, I had opportunities to stay in Istanbul for extended periods of time, and study the Turkish Higher Educational system from close-up. I also had an opportunity to analyse the make-up of the *zeal* of the people living in this magical city, Istanbul which was at the crossroads of civilizations, and where Asia met Europe. Even though I completed my undergraduate studies in Istanbul (1974-78), till joining the Bahcesehir project; I did not have any opportunity to spend any of my adult and professional years here. My feelings were that, Istanbul, having served as the capital of a multi-ethnic, multi-cultural, multi-religious empire for over 600 years, could be used as a location to build a *model* higher educational institution with aspirations of bridging cultures, bringing western and eastern civilizations together, and creating a sincere dialogue of civilizations.

I was appointed the Founding Rector, by the Board of Trustees of the University, in December 1998. One of the first things I did after my appointment was to write a *Fundamental Principles* document for the University (see Appendix A). This document had three parts: Mission Statement; Educational Philosophy; Workplace and Employment Principles. As can be seen from this document, at its onset Bahcesehir University had a broad mission of contributing to the world peace, understanding, and building a curriculum, which addressed the local needs with intercultural emphasis. I am a firm believer in technology-transfer (and know-how and good-will transfer at all levels). In my career in the U.S., I worked on several technology transfer projects from university-to-industry and from an *industrialized country environment* to a *developing-country environment*. Bahcesehir University presented itself as an opportunity to transfer educational know-how (technology) from western higher educational models to Istanbul, with proper renovations, additions, and adaptations. The Fundamental Principles (Appendix A) is written with these thoughts in mind, after spending only a year in Istanbul, following the 20 years I spent in the U.S. with an American dominated professional culture. Though my thoughts have changed in many areas after the writing of this document, and now I find some of the stipulations in this document as invalid or incorrect, I kept the document here in its entirety for the record.

After setting the goals, the next step was to appoint the deans for the four faculties (colleges) with which the University was being inaugurated: Arts and Sciences; Business Administration; Engineering; Communications. Each Deanís candidate was given the *Fundamental Principles* document and asked to react to, in addition to preparing his or her vision for the faculty he/she was asked to set-up.

Mission and Vision Statement

The mission and the vision of the university were finalized in March 1999 together with the four selected founding deans. I am pleased to note that most of the issues addressed, and goals set, in the *Fundamental Principles* document made their way into the Universityís mission and vision statements with unanimous support from the founding deans and the Board of Trustees.

VISION OF THE UNIVERSITY

- To prepare its students not only for a career, but also for life
- To provide total quality in education
- To foster collaboration between the University and Industry
- To adapt a leading and pioneering role in education technology
- To contribute to the peace and stability of the region
- To generate "Think Tanks" and critical thinking

MISSION OF THE UNIVERSITY

To train and educate students who:

- Have discovered the path to information and who can benefit from that information
- Are inquisitive and critical
- Are competent in a second foreign language other than English
- Are competitive but sociable
- Value human virtue; hold a sense of responsibility to society and its problems

- Are willing to do teamwork

- Are willing to respect the opinion of others although they may disagree with them, are democratic and hold in esteem the inviolable rights of others

Implementation of the Vision: MEP-GEP-YEP

Next came time for implementing the vision and taking steps towards fulfilment of the mission. The educational philosophy of the University has **three pillars** which are: *MEP*, *GEP*, and *YEP*. Each one of these is designed to address a special need to address the issues in Appendix A.

GEP, MEP and YEP programs (GMY programs in short) are one of the essential components of the mission of the Bahçesehir University. This program introduces the students to a wide spectrum of perspectives of the intellectual world. The curriculum is designed to develop and equip students not only with knowledge for career enhancement but also to help to fulfill an incomplete education by enhancing their culture and creating socially aware and responsible individuals in our society.

Students of the Bahçesehir University should graduate with an education that

- Provides knowledge about the arts and culture of different societies and times.
- Is well supported with strong historical knowledge.
- Develops an awareness of the international and intercultural world.
- Familiarizes the student with the social institutions and behavior of social groups in Turkey.
- Enriches the comprehension of the meaning and forces of nature.
- Develops the understanding of Turkish culture, language and history.

Such an education will not only equip the graduate with a strong general knowledge but it will also help him/her in understanding how knowledge is acquired.

4.1 MEP Portfolio System (Career Oriented Professional and industrial Education);

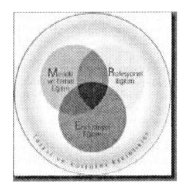

First pillar is the **MEP Portfolio System,** where

M depicts the courses in Major,

E shows the Industrial Education (Internships),

P refers to Professionalism.

MEP portfolio system is one of the cornerstones of the Bah esehir Universityís educational philosophy. The University aims to develop the skills of students by certificate and workshop programs in a world that is increasingly global and competitive. Besides a university diploma, corporations also attach a high priority to viable knowledge and skills when recruiting graduates. Within the context of career planning, the university introduced the MEP Portfolio System. This set of courses, Professionalism for a Career in Industry, introduces the students to a set of "Portfolio" components that we would not ordinarily find in a single set of academic programs. This system enables the students to develop themselves in various areas outside their major field of study and equips the student with three important competitive advantages.

1. Career Oriented Basic Training
2. Professional Education
3. Industrial Training

At the end of four years of university education the students not only obtain a university diploma but also as a result of a systematic approach to Industrial seminars and workshops, they are equipped with reference certificates. By attending certificate programs that will contribute to professional development at professional consultancy firms, they will obtain professional education certificates. Within the framework of this program, the students will get to meet and listen to professionals who are specialists in their fields. This working of the academic with the practitioners will open the doors to the real world of industry, broaden the students vision of what industry entails and shorten the training time that companies will have to invest in the newly graduated student.

This system involves Professionalism. Hence, **MEP** has instruction in professional topics like leadership, time management, organization skills, public speaking, etc. Students earn certificates in these topics, and they must complete a minimum of 14 of these throughout four years. These certificates are given by professional development companies or by diverse centres of the university. For example, our International Institute of Leadership and Public Affairs (IILPA) offered the first leadership development seminar certificate last year for the first time at any university in Turkey. The certificates the students are awarded are placed in their portfolio to be presented to them when they graduate.

The courses they take with us result in a diploma, which process is the same as in most universities. Some universities also have internships and co-op programs. Therefore, what you see in the *ME* portion of the *MEP* system are the components that most universities offer in their curricular design to judge performance progress and, based on that, award a diploma at the end. Here we also include Professionalism to help develop the **common language** and foster the skills in organization, leadership, running meetings, teamwork, etc. -- the kind of things needed to understand the business and professional cultures of the West with a view to **bridging the civilizations.**

More info on the operational characteristics of MEP is given in Appendix B.

4.2 General Education Program (GEP)

THE SECOND PILLAR, WHICH HAPPENS TO BE VERY COMMON IN THE WEST, IS GENERAL EDUCATION PROGRAM.

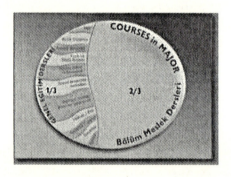

We are the only university in Turkey that has decided to institute a *GE Program*. Most universities in Turkey opted for the easy way out, teaching engineering students only engineering, business students only business, etc. In the U.S., however, **general education** is increasingly becoming a must in all universities. There are 3600 universities; all of them have **GE programs**.

Considering that a university graduate must know certain things, we have blocked one-third of our courses for *GEP*; some of them being Critical Thinking, Analytical Thinking, Sociology, Psychology, etc. We are the only university in Turkey that has implemented such a program so far. However, we do hope that other universities, too, will soon pick this program up to simultaneously instil in the students all three skills:

- Fundamental skills,
- Knowledge skills, and
- Social skills.

At the end of the program, the graduates should have the following qualifications in addition to their majors:

1. Ability to think and write clearly and effectively
2. Depth of knowledge in a certain field
3. Critical appreciation of the Universe, the society and himself/herself
4. Understanding of moral and ethical problems
5. Knowledge of other cultures and times
6. Informed acquaintance with different disciplines

The courses offered by the General Education Program are designed to facilitate an exchange of ideas that will help students broaden their overall knowledge. Such an experience can also aid in developing the studentsí ability to evaluate particular topics in a critical fashion. The common goal of the course is to provide students with skills to organize and present thoughts orally and to stimulate them to higher levels of proficiency and scholarly improvement. The course might also challenge and expand the studentsí interest beyond their primary area of study.

In the first year, students from all departments are obliged to take GEP 101 (General Survey) in the first semester and GEP 102 (Critical Thinking) in the second semester. In the following three years before the graduation, the students choose from a list of courses, one course per semester. The students will be counselled by the GMY Office about their choice of courses. Brief description of the GEP 1001 and 1002 and courses are given in Appendix C.

Study Abroad Program (YEP)

This last pillar, *YEP*, is, in fact, a *study abroad* program.

We have, under *YEP*, incorporated one semester of study abroad program in the U.S. for our students. After they have studied for two years with us, they can do the fifth semester in California, U.S.A. Spending a full semester in California, taking courses together with their American counterparts will help both our students and American students increase their understanding of and widen their horizon to include another worldview or civilization by enriching their education.

While on *YEP*, students are required to take such GE courses as critical thinking, logic, comparative religions, etc. Having these students go through *YEP* will support and accelerate the development of a common understanding, and, of course, **a common language**.

One of the building blocks of the educational philosophy of Bahçesehir University is the opportunity to study abroad for one term and transfer credits back to Bahçesehir University for graduation. This process has been designed based on the specifications of YEP study abroad program. With this program Bahçesehir University wants to broaden the student's vision, increase tolerance and flexibility, and enrich cultural awareness and communication skills.

Students, who have successfully completed the freshman and sophomore years, obtained a TOFEL score of 550 and received a GPA of 2.50/4, can enrol in a university abroad during the 5th semester (1st term of 3rd year), preferably a university that we have a cooperative agreement with.

To be accepted to YEP program, the student must have a GPA of 2.50/4.00 and a TOFEL score of 550.

To enrol in the program, students apply at the end of their freshman year.
Students attending YEP Program take mainly GEP courses in their one semester abroad.

Research Centres to aid Social Advancement

The university has an ambitious mission, which extends beyond providing a quality higher education to its students. We believe that a university should also be actively involved in projects to shed light on contemporary issues and problems of its home country, be it economic or social. The intellectual capital of a university should be put to use to generate ideas and solutions to such problems. Along these lines, our university has established eight applied research centres. These centres have sponsored a total of 51 seminars, conferences and panel discussion during the academic year 2001-2002.

Bah esehir University is only 3 years old, and has only 1200 students. We are a very young and dynamic university with big aspirations and goals.

Among others, we have already established:

- The International Institute of Leadership and Public Affairs (IILPA)

- The Istanbul Strategic Research Centre,
- Nobel Laureate Candidates Research Centre,
- Entrepreneurial and Innovation Management Centre, and
- Southeast Anatolia Project Cooperation Centre.

The International Institute of Leadership and Public Affairs (IILPA)

The International Institute of Leadership and Public Affairs was founded in late 2000 by Dr. Adel Safty, former Head of UN Mission and former President of the United Nations Leadership Conferences as well as Director of the UN Leadership Academy. With the active support of Bahcesehir University and its Chairman of the Board of the Trustees Mr. Enver Yucel, Dr. Safty organized the inaugural conference for the establishment of the IILPA, the Global Leadership Forum, in June 2001, in Istanbul. The Forum brought together distinguished leaders and scholars from all continents in the world, and representatives of over 20 international organizations, including the United Nations, UNESCO, The World Bank and the Organisation of American State, the Organisation of African Unity, as well as distinguished diplomats and parliamentarians.

The Global Leadership Forum also brought distinguished leaders such as Nobel Peace Laureate Oscar Arias, former President of Costa Rica, Mrs. Harriet Fulbright, President Clintonís Executive Director of the Presidentís Committee for the Arts and Humanities, Mr. Jacques Baudot, President of the United Nations Social and Economic Council, the late

Ambassador Tahseen Basheer, and other distinguished leaders from Turkey and the region.

Throughout its first year of operations, the IILPA organized and offered the first Leadership Development Seminar Certificate, ever to be offered at any university in Turkey. It also organized and offered a second certificate on Collaborative Leadership and Team Building. In addition, it organized a public lectures series that included the conference on Clash of civilizations, the conference on the Palestine crisis, the conference on the Threat of Terrorism, and the conference on Turkish-Arab relations.

The IILPA also became a distinguished partner of the International Partnership for Service-Learning in New York, thus joining a list of distinguished universities around the world, committed to combining public service with learning. In that capacity the IILPA can now offer Certificate of Service Learning jointly with the International Partnership in New York.

Moreover, in 2002, Dr. Safty established the High Council of Leadership, that acts as an honorary body of distinguished supporters of the leadership initiative and its underlying commitment to leadership for human development. Dr. Safty brought into that High Council such distinguished names as: Boutros Boutros-Ghali, Lord Frank Judd, Lord Ian Gilmour, Harriet Fulbright, Jacques Baudot, Senator Michel Pelchat (Vice-President of the French Senate Foreign Relations Committee), Mr. Ilter Turkmen, former Foreign Minister of Turkey, Congressman Jose Gomez (Venezuela), Dr. Shoqi Wang (Director General of the Chinese Ministry of Science and Technology), Prof. Hafiza Golandaz (India), Prof. Carol Allais (South Africa), Prof. Marina Tyasto (Russia), and Dr. Mahy Abdel Latif (Foreign Ministry of Egypt).

In addition, a leadership delegation led by Mr. Enver Yucel that included I and Dr. Adel Safty, met with Prince Hassan bin Talal of Jordan in Istanbul, in February 2002. We discussed the Princeís earlier initiative for the establishment of a Research Centre in Istanbul, and agreed to amalgamate Prince Hassanís concept for research with the leadership initiative. Mr. Yucel also offered to the Prince the Presidency of the new Institute of Leadership, and the Prince accepted. This is an exciting initiative that promises, as Harriet Fulbright put it in her introduction to our Leadership Booklet, to benefits all sectors in the society locally, and regionally.

Closure

The goal is to create pragmatic **inter-civilizational educational models** by means of which students shall graduate speaking **a common language** that would be instrumental in establishing **an inter-civilizational dialogue** between the South/East and the North/West.

Accordingly, through such a process, I will try to come up with graduates who are well versed in **a common language** between the South/East and the North/West and ready to take part in **an inter-civilizational dialogue**. Kids would have observed each other, spent time together, and acquired a decent level of knowledge about each otherís culture. I am hoping to have some students from United States visit us as well. I, myself, have had the wonderful experience of being exposed to both civilizations and cultures. I would like, once more, to thank the Fulbright Program for that. Hopefully, through this kind of design involving **an inter-civilizational**

education, I can come up with graduates who do speak **a language common to both civilizations** and who can thus efficiently work on **economic development and social advancement** in this part of world, and who will, I hope, contribute to **human development** itself.

References

Güven, H. Civilizations and Natural Laws: A positive sciences perspective,í **International Leadership Forum**, University of Bahçesehir, Istanbul, June 2002a.

Güven, H. *Dialogue of Civilizations: Paradigms on Economic Development and Social Advancement, International Leadership Forum,* **University of Bahçesehir, Istanbul, June 2002b.**

APPENDIX A: FUNDAMENTAL PRINCIPLES

A. MISSION STATEMENT

A.1 Remove Bottlenecks That Exist In The Higher Education System In Turkey

Due to certain educational and social factors students have been queuing up to be accepted by the universities; the number of students applying to universities are seven fold compared to the ones that get accepted. Even from this point of view, Bah esehir University will be fulfilling this function by partly removing this bottleneck. The university will be helping to fulfill the higher education dreams of a number of students in relation to its quota.

A.2 Provide Well-Educated Graduates To Sectors in Need of Human Resources

One of the biggest problems in Turkish economy is the scarcity of well-educated human resources. Bah esehir University should develop educational programs and models to provide human resources to needed sectors that take priority in Turkey.

A.3 Provide a Suitable Academic Environment for Research

Besides the scarcity of academic staff that does research, it is also very difficult to find well-equipped environments suitable for research. Bah esehir Universty should fulfill the need in this area and create a suitable academic environment for research.

A.4 Contribute to Regional Peace and Prosperity

Turkeyís region accommodates different countries with different race, religion and language and international relations are problematic. All the regionís countries have bilaterally unsolved problems and are endeavouring to dominate each other.

Bah esehir University should assist youngsters from all neighbouring countries to provide them with an education that emphasizes on peace, helping them in to fulfill their dreams of higher education; as well as teaching them to live in peace and friendship. In this way, it will also be contributing to regional peace.

A.5 Contribute To World Peace And Prosperity Within The Framework Of Turkey s Geopolitical Location: Develop A Conflict Resolution Centre, World Peace Centre And Form A Think Tank

Turkey, with respect to its geopolitical location, takes place in the intersection of various races, religions, civilizations and languages.

If Turkey can consolidate its position by proper policies and international relations, it can become a centre for the resolution of conflicts.

Although the majority of its population is Muslim, with its secular and modern structure, it can form a barrier against religious fundamentalist movements.

Situated in Istanbul, the Bahçesehir University should be a world peace centre for the resolution of conflicts in this world and region; it should undertake the task of becoming a think tank (a platform for the production and the development of ideas) specially for the Turkic and the Islamic countries in the middle-east by paving the way for them in becoming a modern, secular and a law abiding state.

B. EDUCATIONAL PHILOSOPHY

B.1 Take the U.S. Universities as a Model Target

In the area of Higher education, it is a fact that the most developed models of education exists in the U.S.A

In the light of this reality, Bahçesehir University should target the model of the most developed U.S universities and should develop and apply educational and managerial policies and models that would not fall below the quality level of its U.S counterparts.

B.2 Be a Pioneer and a Leader in the Field of Educational Technology

Distance education is becoming more and more widespread throughout the world. Classroom dependent higher education is no longer practiced. Through the Internet and computer technology, students can follow lectures from their rooms and can reach out to information and sources of knowledge a lot easier than they used to.

As a requirement of this new age, Bahçesehir University should be equipped with the technological tools; the students should be allowed to make use of these facilities and the university should be able to get them directly experience the electronic univer sity , thus paving the way in Turkey and taking its place among the leading universities in the world.

In this context, collaborating with SDSU, the university should be able to provide the students with the opportunity to participate in such programs as leadership , strategic planning and management , JIT and TQM methods , principles of world class performance , globalization: strategies for twenty-first century , conflict resolution and resource management through the video -conference method that already exist in SDSU.

B.3 Provide a High Quality and Advanced Education in English

Even though they can read, write and understand the biggest problem of those who are learning English as a second language, are that they are not all that successful in having a conversation.

In the Bah esehir University, all lectures and internal communications, excluding lessons that directly concern Turkey, should be in English; all students and staff should be able to read, write and understand and be able to defend their ideas and express themselves well in English. The students should be presented with the opportunity to live for some time in English speaking countries (specially in U.S.A).

B.4 Be Able To Provide a Good Quality and Effective Education

Individuals graduating from Bah esehir University should be fully equipped in their field of study and should attain a high level of education that provides them with specific skills in their specialized area and a broad general knowledge.

B.5 Train Students to Prepare Them to Follow World Developments Closely in Parallel With World Progress

To train students solely towards a profession, to ignore vital changes, has lots of drawbacks when preparing them to a fast changing world.

Bah esehir University should also offer programs that prepare students to life besides the general departmental programs; students must graduate as individuals who can participate in production, follow closely technological changes and developments and sustain their progress, in short, as individuals ready for life.

For example, basic preparatory program / preparation to life program offered in SDSU, should be offered here for a semester. Lectures like leadership , strategic planning and management , JI T and TQM methods , principles of world class performance , globalization: strategies for twenty-first century , conflict resolution and resource management should be available to students.

B.6 Help Students to Acquire Practical Talents besides Theoretical Knowledge Establish and Develop University Industry cooperation

One of the most important problems university graduates face is the lack of work experience when they start a new job.

Bah esehir University should collaborate with the industry and various enterprises so as to provide students with practical training and training opportunities during the period of their education.

C. WORKPLACE AND EMPLOYMENT PRINCIPLES

C.1 Establish Relationships at Work That Depend on Love, Respect and Trust

Like in all other lines of business, success is only possible with mutual understanding and love.

The employees of the Bah esehir University should have a teamwork spirit and an understanding of being part of a team that work in harmony; they should behave in such a way so as to achieve peace among themselves; they should show respect and trust each other. The administrators, employees, lecturers and students (no matter what their job description or what they are entitled to) should all love their work.

C.2 Form a Sense of Belonging to the Bah esehir University

All necessary efforts should be spent for the creation of a sense of belonging to the Bah esehir University; all of university members should share the joys and sorrows of employees and students. Regular social activities should be organized (excursions, dinners, parties, reward ceremonies, etc.) and a monthly newsletter should be published for internal communications and external public relations.

C.3 Attain Social Justice and Equality of Opportunity

In our country, the principles of just distribution of income, equal opportunity of education through social justice, and equality of individuals before justice, were kept only in words and were never put into use.

Social justice, principles of equality and a peaceful work environment should be attained at the Bah esehir University.

All expectations and criteriaís should be in writing. Within the framework of these principles, objective decisions should be taken and choices be made.

Good faith, in Bah esehir University should be accepted as a main principle; everyone should be regarded as innocent until proven guilty.

C.4 Develop Working Principles That Respect Laws And Also Bear In Mind Universal Values

Without ignoring universal rights, laws and basic human rights, Bah esehir University should adopt an education philosophy that is in line with the constitution of the Turkish Republic and Y K regulations. With the understanding that the main aim of all regulations is to enhance the individual, necessary tolerance and flexibility should be granted to all.

C.5 Set The Medium Of Written Or Verbal Communication In English

In this university, where the medium of instruction is in English, all communications, written or verbal, should also be in English.

C.6 When Recruiting, Clearly Define Job Descriptions

Job descriptions should be handed to employees when they are recruited; what is expected of them should also be conveyed clearly. These definitions should be made separately with the following headings:

- What will be the educational and administrative expectations of the management and what will be required of employees?

- What will be expected of employees in terms of individual progress and what will be required of them?

- What will be expected of employees in terms of community service and what will be required of them?

C.7 Develop and Set Up Performance Evaluation Criteria at Work

All performance evaluation should be based on certain criteria. The employees of Bah esehir University should consist of individuals who, within the framework of a universal measures, have no worries of a salary, future prospects and social insurance, who are happy, and for the benefit of their country and in the name of humanity, compete to perform their duties in the best possible way. Employees should also participate vigorously in efforts that will enhance the quality and promotion of the university. Specially, academics should not only lecture but;

- Should carry out applied research, and should also contribute to finding solutions to the problems of the society and the country;

- Should play a role in having an accurate and balanced faculty budget, should be engaged in such work that will increase the portion, the faculty gets from the main university budget, should contribute to the growth of his/her faculty in parallel to the growth of the university;

- Should participate in seminars and university promotion meetings.

APPENDIX B: THE MEP SYSTEM

The MEP program continues during the first three years of a bachelor degree. Students are required to attain a passing mark for every semester. The MEP program is coordinated through a central GEP, MEP, and YEP (GMY) Coordination Office. The faculties organize MEP conferences and workshops and are responsible for taking the attendance. Each faculty announces the conference title, the presenter, the time and place of the conference on the billboards and the university web with the collaboration of the GMY Office. The MEP conferences are held on every Tuesdays and Thursdays. Every student is provided with a MEP card. The MEP card has openings for 10 conferences. For each conference attended, the student writes the name of the conference, the presenter, and the date on the opening and gets it signed by the organizing faculty. First year students take MEP 191 and 192, second year students take MEP 291 and 292, third year students take MEP 391 and 392. Third year students taking MEP 391 and 392 are required to take notes on note pads provided by the university and submit them at the end of the conference.

1. First year students, for every semester are required to attend at least four conferences organized by his/her faculty and four conferences organized by other faculties. If a student attends sixteen conferences in a semester he/she will be awarded with a special certificate of achievement and a gift.

2. Second year students are required to attend at least four conferences organized by his/her faculty and four conferences organized by other faculties for every semester,

making eight conferences in total. They are also required to attend two certificate programs each semester. Evaluation will be as follows:

8 conferences attended per semester (8 x %5) = %40
2 certificate programs per semester (2 x %30) = %60
Total per semester = %100

3. Third year students required to attend at least four conferences organized by his/her faculty, four conferences organized by other faculties and two conferences organized by other universities or institutions, making ten conferences in total. Students have to provide a proof of their attendance of the conferences attended outside of the university.

10 conferences attended per semester (10 x %4) = %40
2 certificate programs per semester (2 x %30) = %60
Total per semester = %100

At the end of the semester, the students will submit their MEP cards to the GMY Office. The GMY Office is responsible for marking the cards and submitting the final grades to Studentís Registry.

The certificate programs are organized through the Rectorís Office and are held twice per semester. The surveillance of the programs is collaborated with the GMY Office.

MEP conferences will also include Learning strategies seminars so as to aid the students on their study schedules. These seminars will be organized in collaboration with Careers Enhancement Centre.

External students from other Turkish universities, subject to a quota, will be allowed to participate to the MEP program.

External students satisfying the conditions mentioned above will be awarded with the relevant certificates. These students will have to register with the GMY Office in the beginning of the semester.

Visiting staff should be seated at the beginning of each row so as to safeguard the discipline of the conference.

APPENDIX C: BAHCESEHIR UNIVERSITY FRESHMEN GEP COURSES

The Freshmen (first year) program offers two compulsory general education courses, GEP 1001 AND GEP 1002:

***GEP 1001 - General Survey* (First year first semester)**
This course is designed to provide the students with an overall introduction to the basic concepts of arts and sciences. The course will cover a different subject every week. The subjects will be Economics, Law, Ancient civilizations, Political Science, Architecture, Sociology, psychology, International Relations, Contemporary Issues in Science, Art and design, Literature, philosophy and Media. A different lecturer according to their relevant field of specialization will lecture subjects. The course will be supported by audio, visual and written material. The students will be required to submit a portfolio and sit for an exam at the end of the semester. Credits: 3

***GEP1002 - Critical Thinking* (First year second semester)**
Critical Thinking is a course designed to help students develop their skills in reasoning, analysis and the use of logical arguments. The goal is to teach the student to better comprehend and evaluate the materials read and to understand and appreciate different viewpoints. One focus of the course will be on learning to see the arguments for both sides of an issue in order to reach more comprehensive conclusions. Class participation and interaction will be an extremely important part of the learning process. Lectures will be kept to a minimum with emphasis upon practical techniques and application of the materials in the readings. Credits: 3

Adel Safty was born in Egypt and educated in France and England before becoming university professor in North America. He holds an undergraduate Bachelor degree in English and French literature from the University of Paris III, France, and a Bachelor Degree in Law, Honours, from the University of London, England. He also holds Masterís Degrees in Political Sociology and in Political Science and a Doctorate Degree in Political Science from the University of Paris I, Sorbonne, France.

Dr. Safty is also a graduate of the Leadership Programme of the Center for Creative Leadership (Greensboro, NC. USA). He is also a graduate of the JFK School of Government Leadership Programme at Harvard University.

Dr. Safty served as a tenured university professor and as Director of the government-funded Institute of International Studies in British Columbia, before joining the United Nations as a diplomat. Professor Safty is author and editor of 10 books. Among his publications, his book From Camp David to the Gulf (Black Rose, University of Toronto Press, Montreal and New York, 1992) was selected Publisherís Choice in 1993 and a second edition appeared in 1997.

Prof. Safty served as Head of United Nations Mission and President of the United Nations Leadership Conferences in the late 1990s that brought together distinguished leaders and delegates from over 100 countries. In 1997, Prof. Safty established the first ever UNESCO Chair in Leadership. In 2002, he established the second UNESCO Chair and was named Permanent UNESCO Chair of International Leadership. Prof. Safty is currently Dean of Leadership and President of the School of Government and Leadership at the University of Bahcesehir, Istanbul.

Printed in the United States
1161500007B/59